Complete Guide to Desktop Publishing with WordPerfect

Complete Guide to Desktop Publishing with WordPerfect

S. Scott Zimmerman
Beverly B. Zimmerman

Scott, Foresman and Company
Glenview, Illinois   London

Cover photo: Courtesy of The Image Bank

Library of Congress Cataloging-in-Publication Data

Zimmerman, S. Scott
    Complete guide to desktop publishing with WordPerfect / S. Scott
Zimmerman, Beverly B. Zimmerman.
       p.   cm.
    Includes index.
    ISBN 0-673-46078-9
    1. Desktop publishing.   2. WordPerfect (Computer program)
I. Zimmerman, Beverly B.   II. Title.
Z286.D47Z56   1990
682.2 ' 2544536 — dc20   89-35165
                                 CIP

1 2 3 4 5 6 MVN 94 93 92 91 90 89

ISBN 0-673-46078-9

Notice of Liability

The information in this book is distributed on an "As Is" basis, without
warranty. Neither the author nor Scott, Foresman and Company shall
have any liability to customer or any other person or entity with
respect to any liability, loss, or damage caused or alleged to be caused
directly or indirectly by the programs contained herein. This includes, but is not limited to, interruption of service, loss of data, loss
of business or anticipatory profits, or consequential damages from
the use of the programs.

Scott, Foresman professional books are available for bulk sales at
quantity discounts. For information, please contact Marketing
Manager, Professional Books Groups, Scott, Foresman and Company,
1900 East Lake Avenue, Glenview, IL 60025.

Trademarks

WordPerfect is a trademark of WordPerfect Corporation. PC, XT, AT, PS/2, PC-DOS, and IBM are trademarks of International Business Machines Corporation. HPLG is a trademark of Hewlett Packard Company. MS-DOS is a trademark of Microsoft Corporation. PostScript is a trademark of Adobe Systems Incorporated. Other brand and product names are trademarks or registered trademarks of their respective holders and are listed in Appendix D, "Directory of Products."

Preface

The war of word processors currently raging in the microcomputer world has spawned new and exciting features in word processing software. Each round of upgrades among the leading word processors has brought newer, faster, and more powerful features. Graphics, styles, macro programming, and desktop publishing are just a few of the recent additions.

WordPerfect Corporation continues to be the world leader in implementing these powerful new features. Its commitment to excellence, innovation, and user support has made WordPerfect the most popular word processor and may eventually make it the most popular desktop publishing software.

Our goal in writing the *Complete Guide to Desktop Publishing with WordPerfect* is to provide a clear, up-to-date, and complete how-to book on desktop publishing using WordPerfect 5.1 for the IBM PC, XT, AT, PS/2, and compatibles. We have provided everything the writer, typist, or publisher needs to start desktop publishing with WordPerfect, including explanations of what desktop publishing is, what it requires, how to set up WordPerfect for desktop publishing, how to design documents, and how to publish many types of documents. We have included step-by-step explanations of WordPerfect's many desktop publishing features—from standard document formatting to complex applications of graphics, styles, and macros. We have given real examples—from creating a letterhead to making flyers, from generating form letters to publishing newsletters.

Unfortunately, the increased popularity of desktop publishing has led to an increased number of gaudy, ugly documents. We hope this book will help new desktop publishers create simple, attractive publications.

Scott and Beverly Zimmerman

Acknowledgments

We are indebted to many people for their help in making this book possible, including the following:

- Our ever-supportive and patient editor, Amy Davis, and the other members of the Professional Books Group of Scott, Foresman and Company.

- The enthusiastic and capable group at PC&F—especially Debbie Truche, Shirley Simmons, Mary Maguire, and Helen Gagnon—who did the copyediting and typesetting of this and several other books we have written.

- Rebecca Mortensen and Paul Eddington, Corporate Communications, WordPerfect Corporation, who supplied us with beta copies of WordPerfect 5.1 and with other WordPerfect Corporation software.

- Those who reviewed the manuscript and made helpful suggestions.

Contents

**CHAPTER   5   Printing Documents   *79*

CHAPTER 16 Publishing Letters **261**

Chapter 1

Introduction

This book is a complete guide to desktop publishing with WordPerfect on the IBM PC/XT/AT, the IBM PS/2, and compatible computers.

WHO WOULD BENEFIT FROM THIS BOOK

Those who would benefit from this book include the following:

- Beginning word processing users, including typists, secretaries, students, writers, business executives, and others who have some experience with WordPerfect but who now want to do desktop publishing.

- Experienced WordPerfect users who now want to learn the principles of design and apply WordPerfect to desktop publishing.

- Office managers who are trying to decide whether or not to use WordPerfect for some or all of their desktop publishing requirements.

WHAT THIS BOOK CONTAINS

The *Complete Guide to Desktop Publishing with WordPerfect* contains nineteen chapters and four appendixes.

- Chapter 1, "Introduction" (this chapter), contains an introduction to desktop publishing with WordPerfect and an explanation of how to use this book.

- Chapter 2, "Using WordPerfect," contains a brief review of key features of WordPerfect and explains how to configure your printer for WordPerfect.

- Chapter 3, "Designing Documents," describes how to design and prepare a document for publication. It gives the six steps in producing a publication and the eight major principles of design.

- Chapters 4 through 6 show you how to apply normal word processing features (formatting, printing, and making columns) to desktop publishing.

- Chapters 7 through 13 demonstrate special desktop publishing features of WordPerfect, including drawing lines and boxes, creating and displaying graphics, installing and using fonts, inserting special characters, and typing tables and formulas.

- Chapter 14, "Using Styles," and Chapter 15, "Using Macros," describe advanced features of WordPerfect that will increase your efficiency and productivity in preparing published material.

- Chapters 16 through 19 give step-by-step procedures for publishing various types of documents, including letters, flyers, forms, and newsletters. These chapters apply the principles and techniques covered earlier in the book to actual publications. You can, in turn, apply these same principles and techniques to *any* of your publishing projects.

The following guidelines show how you might approach this book

With This Experience	*Do This*
Have never used a word processor before and don't have WordPerfect currently installed on your computer system.	This book assumes some knowledge of word processing in general and WordPerfect in particular. See Appendix C, "Additional Reading," for recommended beginning books on WordPerfect.
Have some experience with WordPerfect but little experience with desktop publishing.	Peruse Chapter 2, then carefully read the rest of the book.
Have considerable experience with desktop publishing but only limited experience with WordPerfect.	Read Chapter 2, peruse Chapter 3, and then focus on Chapters 4 through 15.
Know WordPerfect extremely well but have no experience with desktop publishing.	Read Chapter 3, "Designing Documents," then skip to Chapter 16, "Publishing Letters," and read from Chapter 16 to the end of the book.
Know WordPerfect and desktop publishing already but need help with specialized features or particular applications.	Check the table of contents and the index for the particular topics that interest you.

Regardless of your experience or needs, you will benefit from the reference materials found in the appendixes and index.

WHAT THIS BOOK CAN'T DO

This is a complete guide to desktop publishing with WordPerfect in the sense that it covers all the desktop publishing features of Word-Perfect, but it doesn't cover everything about desktop publishing or everything about WordPerfect. You can't expect this book—or any other single book—to do the following:

- *Make you an expert designer/publisher.* Learning and properly applying desktop publishing principles and techniques to the many different types of home and business documents takes time, talent, and training.

- *Make you an expert writer.* Quality publications require good writing. And good writing requires ability, effort, and experience. Your goal as a desktop publisher should be to write (or get someone else to write) simple, clear, lively, warm prose. This book says almost nothing about how to achieve that goal.

- *Make you a computer expert.* Desktop publishing requires the use of many computer hardware components (keyboard, monitor, mouse, scanner, etc.) and software applications (word processor, graphics programs, etc.). This book discusses all of these components and applications, but focuses on the word processor, WordPerfect.

For additional references on desktop publishing, word processing, and writing, see Appendix C, "Additional Reading."

WHAT IS DESKTOP PUBLISHING?

In its simplest definition, desktop publishing is the production of printed matter using a desktop computer system. So how does this differ from normal word processing? It doesn't—necessarily. Almost any document you prepare and print is desktop published material in a limited sense of the phrase.

But desktop publishing usually implies something more, as shown by the documents on pages 6 and 7. Document A (the first page of an annual report) was produced using normal word processing features, while Document B (the same page of the report) is the same document produced with desktop publishing features that provide a more professional look.

The following characteristics are commonly associated with desktop publishing:

- *High print quality.* Desktop publishing usually involves a high-quality printer, such as an ink-jet printer or, more commonly, a laser printer.

- *Variable fonts.* Desktop publishing provides a variety of typeface sizes and appearances.

- *Graphics.* Desktop publishing usually supports computer drawings, digitized photographs, lines, and boxes.

- *Special characters.* Desktop published work uses true em dashes (—), not just double hyphens (--). The bulleted lists display true bullets (•), not just a lowercase o. Desktop published material also contains true left and right quotes ("this," not "this"), left and right single quotes ('this,' not 'this,'), digraphs (Æ, œ), diacriticals (ñ, é), Greek letters (α, β), and other special characters (©, →, £, ¿, ±).

- *Kerning and leading.* Desktop publishing adjusts (kerns) the spacing between letters and adjusts (leads, rhymes with *beds*) the spacing between lines.

- *Columns, headers, footers, superscripts, subscripts, and other formatting features.* Desktop publishing also includes many features (such as columns, headers, footnotes, and superscripts) associated with sophisticated word processors.

WordPerfect 5.1 supports all of the above desktop publishing features—and many others.

WHO NEEDS DESKTOP PUBLISHING?

Corporate America spends billions of dollars annually to publish newsletters, advertisements, reports, forms, pamphlets, manuals, and books. No wonder managers everywhere, in businesses large and small, are excited about the potential of desktop publishing—touted as a low-cost, in-house method for producing high-quality printed material.

So if you need to produce high-quality printed material, you can benefit—in time and money—from desktop publishing.

ANNUAL REPORT

Ocean Breeze Bookstore

February 8, 1989

INTRODUCTION

Ocean Breeze Retail Sales, Inc., with Ocean Breeze Bookstore, San Diego, California as its sole outlet, was organized May 29, 1966, by Ernest Reeder and Manuel Libro.

Mission Statement

The mission of Ocean Breeze Bookstore is:

to serve our customers by providing a wide selection of general and specialized, new and used books, low-priced texts, and periodicals in English and Spanish. Since 1982, the company has also included office supplies and computer software in its retail listings.

Company Philosophy

The Ocean Breeze Bookstore philosophy is summarized in two words--quality service--and is demonstrated by the following company goals which were established at the time of organization:

     o   a clean, attractive, well-organized salesroom.
     o   a large inventory of quality books and magazines.
     o   knowledgeable, enthusiastic employees.

Figure 1.1A A document produced with normal word processing features.

Ocean Breeze Bookstore

ANNUAL REPORT

February 8, 1989

Introduction

Ocean Breeze Retail Sales, Inc., with Ocean Breeze Bookstore, San Diego, California as its sole outlet, was organized May 29, 1966, by Ernest Reeder and Manuel Libro.

Mission Statement

The mission of Ocean Breeze Bookstore is:

to serve our customers by providing a wide selection of general and specialized, new and used books, low-priced texts, and periodicals in English and Spanish. Since 1982, the company has also included office supplies and computer software in its retail listings.

Company Philosophy

The Ocean Breeze Bookstore philosophy is summarized in two words—*quality service*—and is demonstrated by the following company goals which were established at the time of organization:

- a clean, attractive, well-organized salesroom.
- a large inventory of quality books and magazines.
- knowledgeable, enthusiastic employees.

Figure 1.1B A document produced with desktop publishing features.

THE GOOD NEWS AND THE BAD NEWS

Here's the good news of desktop publishing:

- You can do many desktop publishing projects in one-half to one-fourth the time that standard publishing projects take. No more depending on designers, copywriters, typesetters, and printers. You can do all the work yourself with your own computer system on your own time within your own schedule.

- You can use familiar WordPerfect features, add a few desktop publishing techniques, and create attractive, readable documents.

And here's the bad news of desktop publishing:

- Unless you have an artist's eye, a writer's ear, and a typographer's hand, your documents may turn out ugly and unreadable. In the hands of amateurs, the results of desktop publishing are unattractive or banal at best and garish or ostentatious at worst. Desktop publishing personnel need training—lots of it—and that requires time and money.

- With access to fonts, styles, and graphics, many employees waste time and resources (paper, laser printer cartridges, and electricity) making their documents "look better." A three-line memo to a co-worker doesn't need fancy typefaces and illustrations.

- An overzealous (or self-designated) desktop publisher will create all kinds of published "must-haves"—additional report forms, individualized memo pads, department directories, and organizational charts—all in the name of "increased efficiency," "better communications," and "improved company morale." The result is an unproductive employee who creates needless work for people around him.

THE BOTTOM LINE

The bottom line in deciding if you want desktop publishing for your home or business is your answer to this question: Will it save you time and money? The following guidelines, if followed, will help you avoid desktop publishing pitfalls:

- Be prepared to hire a professional designer/artist or to spend the time and money to train current personnel.

- Establish clear guidelines for what you want published and who you want to publish it. An experienced designer using desktop publishing may be able to prepare most of the company publications, especially newsletters, reports, and user's manuals, but you may still want to hire, for example, an advertising agency to prepare your material for a national advertisement campaign.

- Monitor the work of desktop publishers. Make sure they are following established guidelines and avoiding unnecessary projects. If you are the desktop publisher, take a hard look at your own work. Is it prepared according to established principles of design? Is it saving you time and money? Is it necessary?

- Prepare WordPerfect styles and macros (see Chapter 14, "Using Styles," and Chapter 15, "Using Macros") for use throughout the company. This will (1) provide a standard company design, (2) prevent unauthorized personnel from wasting time at page design and layout, (3) discourage proliferation of unnecessary publications.

With awareness and planning, you and your company can benefit substantially from desktop publishing.

WORDPERFECT VS. PAGE LAYOUT PROGRAMS

Until recently, the primary tool for desktop publishing was a page layout program such as PageMaker or Ventura Publisher. With the advent of WordPerfect series 5, desktop publishing and word processing merged into a single software package. WordPerfect supports all the major features required for desktop publishing—graphics (displaying, cropping, rotating, inverting, and scaling figures), lines (horizontal and vertical rules), boxes, fonts (typefaces, sizes, appearances, and colors), and special characters (true quote marks, em dashes, en dashes, mathematical and scientific symbols, etc.).

But can WordPerfect stand up to PageMaker and Ventura Publisher? The answer depends upon your desktop publishing goals and needs. The following are the advantages of WordPerfect over a dedicated page layout program for desktop publishing:

- WordPerfect is familiar. You can use what you already know about WordPerfect, learn additional WordPerfect features specific to desktop publishing, and understand the principles of publication design in order to use WordPerfect for desktop publishing. Learning a page layout program, on the other hand, takes a significant investment of time and money.

- WordPerfect provides free fonts and clip art, and with a modest additional investment, you can purchase other fonts and artwork. Most page layout programs do not supply these items.

- WordPerfect surpasses all page layout programs in working with words and managing documents. For example, WordPerfect checks your spelling, produces tables of contents and indexes, generates footnotes and endnotes, numbers items, and sorts lists. Page layout programs have few, if any, of these features.

- WordPerfect provides other advanced features not normally included with page layout programs: styles, macros, search-and-replace, widow/orphan protection, and automatic document assembly.

- Future versions of WordPerfect will have even more desktop publishing features. At some point, moreover, WordPerfect may match or exceed the page layout features of a PageMaker or Ventura Publisher.

The following are advantages that dedicated page layout programs have over WordPerfect.

- Page layout programs show the document pages while they are being created and edited. This is the greatest advantage of a page layout program over WordPerfect. With WordPerfect, you have to create and edit fonts, special characters, graphics, lines, and boxes without actually seeing what you are doing and then use the View Document feature to see how the page actually looks. With a page layout program, you can see the different fonts, lines, boxes, and so forth, as you create them.

- Page layout programs allow you to *draw* lines, boxes, and circles directly on the screen. With WordPerfect, you don't literally *draw* but rather *create* the objects by specifying their size and location.

- Page layout programs usually support creation of circles, diagonal lines, drop shadows, rounded corners, and other special effects that are absent from or difficult to produce in WordPerfect.

- Page layout programs are more powerful and flexible in managing text that starts on one page and continues on another.

So what should be your choice, WordPerfect or a page layout program? If you are a professional publisher, if desktop publishing is your major job task, or if you need to produce a wide variety of short and long publications, then you should probably use a dedicated page layout program rather than WordPerfect. But if desktop publishing is a small part of your job description, if you have to produce long publications (books and manuals) rather than short documents (advertisements, flyers, etc.), or if you can't afford both a high performance word processor and a page layout program, then WordPerfect is for you. Of course, some individuals and companies will want to purchase both WordPerfect and a page layout program and then use the program that best fits the job: WordPerfect for letterheads, blank forms, annual reports, long catalogs, books, and manuals, and a page layout program for newsletters, flyers, advertisements, short brochures, and short catalogs.

WHAT YOU NEED (OR WANT) IN HARDWARE

In order to do desktop publishing with WordPerfect, you will need the following hardware:

- An *IBM PC/XT/AT or PS/2 or compatible* with 640 Kb (kilobytes) of memory. You can get by with 386 Kb, but 640 Kb or more is highly recommended.

- *Two floppy disk drives, or one floppy disk drive and one hard disk drive.* The floppy drives may be 5.25″ or 3.5″. We strongly recommend that you purchase a hard disk drive.

- A *graphics card and color monitor.* Although you can get by with a monochrome monitor for normal word processing, you must have a graphics card and color monitor for desktop publishing. The color graphics adapter (CGA) is adequate, but the enhanced graphics adapter (EGA) or the new video graphics array (VGA) are preferred.

- A *laser printer.* A dot matrix printer will serve adequately for previewing desktop published material, but if you are serious about desktop publishing, you will need a laser printer.

- *A mouse.* For word processing with WordPerfect, a mouse is nice, but not necessary. For graphics programs, on the other hand, a mouse is essential. See Appendix D, "Directory of Products," for a list of mouse suppliers.

- A *scanner* (digitizer). If you want to include photographs or pictures from other printed material, a graphics scanner or digitizer is required. This is a helpful, but not necessary, hardware accessory for desktop publishing.

WHAT YOU NEED (OR WANT) IN SOFTWARE

You will need (or want) the following software packages for desktop publishing with WordPerfect:

- The *WordPerfect* 5.1 (or later version) word processing software for IBM computers and compatibles.

- *MS-DOS* or *PC-DOS* version 2.0 or later, and preferably version 3.0 or later. DOS is the disk operating system that was shipped with your computer or can be purchased from your local computer dealer.

- A *graphics software* package. Publications require figures, charts, and graphs. If you have to create your own computer graphics, you need a graphics draw or paint program. See Chapter 8, "Creating Graphics."

- *Soft fonts*. Laser printers have anywhere from three to a hundred built-in fonts. For example, the popular Hewlett-Packard Laser-Jet Series II comes standard with six built-in fonts, an insufficient number to do anything but the simplest desktop publishing. If you're serious about desktop publishing and your printer has a limited number of built-in fonts, you need additional fonts that the computer system can transfer (download) from a disk into printer memory. See Chapter 10, "Installing Fonts."

- *Clip art*. One way of getting graphics for your publications is through clip art, software files that include high-quality art of all types for all occasions. See Appendix D, "Directory of Products," for clip art suppliers.

WARNING: PRINTER DIFFERENCES

WordPerfect supports a wide variety of printers: impact printers, 9-pin dot matrix printers, 24-pin dot matrix printers, inkjet printers, non-PostScript laser printers, and PostScript laser printers. This book shows sample documents that will work on some printers but not on others. If your printer doesn't support a feature in exactly the same way as the authors' printer, your documents will not look quite like the figures in the book. In the step-by-step procedures, just try to reproduce the features as best you can.

CONVENTIONAL WISDOM: HOW TO USE THIS BOOK

We will follow a standard convention throughout this book to tell you what you should see on the computer monitor (screen), what keys to press, and what phrases to type:

- Monitor output appears in boldface type:
  Current date is Tue 1-01-1980
  Enter new data (mm-dd-yy):
  Doc 1 Pg 1 Ln 1″ Pos 1″

- Words or phrases that you should type appear in the monospace typeface:

  ```
  2-8-89
  diskcopy a: b:
  the quick brown fox
  ```

- Keys that you should press (i.e., the letters, numbers, and characters, and names of special keys on your keyboard) appear in boldface type:
  A, c, 2, $, Enter, Tab, Home, Up Arrow, Num Lock

- Key combinations are indicated with a hyphen between the two keys:
  Ctrl-V
  Shift-F5

  This means that you should press the first key and hold it down while pressing the second. For example, **Ctrl-Home** means that you should press the key labeled **Ctrl** (Control) and, while holding it down, tap the key labeled **Home.**

- The names of WordPerfect function key commands and pull-down menu options also appear in boldface type (with the actual keystrokes in normal typeface and in parentheses):
  Underline (F8)
  Date/Outline (Shift-F5)
  Spell (Ctrl-F2)
  Macro (Alt-F10)
  Compose (Ctrl-2 or Ctrl-V)

- The key you should press to select a menu item is also given in boldface type (with the menu item name given in parentheses):
  2 (**P**age), **3** (**H**eader), **1** (Header **A**), **2** (Every **P**age)
  The menu item name usually has one character in boldface type;

this is an alternate (mnemonic) key that you can press instead of the number in selecting the menu item.

- Comments, descriptions, or names of commands are often set off with parentheses. Do *not* type the parentheses or the information they enclose unless the phrase appears in monospace type.

- Commas and spaces separating items in a sequence of characters, phrases, and commands, or periods at the end of a sequence should *not* be typed unless you are explicitly told to do so. For example, in this sequence of keypresses **2** (**P**age), **3** (**H**eader), **1** (Header **A**), **2** (Every **P**age) you should type only **2312**, not the parentheses, the information in parentheses, the commas, or the spaces. You may, alternatively, press the bold letter in the command name instead of the number; in this sequence, for example, you could type **PHAP** instead of **2312**.

- When you are told to *enter* a word or phrase, you should type the information and then press **Enter**. You will not necessarily be told to press the **Enter** key but should do so on your own.

Most of these conventions follow the conventions used in the *WordPerfect Workbook* and the WordPerfect reference manual. Even without a knowledge of these conventions, however, you will usually be able to tell from the context of the instruction what you should type.

HOW TO ORDER THE COMPANION DISKS

The authors are making available all the macros, macro programs, styles, keyboard layout files, and publications (documents) in this book. These files have been placed on two 5.25″ disks. In addition, the disks contain the following:

- For business managers and secretaries: a library of styles and macros that you can customize for your own business needs and that will help you automate document preparation.

- For social scientists and educators: a library of styles and macros that will help you format and footnote your reports and professional papers in the standard APA (American Psychological Association) style.

- For scientists: a library of styles and macros that will help you format and footnote your scientific papers in the standard ACS

(American Chemical Society) or APS (American Physical Society) style. You can easily customize the WordPerfect styles and macros for a particular scientific journal.

- The utility program WPMOUT for printing macro programs or converting them to WordPerfect-readable text files that can be formatted and printed. WPMOUT is an indispensable tool for anyone using the WordPerfect macro language to write macro programs.

- Sample macro programs that demonstrate advanced macro techniques and applications. These programs are heavily commented to help you follow the logic and apply programming techniques to your own word processing needs.

To order your *Desktop Publishing with WordPerfect* companion disks, send a check, money order, or credit card number and expiration date, in the amount of $19.95 (U.S. dollars only) for each set of disks. Add $5.00 for shipping and handling outside the U.S. or for UPS shipping within the U.S. Send your name, address (including zip code), telephone number (in case we have questions about your order), and payment to Zimtech, 623 East Heather Road, Orem, UT 84057.

Chapter 2

Using WordPerfect

This book assumes that you have properly installed and have used WordPerfect (version 5.1 or later) on your computer. If you have questions about setting up WordPerfect, upgrading to 5.1, or using the basic features of WordPerfect, consult your WordPerfect user's manual or one of the books listed in Appendix C under "Additional Reading."

This chapter will review some of the important aspects of using WordPerfect. If you are an experienced WordPerfect user, you may skip this chapter and go on to Chapter 3, "Designing Documents."

The chapter covers the following:

- How to use the WordPerfect status line, the function keys, and the repeating keys.

- How to use WordPerfect pull-down menus and a mouse.

- How to cancel commands and get help within WordPerfect.

- How to display WordPerfect codes in the Reveal Codes window.

- How to use WordPerfect's cut-and-paste and block features.

- How to prepare documents.

- How to configure WordPerfect for the printer used by your computer system.

USING THE WORDPERFECT STATUS LINE

When you first start WordPerfect, you see a screen that is blank except for two items—the cursor (the flashing underbar) in the upper left corner of the screen and the status line at the lower right of your screen. The status line indicates where the cursor is located on the page and other important information.

When you first turn *on* WordPerfect, the cursor is located at the top left of the screen, and the status line reads
Doc 1 Pg 1 Ln 1″ Pos 1″

- **Doc 1** indicates that you are typing document 1.

  WordPerfect allows you to work on two documents at once. For now, you should remain in document 1.

- **Pg 1** indicates that you are currently typing on the first page of your document.

  This number will change automatically as you go to the next page.

- **Ln 1″** indicates that the current line is one inch from the top of the paper.

  This number will increase automatically as you proceed to the next line.

- **Pos 1″** indicates that the horizontal position of the cursor is one inch from the left edge of the paper.

  This number changes automatically as you type each character. In addition, the **Pos** number indicates the current font (bold, underline, italics, redline, subscript, etc.) according to the code used by your monitor. Furthermore, when the Caps Lock is *on*, the word **POS** appears in all-capitalized letters; when the Num Lock is *on*, the word **Pos** flashes.

The left edge status line also displays messages when certain WordPerfect features are active, for example:

- **Macro Def** indicates that a macro is being defined and that every key pressed and every command executed will become part of the macro.

- **Block on** indicates that the highlighted text has been defined as a block and will be acted upon as a unit.

- **Typeover** indicates that typed characters will replace existing text rather than be inserted in front of existing text.

- **Merge** indicates that a merge is being executed.

- **C:\WP51\FILENAME.EXT** indicates the pathname of the current document once it has been saved to, or retrieved from, the disk.

More than one of these messages (and/or others) may appear on the status line at a time.

USING THE FUNCTION KEYS

The function keys are used alone or in conjunction with the modifier keys to perform the special WordPerfect features indicated on the function-key template. The position of the feature and the color code indicate which modifier key should be held down with a function key to evoke a specific WordPerfect feature (see Figure 2.1).

For example, the F6 function key activates four separate features: Ctrl-F6 is the Tab Align feature; Shift-F6 is the Center feature; Alt-F6 is the Flush Right feature; and F6 is the Bold feature.

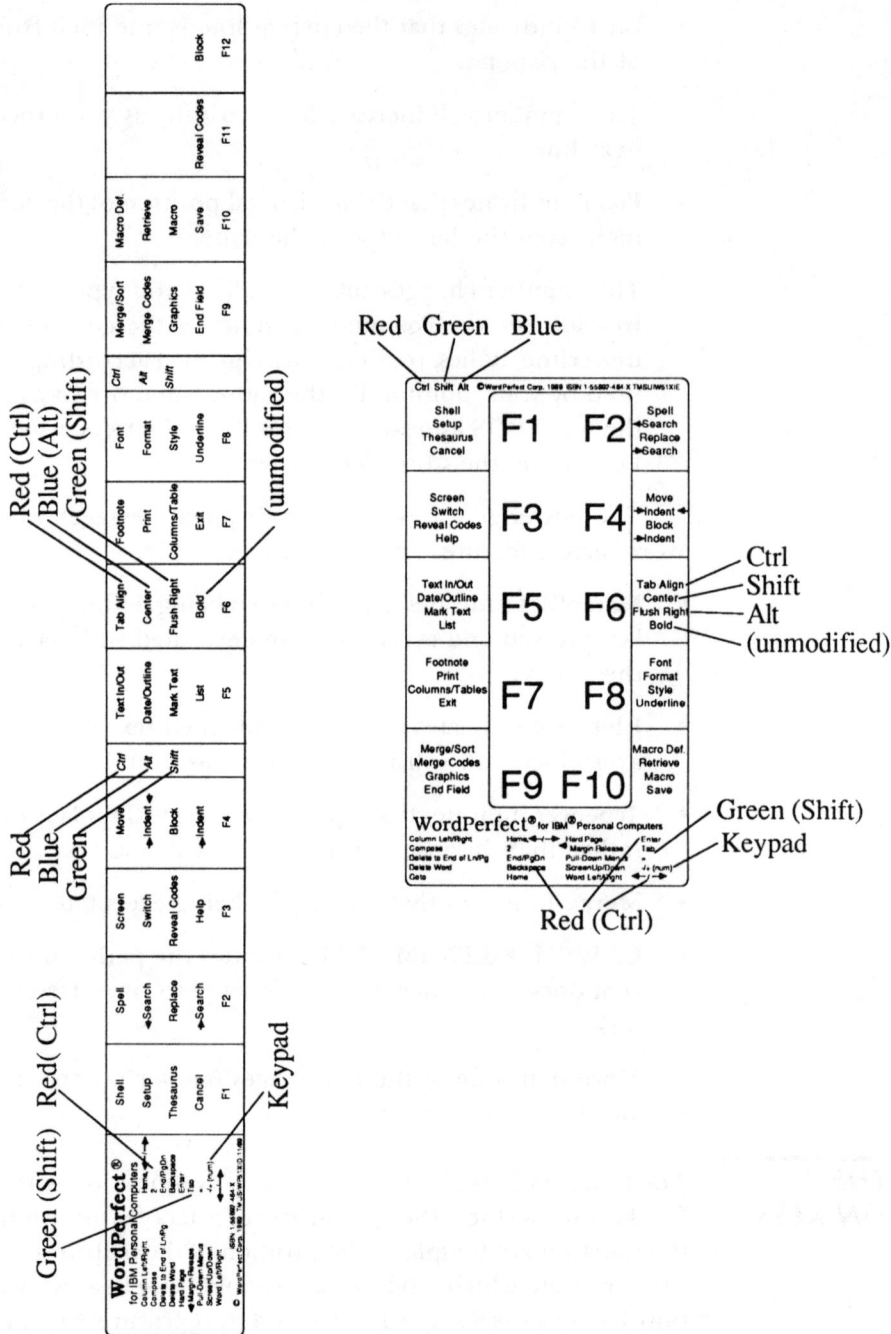

Figure 2.1 The Function Key Template indicating the WordPerfect features.

REPEATING KEY COMMANDS

Most of the keys on the keyboard repeat themselves when you hold them down. This can cause problems for heavy-handed typists. For example, if you depress the **A** key and hold it down, it will continue to print A's across the screen until you release the key. Likewise, if you press and hold down the Backspace key, it will continue to erase until you release it.

You can also cause undesirable results if you hold down a function key too long. Although you must hold down a *modifier* key (Ctrl, Shift, or Alt) while using a function key, you should *not* press and hold down the function key itself. Just tap the key lightly. If you do hold down the function key too long, the screen message will flicker until you release the function key.

In addition, some keys are "toggle" keys. That means you press them to turn a feature *on* and then press them again to turn the feature *off*. For example, holding down the Alt key and tapping F4 will turn the Block feature *on*. Repeating that command (holding down the Alt key and tapping F4) will turn the Block feature *off*.

USING PULL-DOWN MENUS AND THE MOUSE

WordPerfect 5.1 and later versions support pull-down menus and mouse commands. If your computer system comes equipped with a mouse, press the right-hand button of the mouse to activate the main menu. The following appears across the top of the screen:
File **E**dit **S**earch **L**ayout **M**ark **T**ools **F**ont **G**raphics **H**elp
Now move the mouse pointer (a block character) to the desired menu item, and click the left button of the mouse. A pull-down menu appears on the screen. To select an option within a pull-down menu, move the mouse pointer to the item and click the left button again.

Even if you don't have a mouse, you can still use the pull-down menus. To set up this feature, do the following: From within WordPerfect, press **Setup** (Shift-F1), **4** (Menu Options), **4** (Alt Key Selects Pull-Down Menu), **Y** (Yes) to use the Alt key for evoking the pull-down menus, and **Exit** (F7) to return to the main document screen.

Now, to evoke the main menu across the top of the screen, press and release the **Alt** key. Then use the **Right Arrow** and **Left Arrow** to highlight the desired item within the main menu, and press **Enter** or **Down Arrow** to evoke the pull-down menu underneath the main menu item. Finally, press **Up Arrow** or **Down Arrow** to highlight the desired command, and press **Enter**. The command is executed.

Each option within the pull-down menus corresponds to a keyboard command. In this book, we will give you only the keyboard commands to evoke a particular WordPerfect feature, but you can use the pull-down menus any time you wish.

You can also use the mouse to move the cursor. Simply move the mouse pointer to the desired location on the screen and click the left mouse button. The cursor moves to the indicated location.

Pressing both mouse buttons at once is equivalent to pressing **Cancel** (F1).

Finally, you can use the mouse to select a block of text, just as if you had pressed **Block** (Alt-F4) and used the arrow keys to highlight the desired text. To use the mouse, move the mouse pointer to the beginning of the block of text, press and hold down the left button, and drag the mouse over the text you want to highlight. Then you can use either the keyboard commands or the pull-down menus to manipulate the block of text.

You should consult your WordPerfect user's manual for more information on using the mouse.

CANCELING COMMANDS AND GETTING HELP

Two features that are helpful when you are first learning WordPerfect or when you find you do not know which keys to press are Cancel (F1) and Help (F3).

The Cancel Feature

In the normal course of word processing, you will occasionally press the wrong key. You should use Backspace to erase an accidental Enter, Tab, Center, Bold, or Underline command and then continue typing. Use Cancel (F1) to back out of a WordPerfect prompt or message, to cancel a WordPerfect hyphenation request (when hyphenation is *on*), or to recover up to three levels of deleted text.

For example, if you accidentally press Exit (F7), the Save Document prompt appears at the bottom left of the screen. Pressing Cancel (F1) will cancel the Exit feature and return you to your document.

The Help Feature

The Help feature (F3) allows you to access the Help Directory (see Figure 2.2). You can get help on any WordPerfect feature by simply pressing the corresponding function key. Or you can press a letter to get an alphabetical list of WordPerfect features and the keys you use to execute that feature. In addition, pressing those keys will bring a brief explanation of the feature onto the screen.

For example, suppose you need information on how the Retrieve Text feature works. You could press Help (F3) to access the WordPerfect Help Directory and then press Retrieve (Shift-F10). WordPerfect

```
Help                    License #. (number)      WP 5.1  (release date)



     Press any letter to get an alphabetical list of features.

          The list will include the features that start with the letter,
          along with the name of the key where the feature is found.  You
          can then press that key to get a description of how the feature
          works.




     Press any function key to get information about the use of the key.

          Some keys may let you choose from a menu to get more information
          about various options.  Press HELP again to display the template.




     Press Enter or Space bar to exit Help.
```

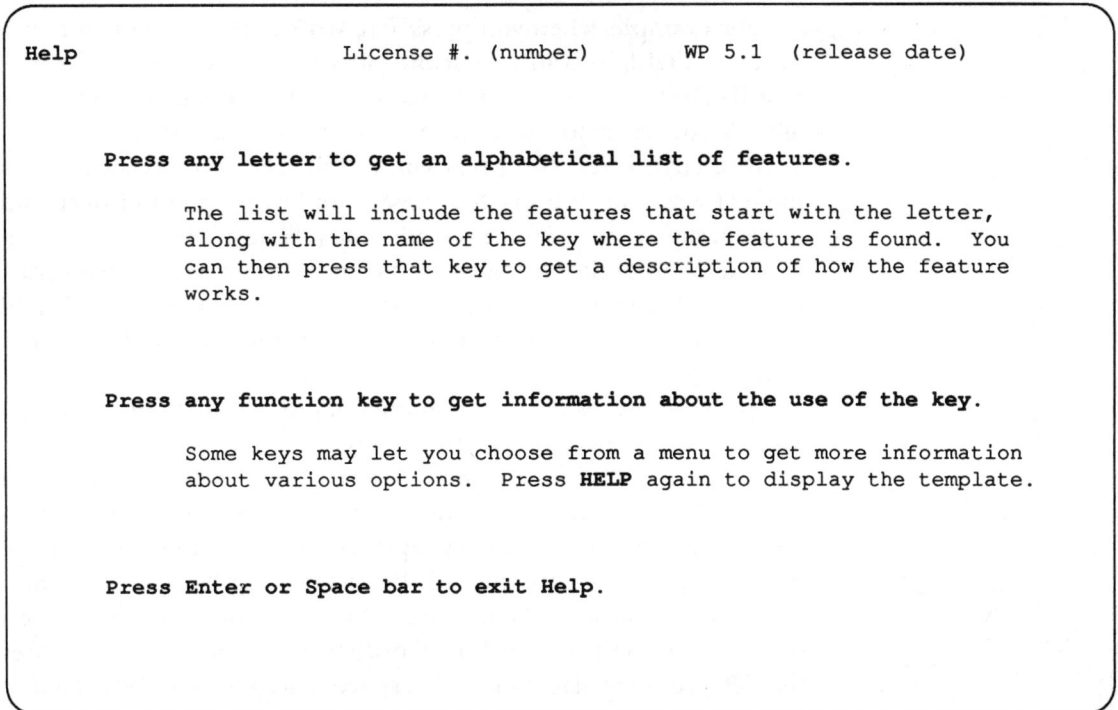

Figure 2.2   The WordPerfect Help feature.

would display an explanation of Retrieve Text. Or, you could press Help (F3) to access the Help Directory and then press **R**. WordPerfect would display a list of features beginning with the letter R and would indicate that information on Retrieve could be found by pressing Shift-F10.

After you get the information you want, you should press the Space Bar to exit the Help Directory and return to your document.

REVEALING FORMAT CODES

As you type words and perform word processing functions, Word-Perfect places special *codes* in your document to indicate such things as the end of a line, the end of a page, a change in the margins, and a figure or line. These codes, which are normally hidden from view, also mark the text to center a title, boldface a heading, underline a phrase, indent a paragraph, and do all the other necessary formatting chores. Whenever WordPerfect displays your document on the monitor screen or sends it to the printer, the hidden codes serve as signals to tell WordPerfect how the text should appear.

For example, when you press Tab, WordPerfect places an invisible code, **[Tab]**, in your text at the cursor. From then on, whenever WordPerfect displays or prints that part of your document, the code tells WordPerfect to move the text to the next tab stop.

Similarly, when you press Underline (F8), WordPerfect marks the text with the codes **[UND]** (begin underlining) and **[und]** (end underlining). When you press Underline (F8) again, the cursor moves beyond the underlining code and the underlining ends. Other codes, for example, mark the beginning and end of bold type **[BOLD]** and **[bold]**, and the beginning and end of centered text **[Cntr]** and **[C/A/Flrt]**.

Some codes result from user commands, while others occur automatically. For example, when you press Enter at the end of a paragraph, you are marking the text with the code **[HRt]**, meaning "Hard Return." On the other hand, when your typing reaches the right margin, WordPerfect automatically replaces the space after the last word that fits on the line with the code **[SRt]**, meaning "Soft Return," causing the text to wrap to the next line. If you later delete or add a word or phrase in the previous line, WordPerfect automatically removes the **[SRt]** code (replacing it with a space) and places a **[SRt]** at a new location in your text to maintain the proper line length. The **[HRt]** code, on the other hand, remains at the same location in your text until you delete it.

Displaying the Reveal Codes Window

Fortunately, these codes do not appear on the normal WordPerfect screen. Instead, you see the text more or less as it will appear on the printed page. When you want to see the codes, press Reveal Codes (Alt-F3) and the Reveal Codes window appears. Figure 2.3 shows the normal text window on the top half of the screen and the Reveal Codes window at the bottom of the screen as it appears for the document OWLBOOKS.INV.

Note the following about the Reveal Codes window:

- The cursor is shown in reverse video.

- The Document and Reveal Codes windows are approximately the same size and are divided by a reverse-video bar marked with triangles that represent the tab settings.

- You can move through text and codes with any of the cursor keys.

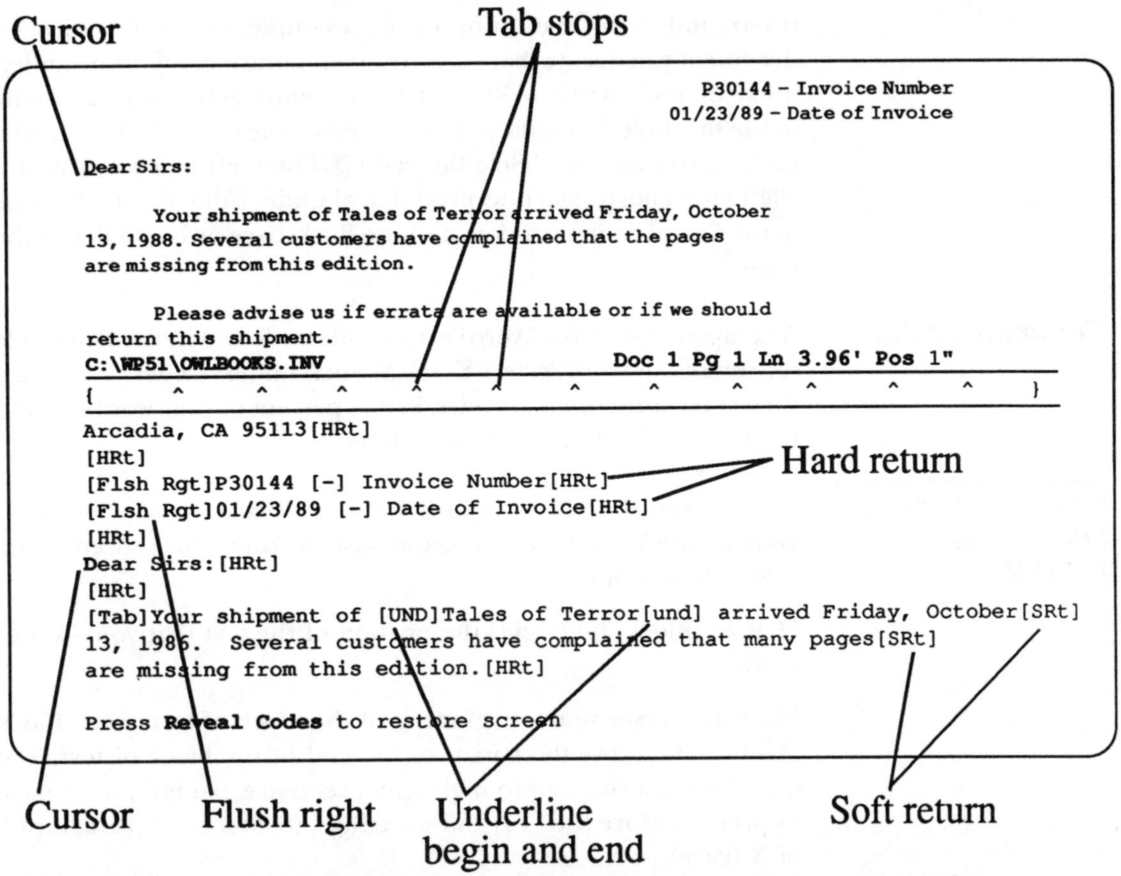

Cursor   **Tab stops**

```
                                              P30144 – Invoice Number
                                              01/23/89 – Date of Invoice


Dear Sirs:

        Your shipment of Tales of Terror arrived Friday, October
13, 1988. Several customers have complained that the pages
are missing from this edition.

        Please advise us if errata are available or if we should
return this shipment.
C:\WP51\OWLBOOKS.INV                          Doc 1 Pg 1 Ln 3.96' Pos 1"
{      ^      ^      ^      ^      ^      ^      ^      ^      ^      ^      }
```

```
Arcadia, CA 95113[HRt]
[HRt]
[Flsh Rgt]P30144 [-] Invoice Number[HRt]          Hard return
[Flsh Rgt]01/23/89 [-] Date of Invoice[HRt]
[HRt]
Dear Sirs:[HRt]
[HRt]
[Tab]Your shipment of [UND]Tales of Terror[und] arrived Friday, October[SRt]
13, 1988.  Several customers have complained that many pages[SRt]
are missing from this edition.[HRt]

Press Reveal Codes to restore screen
```

Cursor   Flush right   Underline   Soft return
                           begin and end

Figure 2.3   The Reveal Codes window as it appears for the document OWLBOOKS.INV.

- You can use any WordPerfect feature (such as Underline) while in the Reveal Codes screen.

- You can delete text and codes within the Reveal Codes window by using Backspace or Del. When the Reveal Codes window is hidden, WordPerfect asks you to verify the deletion of most codes, but when the Reveal Codes window is on the screen, WordPerfect does not ask for verification.

- You must press Reveal Codes (Alt-F3) to exit the Reveal Codes screen and return the document screen to its normal size.

Deleting and Inserting Codes

Understanding the codes in WordPerfect is important, because you can edit (delete, insert, and move) codes just as you can edit (delete, insert, and move) text. Suppose, for example, that while editing a document you decide that an underlined phrase shouldn't be underlined after all. With the Reveal Codes window active, you can easily delete the underline code **[UND]** and eliminate the underlining. Similarly, if you want to delete the code **[HLine:Left & Right,6",0.01", 100%]** for a horizontal line, press Reveal Codes (Alt-F3), find the code in the Reveal Codes window, and use Backspace or Del to delete the code.

Common Codes

A complete list of the WordPerfect codes is found in the Reference section of the WordPerfect User's Manual under "Codes." Figure 2.4 shows the more common codes. Eighty percent of your word processing will involve the codes listed here.

MOVING TEXT, LINES, AND FIGURES

To move text, lines, and figures from one place in a document to another, use WordPerfect's cut-and-paste feature. This procedure involves three steps:

Step 1. Block (highlight) the portion of the text that you want to move.

Move the cursor to the beginning of the block of text, press **Block** (Alt-F4), and move the cursor to the end of the block of text. You can also use a shortcut to highlight a sentence, paragraph, or page by pressing **Move** (Ctrl-F4) and selecting **1** (**Sentence**), **2** (**Paragraph**), or **3** (**Page**).

Step 2. Cut (remove) the selected block of text from the document.

With Block *on*, press **Move** (Ctrl-F4), **1** (**Block**), and **1** (**Move**). With a sentence, paragraph, or page selected, just press **1** (**Move**).

Step 3. Move the cursor to a new location and then press **Enter** to paste (insert) the selected text back into the document at the new location.

To move a figure or line, press **Reveal Codes** (Alt-F3), move the cursor to the left of the figure or line code, press **Block** (Alt-F4), **Right Arrow** (to highlight the code), **Move** (Ctrl-F4), **1** (**Block**), and **1** (**Move**), move the cursor to the desired new location, and press **Enter**.

You can also copy text, figures, or lines by using the same three steps given above except, in step 2, press **Move** (Ctrl-F4), **2** (**Block**), and **2** (**Copy**).

Common WordPerfect Codes	
[ ]	Hard space
[-]	Hyphen
-	Soft hyphen
/	Cancel hyphenation
[Dec Tab]	Decimal align in Tab
[BOLD] [bold]	Bold begin and end
[Block]	Block begin
[Center]	Center begin and end
[Center Pg]	Center page top to bottom
[Col Def]	Column definition
[Col On] [Col Off]	Text columns beginning and end
[Fig Box]	Figure box
[HPg]	Hard page
[HRt]	Hard return
[HLine]	Horizontal line
[Hyph On/Off]	Hyphenation on and off
[→Indent]	Indent
[→Indent←]	Indent left and right
[Just:Right]	Right justification
[L/R Mar:n,n]	Left and right margins
[Footnote:n;[Note Num]...]	Footnote reference
[Ln Spacing:n]	Spacing ($n = 1$ for single, etc.)
[SPg]	Soft new page
[SRt]	Soft return
[SUBSCPT] [subscpt]	Subscript
[SUPRSCPT] [suprscpt]	Superscript
[Tab]	Move to next tab stop
[T/B Mar:n,n]	Top and bottom margins
[Text Box]	Text box
[UND] [und]	Underlining
[Usr Box]	User-defined box
[VLine]	Vertical line
[W/O]	Widow/ Orphan

Figure 2.4 A list of common WordPerfect codes.

USING BLOCKS

Desktop publishers will find WordPerfect Block features especially valuable for changing, centering, and deleting text. A complete list of the block features is shown in Figure 2.5. To use the block features, highlight a block of text with the Block (Alt-F4) command or with the mouse and then select the appropriate WordPerfect command to execute those features.

PREPARING DOCUMENTS

To prepare a document, follow these general steps:

Step 1. Specify the general format of the document by using the features on the **Format** (Shift-F8) command and on other WordPerfect commands.

Step 2. Specify the base font by pressing **Font** (Ctrl-F8), **4** (Base Font), and selecting the desired typeface.

Block Features	
Append	Add block to the end of an existing file
Bold	Boldface block
Case Convert	Switch all characters in block to uppercase or lowercase
Center	Center block horizontally
Copy	Make a copy of block at another location in document
Cut	Remove block and insert it at another location in document
Delete	Erase block
Flush Right	Align block against the right margin
Font	Change the size and appearance of block
Macro	Macro acts upon block
Mark Text	Mark block for lists, index, table of contents
Move	Move block to another location in document
Print	Send block to the printer
Replace	Replace words, phrase, or codes within block
Save	Save block to the disk
Search	Search for text or codes within block
Shell	Append or save block to the clipboard
Sort	Sort the lines or records within block
Spell	Check the spelling of block
Style	Insert formatting codes within block
Switch	Same as case conversion
Text In/Out	Save block as a text file
Underline	Underline block

Figure 2.5   A list of the WordPerfect Block features.

Step 3. Within WordPerfect, type the text of the document and insert desired symbols, lines, text boxes, and graphics.

Step 4. Make any desired format changes as you type the document.

Step 5. Edit the document using standard edit keys and cut-and-paste operations; check the spelling with **Spell** (Ctrl-F2); and insert page numbers, headers, footers, table of contents, index, lists, etc., as desired.

Step 6. Save the document to the disk with the **Save** (F10) command.

Step 7. Print the document with the **Print** (Shift-F7) command (see the next section, "Configuring Your Printer").

The remainder of this book will provide detailed examples of how to apply these steps specifically for desktop publishing.

CONFIGURING YOUR PRINTER

Your task now is to tell WordPerfect which printer you are using. We assume that you have only one printer and that it is connected to your computer in the normal way. (If you have more than one printer, check with your dealer, if necessary, to find out the printer port through which each printer is attached to your computer.)
   To tell WordPerfect about your printer, you need the following:

• WordPerfect 5.1 installed on your hard disk.

• The printer disks—labeled *Printer 1*, *Printer 2*, etc. (or backups of these disks).

• A knowledge of the brand and model of your printer. You may need to check your printer user's manual to get this information.

Get into WordPerfect, then follow these steps to configure your printer:

Step 1. Press **Print** (Shift-F7).

WordPerfect displays the Print and Options menu, as shown in Figure 2.6.

Step 2. Press **S** (Select) to select a printer.

WordPerfect displays the following menu at the bottom of the screen: **1 S**elect; **2 A**dditional Printers; **3 E**dit; **4 C**opy; **5 D**elete; **6 H**elp; **7** Update: **1**

```
Print

     1 - Full Document
     2 - Page
     3 - Document on Disk
     4 - Control Printer
     5 - Multiple Pages
     6 - View Document
     7 - Initialize Printer

Options

     S - Select Printer
     B - Binding Offset              0"
     N - Number of Copies            1
     U - Multiple Copies Generated by    WordPerfect
     G - Graphics Quality            Medium
     T - Text Quality                High




Selection: 0
```

Figure 2.6   The WordPerfect Print and Options Menu, displayed after pressing **Print** (Shift-F7).

These menu items have the following meanings:

1 (Select) chooses the printer currently highlighted as the printer in use. Since you haven't specified a printer yet, no printer is listed (or highlighted), and therefore no printer can be selected at this point.

2 (Additional Printers) adds printers to the current list.

3 (Edit) allows you to change the current printer options, such as the printer name, output port, and initial font.

4 (Copy) copies the current printer definition to another file.

5 (Delete) removes the highlighted printer from the list of printers.

6 (Help) displays helpful information and hints about using the highlighted printer.

Step 3.   Place the *Printer 1* disk into drive A (or B if you have a floppy-drive system), press **2** (**A**dditional Printers), press **2** again (**O**ther Disk), type a: (or b: if you have a floppy-drive system) and press **Enter**.

WordPerfect displays a list of printer brands and models.

Step 4.   Press **Down Arrow** to move the highlight bar down the list of printers. Continue pressing **Down Arrow** until your printer is highlighted or until you have reached the end of the list.

Step 5.   If your printer is not listed on the screen, remove the current printer disk from drive A (or B), press **2** (**O**ther Disk), type a: (or b: if you have a floppy-drive system), press **Enter**, and go back to step 3.

If your printer is listed on the screen, make sure it is highlighted (use the Up Arrow or Down Arrow keys), and go on to the next step. If you have gone completely through all of the printer disks and your printer appears on none of them, call WordPerfect customer support at (800) 321-5097 (toll free) or (801) 226-7977 (*not* toll free). The WordPerfect representative may be able to suggest a printer that is compatible with your brand and model.

Step 6.   Press **1** (**S**elect).

WordPerfect displays the name of the printer file. For example, **Printer filename: HPLASEII.PRS** or some other filename with the .PRS extension.

Step 7.   Press **Enter** to accept the displayed printer filename.

WordPerfect loads the printer definition file into your WordPerfect directory or onto your *WordPerfect 1* disk and then displays the Printer Helps and Hints screen for your printer.

Step 8.   Press **Exit** (F7) to exit the Printer Helps and Hints screen.

WordPerfect then displays the Select Printer: Edit menu. You usually do not need to make any changes here. However, if your printer port is not LPT1:, for example, you should press **2** (**P**ort) and enter the proper printer port. Moreover, if your printer supports different fonts, you may wish to press **6** (**I**nitial fonts) and follow the directions to change the initial font to Times Roman, for example.

Step 9.   Press **Exit** (F7) to exit the Select Printer: Edit menu and return to the Print: Select Printer menu.

Step 10.   With the name of your printer highlighted, press **1** (Select).

WordPerfect returns you to the Print menu.

Step 11.   Press **Exit** (F7) or **0** to exit the Print menu and return to the document screen.

Your WordPerfect is now ready to go. You may wish, however, to use the WordPerfect **Setup** (Shift-F1) feature to make any other changes to WordPerfect before you type documents and create publications.

SUMMARY

In this chapter you have reviewed how to start WordPerfect; how to use the WordPerfect status line, the keyboard, the function keys, the pull-down menus, and the repeat features of the keyboard; how to cancel commands and get help; how to use the Reveal Codes window; how to cut-and-paste text and use WordPerfect block features; how to prepare documents; and how to configure your printer.

Chapter 3

Designing Documents

The goal of desktop publishing is to enhance the appearance and readability of printed matter. To reach this goal, you must follow certain basic elements of design. Ignoring these elements will result in either drab or gaudy documents that detract from, rather than enhance, your message.

This chapter will cover the following:

- The six steps in preparing a publication.

- The eight elements of design that help you produce attractive and readable publications.

PREPARING A PUBLICATION

Figure 3.1 shows the six steps required to prepare a publication.

Design the Document

Your first step is to design the document. You must answer such questions as:

- What will be the overall layout, including the margins, column widths, and placement of figures?

- What will be the font typeface, font size, and font appearance of the main body of text and of the titles, heads, and captions?

- What will be the content, including text and figures?

The principles of design are covered below in detail.

Write the Copy

You or someone else in your company or family has to write the copy (the main text) of the publication. You have to decide:

- What should the publication include? The answer will depend, of course, on whether the publication is company correspondence, a newsletter, an advertisement brochure, a training manual, or something else.

- Who should write the copy? If you're doing a family newsletter, you will probably have to do most of the writing. If it's a company newsletter, it might have many writers, from company management to employees.

- What will be the writing style? The answer depends on the type of document and the audience. If you are producing a newsletter for fellow employees, the tone may be light and casual. If

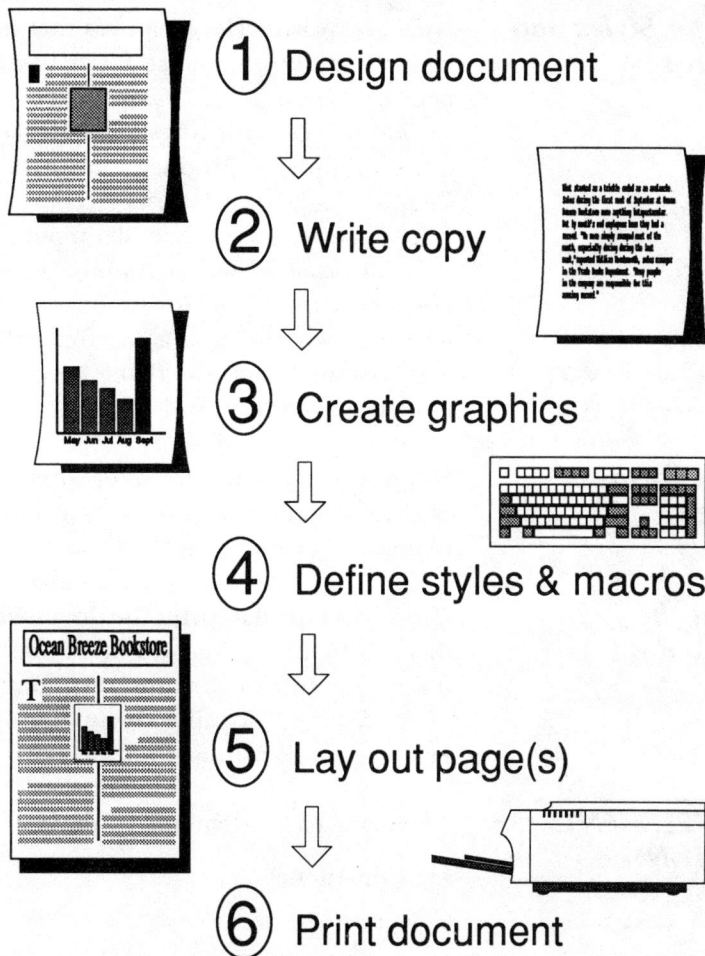

Figure 3.1 The six steps for preparing a publication.

it's for stockholders, you may want the writing to be more formal. Regardless of the style, the writing should be simple, clear, lively, and warm.

Create the Graphics

What is a publication without graphics? A picture may not be worth a thousand words, but it does create interest and help explain a point. Chapters 8 ("Creating Graphics") and 9 ("Displaying Graphics") will help you with this part of your publication.

Define Styles and Macros

Styles are WordPerfect features that help you create formats, titles, heads, lines, boxes, and so forth, in a consistent and efficient manner. See Chapter 14, "Using Styles."

Macros are recordings of keystrokes. They will make your publications simpler to produce, more accurate, and more consistent. See Chapter 15, "Using Macros."

Of course you *can* do desktop publishing without styles or macros, and you *should* do desktop publishing without them if you don't know how to use them. Obviously, one of the purposes of this book is to improve your ability as a desktop publisher by showing you how to use styles and macros so that eventually they will become two of your most used publishing tools.

Lay Out the Page(s)

You now have to put it all together in final document form. Most of the chapters in this book deal with using WordPerfect for page layout.

Print the Document

Finally, you need to print the document. This is not to say, of course, that the first printing will be the last. Usually you will have to do several revisions to get the text, graphics, and layout just right.

Chapter 5, "Printing Documents," will help you with the task of printing publications.

THE ELEMENTS OF DESIGN

The eight basic elements of design are as follows:

- Consistency
- Simplicity
- Variety
- White space
- Headlines
- Graphics
- Fonts
- Typography

The sections that follow treat these elements of design in detail.

CONSISTENCY

Nothing detracts more from the overall look of your document than inconsistency. Consistency gives the reader a feeling of order; inconsistency gives the reader a feeling of confusion.

Keep your document design consistent by doing the following:

- Establish a base font and, except for special cases, stick to it.

  See Chapter 11, "Using Fonts," for more information on choosing appropriate fonts.

- Set the margins, tabs, justification, line spacing, and other formatting features at the beginning of your document and don't change them except for special effects.

- Designate a style for chapter titles, section headings (so-called A-heads), and subsection headings (so called B-heads), and maintain the same style throughout the document. Using WordPerfect styles assures consistency in these items. (See Chapter 14, "Using Styles".)

- Establish conventions on how to display emphasized text (boldface? underline? italics? different font?), how to present lists (bullets? numbers? hanging paragraphs? left and right indent?), how to use symbols and abbreviations ($"$ or *in.* or *inches*? ° or *degrees*? × or x or *times*?, " . . . " or " . . . "), and so forth; then always adhere to your conventions.

  Figure 3.2A shows the effect of consistency in the design of the "Ocean Breeze Bookstore Employee Policies." The page looks organized and appealing. Employees will read it. Figure 3.2B, on the other hand, has inconsistencies that distract the reader.

SIMPLICITY

Use a simple design to attract readers and assist them through the text. Complex designs, regardless of how consistent they are, appear cluttered and unattractive.

Compare Figure 3.3A with Figure 3.3B. The simple design of Figure 3.3A invites readers and helps them move from one idea to the next. The complex design of 3.3B discourages readers before they start, and hinders their progress through the text.

Ocean Breeze Bookstore Employee Policies

This pamphlet is a summary (in nonlegal terms) of policies established by the Ocean Breeze Bookstore board of directors to help further your goals and the goals of the company. Your employment at Ocean Breeze Bookstore indicates your agreement to abide by these policies.

1. Your base salary is determined by your immediate supervisor, within the broad guidelines established by the board of directors.

   a. You will be rewarded with regular salary increases according to your experience and productivity.

   b. Your salary will be reviewed at least quarterly.

   c. You may discuss any questions regarding the fairness of your salary with the store manager, who will treat all such matters with promptness and fairness.

Annual Bonus

2. In addition to your base salary, you will receive an annual bonus.

   a. Bonuses are calculated as a percentage of your base salary.

   b. Bonus percentages will be determined by the board of directors.

   c. Bonuses are paid in February for the profits received during the preceding year.

Service and Respect

3. You should maintain an attitude of service and respect to all customers and potential customers.

   a. "The customer is always right" is not just a platitude; it is a company policy.

   b. You are expected to be courteous and cheerful at all times.

   c. Failure to follow company policy regarding customer relations is grounds for dismissal from Ocean Breeze Bookstore.

Figure 3.2A   The Ocean Breeze Bookstore Policy Statement with consistent design.

Ocean Breeze Bookstore Employee Policies

Annual Bonus

Service and Respect

This pamphlet is a summary (in nonlegal terms) of policies established by the Ocean Breeze Bookstore board of directors to help further your goals and the goals of the company. Your employment at Ocean Breeze Bookstore indicates your agreement to abide by these policies.

1. Your base salary is determined by your immediate supervisor, within the broad guidelines established by the board of directors.

   (a) You will be rewarded with regular salary increases according to your experience and productivity.

   (b) Your salary will be reviewed at least quarterly.

   (c) You may discuss any questions regarding the fairness of your salary with the store manager, who will treat all such matters with promptness and fairness.

2. *In addition to your base salary, you will receive an annual bonus.*

   a. Bonuses are calculated as a percentage of your base salary.

   b. Bonus percentages will be determined by the board of directors.

   c. Bonuses are paid in February for the profits received during the preceding year.

3. You should maintain an attitude of service and respect to all customers and potential customers.

   a. "The customer is always right" is not just a platitude; it is a company policy.

   b. You are expected to be courteous and cheerful at all times.

   c. Failure to follow company policy regarding customer relations is grounds for dismissal from Ocean Breeze Bookstore.

Figure 3.2B The Ocean Breeze Bookstore Policy Statement with inconsistent design.

The Age of Word Processing

Nowhere is our nation's heralded emergence into the Information Age more apparent than in the use of the computer in written communication. Ten years ago, the term "word processor" was rarely used and even more rarely understood. Now, as a result of the widespread acceptance of the personal computer, the term is part of our everyday vocabulary: the help-wanted section of the newspaper lists word processing skills as required for secretaries; television ads declare the skill as essential for college students; and Keyboarding and Word Processing have replaced Type I and Type II in our children's curriculum.

What was once a tremendous capital outlay ($15,000–$20,000 for a "dedicated" word processing machine) is now a modest purchase (under $2,500 for a personal computer, which can do word processing and perform other functions as well). Indeed, word processing is a primary force in the validation of the personal computer as "the tool" rather than "the toy". Homes as well as businesses now find that using the personal computer for word processing is an efficient and cost-effective approach to written communication needs.

The dream of all writers—whether an author creating a manuscript, a secretary typing a memo, a college student composing a term paper, or a homemaker writing a letter—is to produce clean, error-free text...quickly.

A word processor can fulfill that dream. It modifies, corrects, and revises with little effort. It corrects spelling, adjusts margins, inserts or erases passages...all at the touch of a key. It centers headings and aligns columns with ease. And smeared carbon copies, erratic margins, and misplaced page numbers are gone forever!

Figure 3.3A   The Age of Word Processing with simple design.

The *Age* of *Word Processing*

♦ ♦ ♦

•   Nowhere is our nation's heralded emergence into the Information Age more apparent than in the use of the computer in written communication. Ten years ago, the term "word processor" was rarely used and even more rarely understood. Now, as a result of the widespread acceptance of the personal computer, the term is part of our everyday vocabulary: the help-wanted section of the newspaper lists word processing skills as required for secretaries; television ads declare the skill as essential for college students; and Keyboarding and Word Processing have replaced Type I and Type II in our children's curriculum.

•   What was once a tremendous capital outlay ($15,000–$20,000 for a "dedicated" word processing machine) is now a modest purchase (under $2,500 for a personal computer, which can do word processing and perform other

functions as well). Indeed, word processing is a primary force in the validation of the personal computer as "the tool" rather than "the toy". Homes as well as businesses now find that using the personal computer for word processing is an efficient and cost-effective approach to written communication needs.

•   The dream of all writers—whether an author creating a manuscript, a secretary typing a memo, a college student composing a term paper, or a homemaker writing a letter—is to produce clean, error-free text...quickly.

•   A word processor can fulfill that dream. It modifies, corrects, and revises with little effort. It corrects spelling, adjusts margins, inserts or erases passages...all at the touch of a key. It centers headings and aligns columns with ease. And smeared carbon copies, erratic margins, and misplaced page numbers are gone forever!

♦ ♦ ♦

Figure 3.3B   The Age of Word Processing with complex design.

VARIETY

Variety adds pizazz to an otherwise dull document. For an extreme example, compare Figures 3.4A and 3.4B. The first copy of the report (3.4A) uses different font typefaces and sizes, includes graphics (for accent and additional information), displays horizontal and vertical rules (lines), marks a list of items with bullets, and uses white space (blank areas). The second copy of the same report (3.4B) looks plain and unexciting; the author is likely to be the only one to read it.

Variety does not, however, mean complexity or inconsistency. Notice the orderly format of Figure 3.4A. It has variety, but not at the expense of consistency.

WHITE SPACE

Blank areas—called *white space*—give rest to the reader's eye and balance to the page layout. Notice how the white space at the top and along the left edge of the page in Figure 3.4A balances the two figures along the right side. The column of heads ("Beginnings," "Gross Receipts," and "Best-Sellers") on the left are separated by large white spaces, focusing the reader's attention to the heads and balancing the text on the right. Even the small white space to the right of each bullet helps emphasize the three types of items in the software division of Ocean Breeze Bookstore.

HEADLINES

A strong headline (or title) grabs the reader's attention and makes the statement, "This article is important. Read it!"

Compare, for example, the A versions in Figures 3.3 and 3.4 with the corresponding B versions. The headings in the A version catch attention and get the reader interested in the text material. The B versions have weak headings, which effectively say, "This material isn't all that important, really. Don't take the time to read it."

You can, however, take this strength to an extreme. The headline in Figure 3.5, as a case in point, is simply too big and overpowering. Exceptionally large and bold headlines are appropriate only in flyers and other advertisements that rely on special effects and gimmicks.

GRAPHICS

Graphics (also called *artwork* or *art*) includes anything on the page that isn't text: figures, charts, diagrams, logos, photographs, lines, and boxes. Appropriate graphics can do the following:

- Catch the reader's attention.

- Add interest to the page.

- Provide variety in the page organization.

- Make the text more understandable.

Notice, for example, the graphics in Figure 3.4A. The thick horizontal rule (line) at the top of the page adds interest to the title. The logo (book and disk) help identify the document with Ocean Breeze Bookstore. The vertical rule helps separate the heads on the left from the main text on the right and adds interest to the page. The bar chart graphically shows the gross income of the software division of Ocean Breeze Bookstore.

See Chapter 8, "Creating Graphics," and Chapter 9, "Displaying Graphics," for more information on using art in desktop publishing.

FONTS

The appropriate selection and variation of font typeface, size, and attribute make your documents more interesting and informative.

Figure 3.2A demonstrates the appropriate use of fonts:

- The title is 36-point bold Helvetica.

  This presents a strong headline for the document.

- The heads are 14-point bold Helvetica.

  These stand out from the main body of text.

- The main text is Palatino (an easy-to-read serif font).

- The typefaces are simple and effective.

  Helvetica and Palatino are the only fonts on the entire page.

The cluttered, disorganized appearance of Figure 3.2B, on the other hand, is partially due to the lack of consistency in using typefaces. Rather than helping the reader, the irregular and excessive font changes distract the reader from the document's message.

For more information and guidelines on using fonts, see Chapter 10, "Installing Fonts," and Chapter 11, "Using Fonts."

Ocean Breeze Bookstore

Software Division

Beginnings

In July of 1982, Ocean Breeze Bookstore inaugurated its Software Division, which manages the acquisition and sale of the following:

- *Computer software.* Home, business and entertainment software for use on the Apple II, Macintosh, and IBM computers.

- *Computer books.* For word processing, spreadsheets, database management, operating systems, programming, and other specialized applications.

- *Computer supplies.* Computer paper, printer ribbons and toner, disks, and miscellaneous items.

The division does not include computer equipment in its inventory.

Gross Receipts

Gross receipts for the first full year of operation of the Software Division were $116,000. The second year's sales were $162,000, and the third year's sales were $185,000. Since 1986, gross sales have held steady at about $200,000 per year.

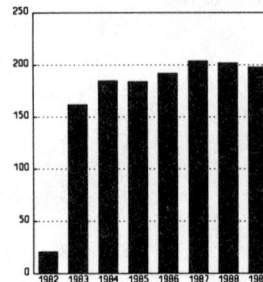

Best-Sellers

Our best-selling software items currently are *Lotus 1-2-3*, *WordPerfect for the IBM* (WordPerfect Corporation), *dBASE IV* (Ashton-Tate), *Word-Perfect for the Macintosh*, *Quicken* (Intuit), and *PC Tools Deluxe* (Central Point Software), in that order. Books dealing with these software products are, not surprisingly, the best-selling titles.

The Software Division continues to compete successfully against local computer stores, including Software, Etc. and Egghead Computer, both national chains. Our success is due to the following: knowledgeable and enthusiastic sales personnel, superior customer support, a large inventory, direct mail advertising to preferred customers, advertisements in local periodicals, and name recognition.

Figure 3.4A   Report of the Software Division of Ocean Breeze Bookstore with variety.

The Ocean Breeze Bookstore

Software Division

In July of 1982, Ocean Breeze Bookstore inaugurated its Software Division, which manages the acquisition and sale of computer software (including home, business and entertainment software for use on the Apple II, Macintosh, and IBM computers), computer books (on word processing, spreadsheets, database management, operating systems, programming, and other specialized applications), and computer supplies (including computer paper, printer ribbons and toner, disks, and miscellaneous items). The division does not include computer equipment in its inventory.

Gross receipts for the first full year of operation of the Software Division were $116,000. The second year's sales were $162,000, and the third year's sales were $185,000. Since 1986, gross sales have held steady at about $200,000 per year.

Our best-selling software items currently are *Lotus 1-2-3*, *WordPerfect for the IBM* (WordPerfect Corporation), *dBASE IV* (Ashton-Tate), *WordPerfect for the Macintosh*, *Quicken* (Intuit), and *PC Tools Deluxe* (Central Point Software), in that order. Books dealing with these software products are, not surprisingly, the best selling titles.

The Software Division continues to compete successfully against local computer stores, including Software, Etc. and Egghead Computer, both national chains. Our success is due to the following: knowledgeable and enthusiastic sales personnel, superior customer support, a large inventory, direct mail advertising to preferred customers, advertisements in local periodicals, and name recognition.

Figure 3.4B Report of the Software Division of Ocean Breeze Bookstore without variety.

Ocean Breeze Bookstore
Software Division

In July of 1982, Ocean Breeze Bookstore inaugurated its Software Division, which manages the acquisition and sale of computer software (including home, business and entertainment software for use on the Apple II, Macintosh, and IBM computers), computer books (on word processing, spreadsheets, database management, operating systems, programming, and other specialized applications), and computer supplies (including computer paper, printer ribbons and toner, disks, and miscellaneous items). The division does not include computer equipment in its inventory.

Gross receipts for the first full year of operation of the Software Division were $116,000. The second year's sales were $162,000, and the third year's sales were $185,000. Since 1986, gross sales have held steady at about $200,000 per year.

Our best-selling software items currently are *Lotus 1-2-3*, *WordPerfect for the IBM* (WordPerfect Corporation), *dBASE IV* (Ashton-Tate), *WordPerfect for the Macintosh*, *Quicken* (Intuit), and *PC Tools Deluxe* (Central Point Software), in that order. Books dealing with these software products are, not surprisingly, the best selling titles.

The Software Division continues to compete successfully against local computer stores, including Software, Etc. and Egghead Computer, both national chains. Our success is due to the following: knowledgeable and enthusiastic sales personnel, superior customer support, a large inventory, direct mail advertising to preferred customers, advertisements in local periodicals, and name recognition.

Figure 3.5   An oversized heading. Headlines should be strong, but not overpowering.

TYPOGRAPHY

Desktop publishing requires that you break some old habits and develop some new ones. The following list of rules will help you get started in the world of professional typesetting:

- Use true left and right quote marks: "this" instead of "this".

  Example: I told my boss, "A truck backed into your new car." **Not**: I told my boss, "A truck backed into your new car."

- Use true left and right single quote marks: 'this' instead of 'this'.

- Use an em dash (—) to separate a dependent clause.

  Example: My boss—a man you wouldn't want to meet in a dark alley—began to cry. **Not**: My boss--a man you wouldn't want to meet in a dark alley--began to cry.

- Use an en dash to mean "to" or "through."

  Example: The car's value was $16,000–22,000. **Not**: The car's value was $16,000-22,000.

- Use a true inch symbol (″), not just double quotes (").

  Example: The dent in the car door was 16″ × 24″. **Not**: The dent in the car door was 16" x 24".

- Use a true times symbol (×) to mean "times" (in multiplication) or "by" (in area measurements).

  Example: The dent in the car door was 16″ × 24″.

- Single space between sentences.

  Example: The truck was mine. My boss fired me. **Not**: The truck was mine. My boss fired me.

- Use italics, not underlining, for titles.

  Example: I'm now reading *When Bad Things Happen to Good People*. **Not**: I'm now reading When Bad Things Happen to Good People.

- When appropriate, use leading (rhymes with *bedding*) and kerning.

  Leading is the adjustment of the spacing between lines of text, and *kerning* is the adjustment of the spacing between letters. See Chapter 4, "Formatting Documents."

  For further typographic rules and an explanation of how to insert the above special characters into a document, see Chapter 12, "Inserting Special Characters."

MAKING EXCEPTIONS

The elements of design discussed in this chapter were gleaned from experts (see Appendix C, "Additional Reading") and from personal experience, but they should *not* be considered as edicts engraved on stone tablets. Once you understand and feel comfortable with those elements of design, go ahead and break the rules. So . . .

If you *want* an oversized title, go ahead and make one.

If you *want* plain, dull text, go ahead and leave the text plain and dull.

If you *want* an outlandishly complex format, go ahead and make your document outlandish.

If you don't *want* graphics in your document, okay, don't use graphics.

The elements of style are meant to help you, not to inhibit you. You are limited only by your creativity.

When can you break the rules? Here are two suggestions:

- Don't break a rule until you understand the rule.

- Don't break a rule except in informal documents such as flyers and advertisements, and even then break the rule only for occasional special effects.

GUIDING READERS

The elements of design should guide the readers by helping them *want* to read your material, assisting them in understanding the message, and directing their attention to the key points.

How do you provide this guidance? Try reading Figure 3.6. You *can* make some sense of it, but only with much effort. Obviously, the text lacks the common visual cues that help a reader, such as space between words, punctuation, uppercase characters, and paragraphs.

Now look at Figure 3.4A, which contains the same text as Figure 3.6. The report not only provides the normal visual cues that guide readers but also uses the "advanced" cues we have discussed in this chapter. For example, Figure 3.4A contains:

- A strong masthead (title), which informs the reader that the document is about the Ocean Breeze Bookstore Software Division.

- Heads (**Beginnings**, **Gross Receipts**, and **Best-Sellers**), which give the reader an overview of the organization of the report.

- Bulleted items, which mark important points.

- Variation in font size and attributes (outline, boldface, italic).

- Graphics, which catch the readers attention, add interest to the page, provide variety in the page organization, and make the text more understandable.

Guide your readers by providing advance visual cues such as titles, headings and subheadings, numbered and bulleted lists, variation in fonts, and graphics. Just remember not to overdo it. Excesses will distract rather than guide your readers.

injulyof1982oceanbreezebookstoreinaugurateditssoftwaredivisionwhichmanagestheacq
uisitionandsaleofthefollowingcomputersoftwarehomebusinessandentertainmentsoftwaref
oruseontheappleiimacintoshandibmcomputerscomputerbooksforwordprocessingspreads
heetsdatabasemanagementoperatingsystemsprogrammingandotherspecializedapplicati
onscomputersuppliescomputerpaperprinterribbonsandtonerdisksandmiscellaneousitems
thedivisiondoesnotincludecomputerequipmentinitsinventorygrossreceiptsforthefirstfullye
arofoperationofthesoftwaredivisionwere$116000thesecondyearssaleswere$162000andt
hethirdyearssaleswere$185000since1986grosssaleshaveheldsteadyatabout$200000per
yearourbestsellingsoftwareitemscurrentlyarelotus123wordperfectfortheibmwordperfectc
orporationdbaseivashtontatewordperfectforthemacintoshquickenintuitandpctoolsdeluxec
entralpointsoftwareinthatorderbooksdealingwiththesesoftwareproductsarenotsurprisingly
thebestsellingtitlesthesoftwaredivisioncontinuestocompetesuccessfullyagainstlocalcomp
uterstoresincludingsoftwareetcandeggheadcomputerbothnationalchainsoursuccessisdue
tothefollowing:knowledgeableandenthusiasticsalespersonnelsuperiorcustomersupportal
argeinventorydirectmailadvertisingtopreferredcustomersadvertisementsinlocalperiodical
sandnamerecognition

Figure 3.6   The Software Division report without space between words, punctuation, and so forth.

SUMMARY

The six steps required to prepare a publication are (1) design the document, (2) write the copy (text), (3) create the graphics, (4) define styles and macros, (5) lay out the pages, and (6) print the document.

See Figure 3.7 for a summary of the proper use of elements of design. You can, of course, make exceptions to these rules under special circumstances.

An important point in designing documents is that you should guide readers in, not distract them from, understanding the main point of the publication.

The Elements of Design

- Give your document a consistent overall design.
- Keep your design simple.
- Include **V**ariet**Y**.
- Use Ample White Space.
- Create **Forceful** mastheads and headlines.
- Employ graphics ◈ effectively.
- Choose appropriate *fonts*.
- Use typographic symbols and features (—, "...", ×, etc.).

Figure 3.7   The elements of design. This document demonstrates that for special effects you can ignore some of the rules.

Chapter 4

Formatting Documents

The *format* of a document is the arrangement of text on the printed page, including such features as the left and right margins, the top and bottom margins, the tab stops, justification, line spacing, indentations, hyphenations, line height, and word spacing.

Most writers or typists take these features for granted; they just get into WordPerfect and start typing. Desktop publishers, on the other hand, must take formatting features very seriously.

USING DEFAULTS

The WordPerfect *defaults* are the initial format settings in WordPerfect. Figure 4.1 lists the major initial default settings. Figure 4.2 shows a document with the initial default format settings.

You can change the default settings by following these steps:

Step 1. Press **Setup** (Shift-F1), **4** (Initial Settings), and **5** (Initial Codes).

WordPerfect displays the Initial Codes edit screen.

Step 2. Use the standard WordPerfect format functions to create initial format codes.

Initial Default Settings	
Left Margin	1"
Right Margin	1"
Top Margin	1"
Bottom Margin	1"
Justification	Full
Line Spacing	1 (Single spacing)
Paper Size	8.5" x 11"
Tabs	Every .05 "
Character size	Usually elite or 10 pt. (depends on printer)
Font	Courier (depends on printer)
Page Numbering	None
Hyphenation	Off
Repeat Value	8
Date Format	Month day, year
Fast Save	Off
Widow/Orphan	Off
Units of Measure	" (inches)

Figure 4.1   Initial default settings.

Font: Courier
Pitch: 10 (elite)

8 1/2 inches

Tabs: 0.5 inch intervals

1 inch

When in the Course of human Events, it becomes necessary for one People to dissolve the Political Bands which have connected them with another, and to assume among the Powers of the Earth, the separate and equal Station to which the Laws of Nature and of Nature's God entitle them, a decent Respect to the Opinions of Mankind requires that they should declare the causes which impel them to the Separation.

We hold these Truths to be self-evident, that all Men are created equal, that they are endowed by their Creator with certain unalienable Rights, that among these are Life, Liberty, and the Pursuit of Happiness--That to secure these Rights, Governments are instituted among Men, deriving their just Powers from the Consent of the Governed, that whenever any Form of Government becomes destructive of these Ends, it is the Right of the People to alter or to abolish it, and to institute new Government, laying its Foundation on such Principles, and organizing its Powers in such Form, as to them shall seem most likely to effect their Safety and Happiness. Prudence, indeed will dictate that Governments long established should not be changed for light and transcient Causes; and accordingly all Experience hath shewn, that Mankind are more disposed to suffer, while Evils are sufferable, than to right themselves by abolishing the Forms to which they are accustomed. But when a long Train of Abuses and Usurpations, pursuing invariably the same object, evinces a Design to reduce them under absolute Despotism, it is their Right, it is their Duty, to throw off such Government, and to provide new Guards for their future Security. Such has been the patient sufferance of these Colonies; and such is now the Necessity which constrains them to alter their former System of Government. The History of the present King of Great-Britain is a History of repeated Injuries and Usurpations, all having in direct Object the Establishment of an absolute Tyranny over these States. To prove this, let Facts be submitted to a candid World.

He has refused his Assent to Laws, the most wholesome and necessary for the public Good.

He has forbidden his Governors to pass Laws of immediate and pressing Importance, unless suspended in their Operation till his Assent should be obtained; and when so suspended, he has utterly neglected to attend them.

He has refused to pass other Laws for the Accommodation of large Districts of People, unless those People would relinquish the Right of Representation in the Legislature, a Right inestimable to them, and formidable to Tyrants only.

He has called together Legislative Bodies at Places unusual, uncomfortable, and distant from the Depository of their public Records, for the sole Purpose of fatiguing them into Compliance with his Measures.

He has dissolved Representatives Houses repeatedly, for opposing with manly Firmness his Invasions on the Rights of the People.

Single Space

11 inches

1 inch

1 inch

1 inch

Justified

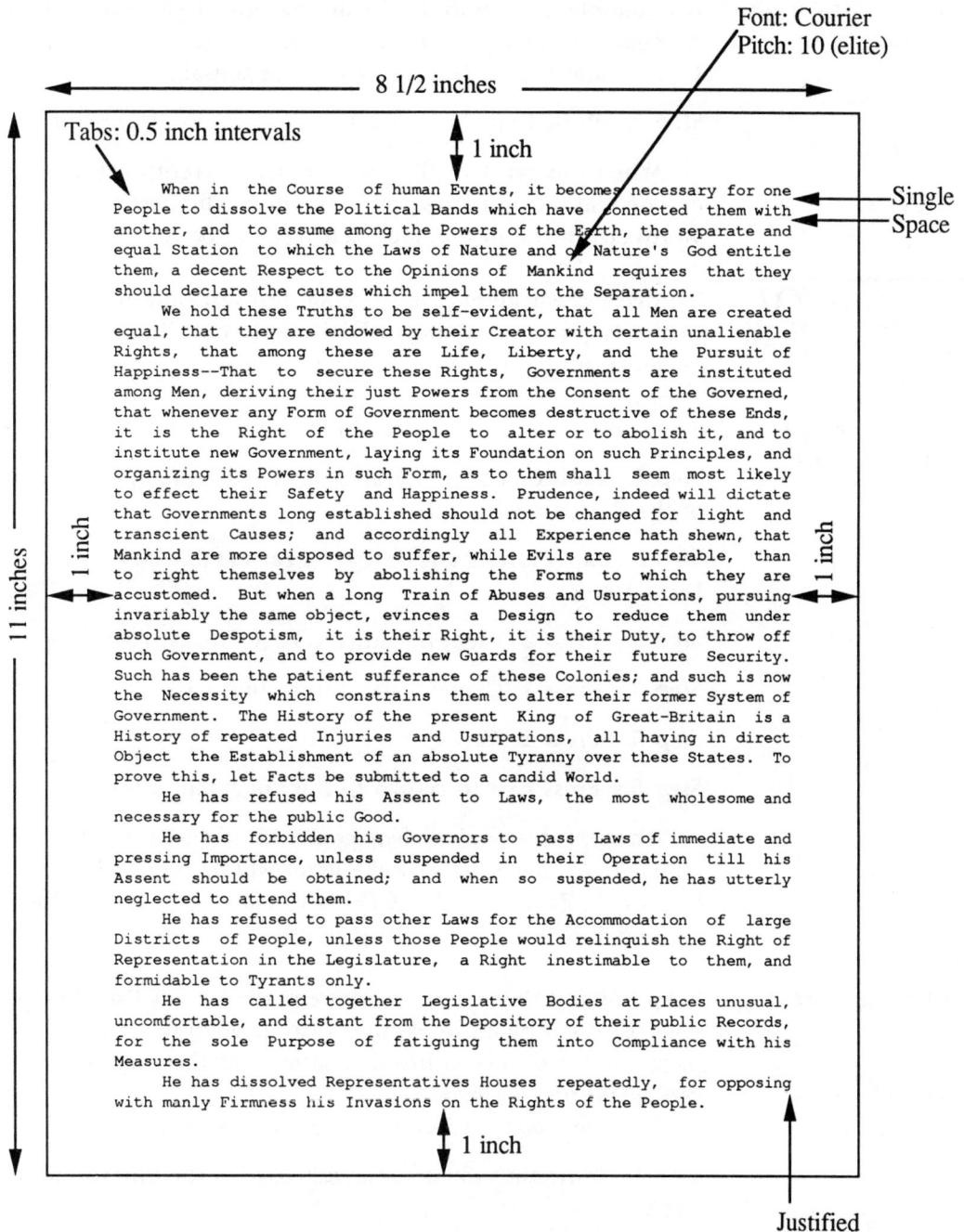

Figure 4.2 A printed document using the initial default settings.

For example, if you want justification (right alignment) *off* as an initial default format, press **Format** (Shift-F8), **1** (**L**ine), **3** (**J**ustification), **1** (**L**eft), and **Exit** (F7) to return to the Initial Codes edit screen.

Step 3. Press **Exit** (F7) twice to return to the document screen.

When you exit WordPerfect after the current work session, the new default settings are saved to the disk. The next time you enter WordPerfect, the new default settings will be in effect.

CENTERING TEXT ON A PAGE OR A LINE

WordPerfect will automatically center text vertically on a page (called Center Page top to bottom) or horizontally on a line (called Center), as shown in Figure 4.3.

Centering Page Top to Bottom

To center text top to bottom, follow these steps:

Step 1. Position the cursor at Ln 1″ Pos 1″ (the upper left corner of the document text).

Step 2. *Before* typing any text, press **Format** (Shift-F8) to invoke the Format menu.

Step 3. Press **2** (**P**age) to indicate Page Format commands.

Step 4. Press **1** (**C**enter Page (top to bottom)).

Step 5. Press **Y** (**Y**es)

Step 6. Press **Exit** to return to the document screen.

The text does not appear centered on the normal document screen, but you can see how the letter will be centered on the page by pressing **Print** (Shift-F7), **6** (**V**iew Document) to preview the document as it will appear when printed.

Centering Text

Keep in mind the difference between the Center Page (top to bottom) feature, which centers the entire page of text *vertically* on the page, and the Center (Shift-F6) feature, which centers a line of text *horizontally* on the page.

To center text on a line, follow these steps:

Step 1. Move the cursor to the left edge of the line you want centered.

**Center
Page
Top
to
Bottom**

Center Text

JUST SAY NO

Is desktop publishing worth the effort?
Not unless you are willing to learn the
basic principles, take the time to
apply them in your own document, use an
expert graphics designer and professional publisher when needed, and avoid
wasting time on routine documents. If
you have a compulsion to "publish"
everything you type, including memos to
the worker in the office next door,
then desktop publishing is for you more
an addiction than an advantage.

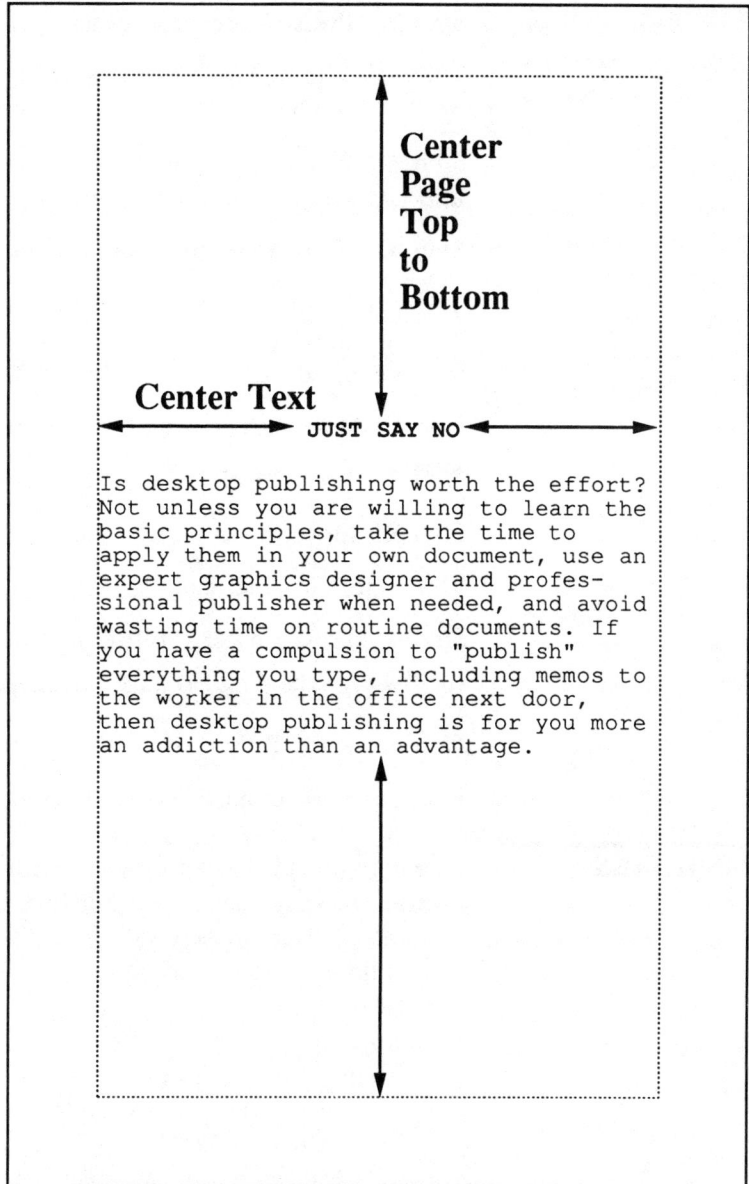

Figure 4.3 Centered text.

Step 2. Press **Center** (Shift-F6).

The cursor jumps to the center of the page. If you have typed text on the line already, the text slides to the right.

Step 3. Type the text, or if the text is already on the screen, press **End** to move the cursor to the right of the text.

Step 4. Press **Enter** to move the cursor down to the next line.

The text becomes centered on the line.

If you have already typed one or more lines of text that you now want centered, follow these steps:

Step 1. Move the cursor to the beginning of the text to be centered.

Step 2. Press **Block** (Alt-F4) to turn *on* Block mode.

Step 3. Move the cursor to the end of the text to be centered.

This highlights the text.

Step 4. Press **Center** (Shift-F6).

WordPerfect prompts **[Just:Center]? (Y/N)**.

Step 5. Press **Y** (Yes) to center the text.

Block mode is automatically turned *off* and the text becomes centered.

USING TABS

In the good old days of typewriters and impact printers, you just pressed the space bar to set your location on a line and started typing. This method worked well for creating charts and tables, because you could line up text as you saw it on the paper or on the computer screen.

Those days are gone. The space bar method no longer works, because most of the WordPerfect fonts used in desktop publishing are *proportional*. An *i*, for example, takes up much less space than an *M*. (See Chapter 11, "Using Fonts.") If you use the space bar to line up characters on the WordPerfect screen, they probably will *not* line up on the printed page. So you must use tabs to set your location.

The default setting for tab stops in WordPerfect is every 0.5″ starting from the left edge (position − 1″) of the paper, proceeding to − 0.5, 0.0 (the left margin), + 0.5, + 1.0, and so forth, where the values are relative to the left margin. If you change the left margin, the tab stops will automatically change also. When you press Tab, the cursor jumps to the next 0.5″ location.

But suppose you want tab stops at every 0.25″. You must change the tab settings as follows:

Step 1. Move your cursor to the location in the document where you want the next tab stops and press **Format** (Shift-F8), **1** (Line) to view the Format: Line menu.

Step 2. Press **8** (Tab Set).

WordPerfect displays the tab ruler at the bottom of the screen.

Step 3. Type –1 and **Enter** to move the cursor to the – 1″ spot on the tab ruler, one inch to the left of the left margin.

Step 4. Press **Delete to EOL** (Ctrl-End) to clear the tabs from the cursor position (at – 1″) to the end of the line.

The left tab symbols (**L**) are cleared from the tab ruler.

Step 5. Type –1,0.25 and press **Enter** to set the tabs to every one-fourth inch.

When you type two numbers separated by a comma, WordPerfect interprets the first number as the starting position and the second number as the increment. Thus, –1,0.25 starts the tab stops at – 1″ and puts a tab stop every 0.25″ from then on.

Step 6. Press **Exit** (F7) twice to exit the tab ruler and return to your document.

WordPerfect supports eight types of tab stops:

- **L** (or **Tab)** creates the normal left tab stop. When you press Tab to move the cursor to a left tab stop and then type text, the text moves to the right.

- **C** creates a *center* tab stop. When you press Tab to move the cursor to a center tab stop and then type text, the cursor stays in the same location (in the center of the text), and the characters scroll both left and right to keep the line centered at the tab stop.

- **R** creates a *right* tab stop. When you press Tab to move the cursor to a right tab stop and then type text, the cursor stays in the same location (to the right of the text), and the characters scroll to the left.

- **D** creates a *decimal* aligned tab stop. When you press Tab to move the cursor to a decimal tab stop and then type text, the cursor stays in the same location (to the right of the text) until you press a decimal point (.), after which the typed characters move to the right. This is used to type, for example, a list of prices.

- You can modify each of the four tab stop types above by moving the cursor with the Right Arrow and Left Arrow keys along the tab ruler to the location of the desired tab stop and pressing period (.). This causes WordPerfect to insert a dot leader preceding the text typed at the tab stop.

Figure 4.4 demonstrates these types of tab stops. In the figure, all tab stops are set at 4.5″, some with and some without dot leaders, as indicated.

You will see uses for these various types of tab stops in sample documents later in this book.

```
                     Tab Stops at 4.5"

                              ↓
                         L (left) tab stop.

                              ↓
                     C (center) tab stop.

                              ↓
                 R (right) tab stop.

                              ↓
              D (decimal) tab at 4.5 inches.

Without dot leader    $51.77
Second value          218.22
Total                 $269.99

                              ↓
With dot leader . .   $51.77
Second value . . .    218.22
Total . . . . . . . . $269.99
```

Figure 4.4   The types of tab stops.

JUSTIFYING TEXT

The initial default in WordPerfect is for text to be justified, which means that the text is aligned along both the left and right margins.

Justification

To turn *off* justification (which, in WordPerfect terminology, is Full Justification), follow these steps:

Step 1.   Move the cursor to the beginning of your document or to the location in the document where you want justification to end.

Step 2.   Press **Format** (Shift-F8), **1** (Line), **3** (Justification), **1** Left, and **Exit** (F7).

To turn justification back *on*, follow the same two steps, but press **Y** (Yes) instead of **N** (No) in the Format: Line Menu.

Figure 4.5 demonstrates the different types of justification.

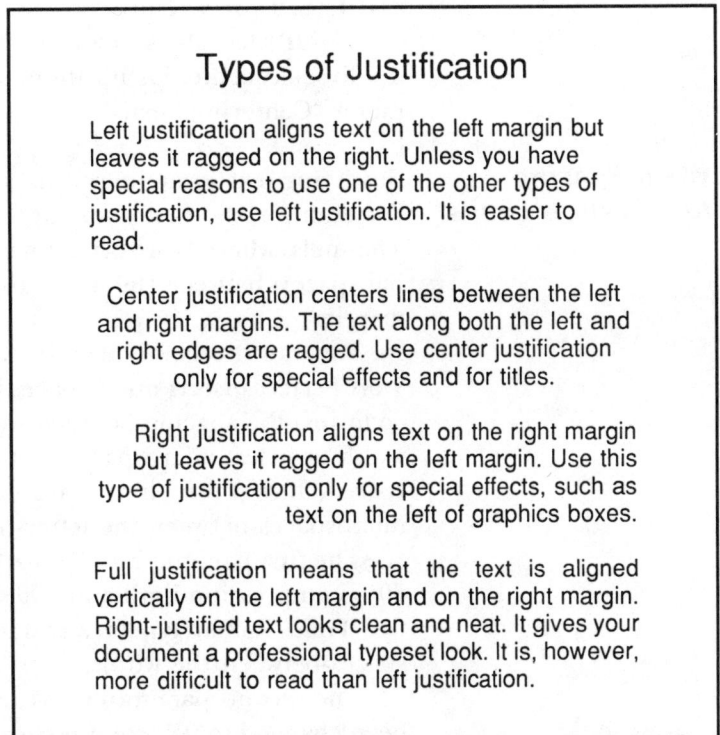

Types of Justification

Left justification aligns text on the left margin but leaves it ragged on the right. Unless you have special reasons to use one of the other types of justification, use left justification. It is easier to read.

Center justification centers lines between the left and right margins. The text along both the left and right edges are ragged. Use center justification only for special effects and for titles.

Right justification aligns text on the right margin but leaves it ragged on the left margin. Use this type of justification only for special effects, such as text on the left of graphics boxes.

Full justification means that the text is aligned vertically on the left margin and on the right margin. Right-justified text looks clean and neat. It gives your document a professional typeset look. It is, however, more difficult to read than left justification.

Figure 4.5   Text justification and alignment.

Right Justification

Figure 4.5 also shows a third type of text alignment—flush right or Right Justification. A line or paragraph that is flush right is aligned on the right margin but ragged along the left margin.

To make a paragraph, follow these steps:

Step 1.   Move the cursor to the beginning of the paragraph that you want right justified.

Step 2.   Press **Format** (Shift-F8), **1** (Line), **3** (Justification), and **3** (**Right**).

Step 3.   Press **Exit** (F7) twice to return to the WordPerfect document screen.

The text from that point on will be right justified. To return to left or full justification, move the cursor to the end of the text that is right justified, press **Format** (Shift-F8), **1** (Line), **3** (Justification), and **1** (**Left**) or **4** (**Full**).

WordPerfect also supports center justification, as shown in Figure 4.5. To select center justification, use the procedure described above under "Centering Text."

Word Spacing Justification Limits

Justifying text sometimes causes unsightly spaces between words. For example, the first paragraph in Figure 4.6 shows big gaps and "channels" where WordPerfect has inserted microspaces (small partial spaces) between the words to make the text align on the right margin.

You can overcome most of the problem by changing the way WordPerfect inserts microspaces between words. WordPerfect may compress the spacing between words down to 60% of the normal width or insert microspaces up to 400% of the normal width of a space. Once those limits are reached, WordPerfect then adds microspaces between the letters of the words.

The first paragraph in Figure 4.6 uses the WordPerfect defaults: 60% compression limit and 400% expansion limit. For fully justified Times Roman typeface, this is unattractive because of the large spaces between the words.

The second paragraph isn't much better. Here, the limits have been changed to 0% compression (meaning that WordPerfect can compress the spacing between words down as low as it wants, without limit) and 100% expansion (meaning that the spacing between the words can't be expanded at all). Now the spacing between characters is too great compared to the spacing between words.

Word Spacing in Justified Text

60/400

This paragraph is an example of the serious problem encountered with justification *on*. To keep the text aligned on the right margin, WordPerfect inserts microspaces between the words. This causes unsightly gaps and white channels between the words. To help overcome the problem, you can reset the "Word Spacing Justification Limits" found in the "Printer Functions" menu within the "Format: Other" menu.

0/100

This paragraph is an example of the serious problem encountered with justification *on*. To keep the text aligned on the right margin, WordPerfect inserts microspaces between the words. This causes unsightly gaps and white channels between the words. To help overcome the problem, you can reset the "Word Spacing Justification Limits" found in the "Printer Functions" menu within the "Format: Other" menu.

50/150

This paragraph is an example of the serious problem encountered with justification *on*. To keep the text aligned on the right margin, WordPerfect inserts microspaces between the words. This causes unsightly gaps and white channels between the words. To help overcome the problem, you can reset the "Word Spacing Justification Limits" found in the "Printer Functions" menu within the "Format: Other" menu.

Figure 4.6   The effect of changing the word spacing justification limits. Times Roman font.

The third paragraph is just right. With the settings at 50% compression limit (meaning that WordPerfect can compress the spacing between words down to 50% of the normal width) and 150% expansion limit (meaning the spacing between words can increase up to 1.5 times the normal width), the relative size of the spacing between characters and words makes the text attractive and readable.

Other typefaces (fonts) may have different optimal settings. You just have to experiment with different values until you find ones that look right.

To change the word spacing justification limits, follow these steps:

Step 1.   Move the cursor to the beginning of the text or to the location where you want to change the justification limit.

Step 2.   Press **Format** (Shift-F8), **4** (**O**ther), **6** (**P**rinter Functions).

WordPerfect displays the Format: Printer Functions menu shown in Figure 4.7.

Step 3.   Press **4** (Word Spacing **J**ustification Limits).

Step 4.   Opposite Compressed to (0% · 100%), type a value (such as **50**) and press **Enter.**

Step 5.   Opposite Expanded to (100% · unlimited), type a value (such as **150**) and press **Enter.**

```
Format: Printer Functions

    1 - Kerning                                          No

    2 - Printer Command

    3 - Word Spacing                                     Optimal
        Letter Spacing                                   Optimal

    4 - Word Spacing Justification Limits
        Compressed to (0% - 100%)                        60%
        Expanded to (100% - unlimited)                   400%

    5 - Baseline Placement for Typesetters               No
        (First baseline at top margin)

    6 - Leading Adjustment
        Primary   - [SRt]                                0"
        Secondary - [HRt]                                0"




Selection: 0
```

Figure 4.7   The Format: Printer Functions menu.

Step 6. Press **Exit** (F7) to return to your document.

For more on spacing between characters, see the section on "Kerning" later in this chapter.

HYPHENATING WORDS

WordPerfect establishes the length of each line by wrapping words that extend beyond the margin onto the next line. If the word contains many characters, this may result in a very ragged margin. If the lines are justified, WordPerfect aligns the right edges, but the spacing between words may be extensive and uneven. Turning *on* the hyphenation feature (part of the Format: Line menu) allows WordPerfect to hyphenate longer words, thereby evening out the ragged margin and improving the spacing in justified text.

Turning On Hyphenation

Although you may turn hyphenation *on* at the beginning of a document, it is usually more convenient to type the initial draft of the document with the hyphenation *off*; then, after completing the draft, return to the beginning of the document, turn the hyphenation *on*, and let WordPerfect hyphenate all the words at once.

WordPerfect supports several types of hyphenation. If you just want to hyphenate one word, move the cursor to the location where you want the hyphen, and press **Ctrl**-(dash). The hyphen does *not* actually appear on the screen or on the printed document *unless* the word occurs at the end of a line where it can be split. Otherwise, the hyphen remains invisible.

You can also tell WordPerfect to automatically hyphenate words within a document, using one of two methods. To set the desired hyphenation method, do the following:

Step 1. Press **Setup** (Shift-F1), **3** (Environment), and **6** (Hyphenation). WordPerfect displays the menu **Hyphenation: 1** External Dictionary/Rules; **2** Internal Rules: **1.** The External Dictionary/Rules uses the dictionary files WP{WP}US.LEX and WP{WP}US.HYC. The Internal Rules uses a dictionary built into WordPerfect itself. The External Dictionary/Rules is the best option if you have the disk space because it contains many more words and rules than the internal dictionary.

Step 2. Press **1** (External Dictionary/Rules) if you have the disk space. Otherwise, press **2** (Internal Rules).

Step 3. Press **Enter** to return to the setup menu and **6** (Location of Files).

Step 4.   Press **3** (Thesaurus/Spell/Hyphenation) and type the directory where your thesaurus, spell, and hyphenation files are kept, for example, `C:\wp51`.

This procedure tells WordPerfect what kind of hyphenation dictionary/rules you're going to use and the location of the hyphenation files, but it doesn't actually turn *on* hyphenation. To use the hyphenation feature, follow these steps:

Step 1.   Move the cursor to the location in the document where you want hyphenation to start (usually at the beginning of the document).

Step 2.   Press **Format** (Shift-F8), **1** (**Line**), **1** (**Hyphenation**), **Y** (**Yes**), and **Exit** (F7).

Hyphenation can be temporarily turned *off* by moving the cursor to the top or bottom of the document and pressing **Exit** at the first word to be hyphenated.

To turn hyphenation *off* for the remainder of the document, move the cursor to where you want hyphenation terminated, press **Format** (Shift-F8), **1** (**Line**, **1** (**Hyphenation**), **N** (No), and **Exit** (F7).

Setting the Hyphenation Zone

The *hyphenation zone* is a formatting feature that lets you adjust the amount of hyphenation. When hyphenation is *on*, WordPerfect uses a hyphenation zone to decide whether a word extending past the right margin should be hyphenated or wrapped to the next line. Similarly, the hyphenation zone determines how far the hyphen can move during the hyphenation help. The hyphenation zone consists of a left zone (preset at 10% of the text width), and a right zone (preset at 4% of the text width).

Figure 4.8 demonstrates the four possible situations for words that extend beyond the right margin:

1. The word begins before the left H-zone and ends before the right H-zone: the word wraps to the next line.

2. The word begins after the left H-zone and ends before the right H-zone: the word wraps to the next line.

3. The word begins after the left H-zone and extends beyond the right H-zone: the word wraps to the next line.

4. The word begins before the left H-zone and extends beyond the right H-zone: the word is hyphenated.

Right Margin

① . . . an example of the serious problem

Wraps to next line

② . . . an example of the serious problem

Wraps to next line

③ . . . initiation into desktop publishing

Wraps to next line

④ . . . WordPerfect inserts microspaces

Hyphenation

Left H-Zone   Right H-Zone

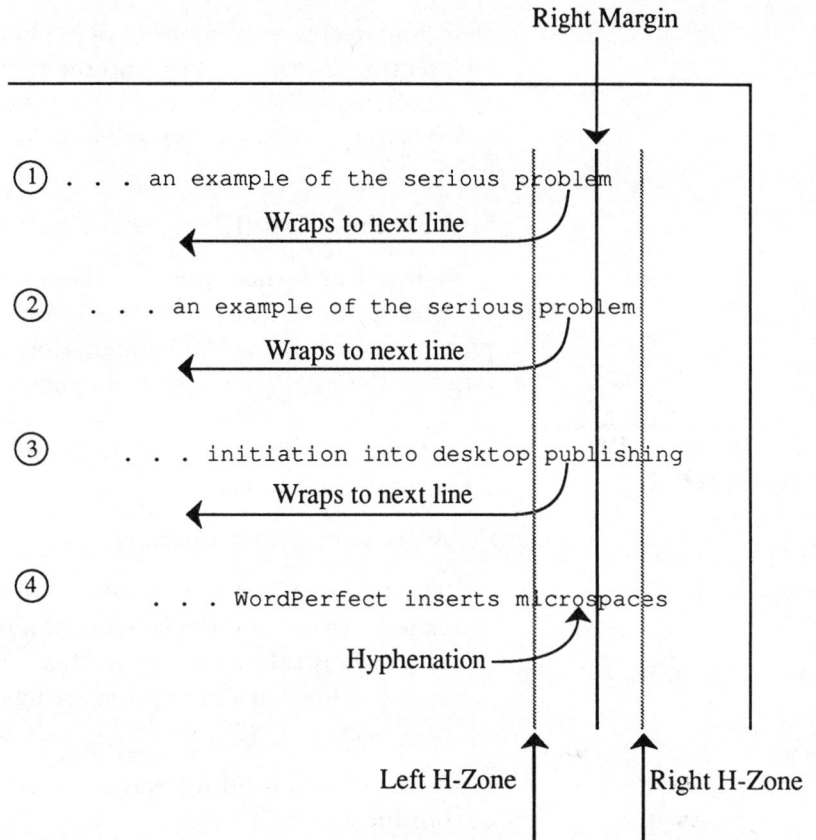

Figure 4.8 The hyphenation zone. The narrower the zone, the greater the amount of hyphenation.

You can make the hyphenation zone larger or smaller. A smaller hyphenation zone increases the amount of hyphenation and decreases the raggedness of the right margin (especially recommended for text columns or when right justification is off). A larger hyphenation zone decreases the amount of hyphenation and increases the raggedness of the right margin.

To adjust the hyphenation zone, follow these steps:

Step 1. Press **Format** (Shift-F8), **1** (**Line**), and **2** (Hyphenation **Z**one).

Step 2. Enter the hyphenation zone settings.

The hyphenation zone is preset to left 0.65″ (10%) and right .26″ (4%), if the line width is the typical 6.5″. To increase the hyphenation zone (and decrease the amount of hyphenation) to left 1″ and right 0.5″, set the left zone to 15% and the right zone to 8%. To decrease the hyphenation zone (and increase the amount of hyphenation) to left 0.4″ and right 0.2″, set the left zone to 6% and the right zone to 3%.

Step 3.   Press **Exit** (F7) to return to the document screen.

When you format your document into narrow columns (see Chapter 6, "Generating Columns"), you will see even more the importance of adjusting the hyphenation zone to the right values to improve the appearance of your document.

KEEPING TEXT TOGETHER

In ordinary as well as desktop published material, you should observe the following rules:

- Avoid widows and orphans.

  The first line of a paragraph alone at the bottom of a page is called a *widow*, and the last line of a paragraph alone at the top of a page is called an *orphan*. Make sure that, when possible, at least two lines of a paragraph are together at the top or bottom of a page.

- Never allow a heading (A-head or B-head) to be printed on the bottom line of a page.

  You should follow a heading with at least two lines of text.

- Keep an entire table (if it fits) on one page.

  Don't allow a table to be split in two.

- Keep other text elements together on a page if splitting a phrase, sentence, or part between two pages will cause confusion.

  WordPerfect provides several methods to assist you in following these rules.

Widows and Orphans

WordPerfect's widow/orphan protection automatically solves the problem of widow and orphans. After turning *on* widow/orphan protection at the beginning of your document, you won't have to worry about the problem again.

Follow these steps to turn *on* widow/orphan protection:

Step 1. Move the cursor to the point in your document where you want widow/orphan protection to begin, usually at the beginning of the document.

Step 2. Press **Format** (Shift-F8), **1** (Line), **9** (Widow/Orphan Protection), **Y** (Yes).

Step 3. Press **Exit** (F7) to return to the document screen.

WordPerfect will now automatically keep at least two lines of a paragraph together (where possible) at the beginning and end of each page throughout the entire document.

You can select ranges of text in which the protection is *on* or *off* by turning widow/orphan protection *on* at the beginning of a range of text and turning it *off* at the end of the range.

Conditional End of Page

WordPerfect's widow/orphan protection will not keep paragraph headings from becoming widows, nor will it prevent short lines (such as those on a list) from being separated by a page break. You can, however, use the Conditional End of Page command to keep a certain number of lines together without being split by a page break.

Follow these steps to set the conditional end of page:

Step 1. Position the cursor on the line *above* the block of lines that should be kept together.

Step 2. Press **Format** (Shift-F8), and **4** (Other).

The Format: Other menu appears on the screen.

Step 3. Press **2** (Conditional End of Page). The prompt **Number of Lines to Keep Together:** appears at the bottom of the screen.

Step 4. Enter the number of lines that you wish to keep together.

For headings in a single-spaced document, we suggest 4 to 6 as the number of lines to be kept together. In a double-spaced document, the number should be 6 to 14, depending upon your personal preference.

Step 5. Press **Exit** (F7) to return to the document screen.

Marking a conditional end of page at every major heading and subheading is advisable, but it is also a nuisance. The solution is to include the conditional end of page protection as part of a heading style; see Chapter 14, "Using Styles." Then you are assured that a heading will never be isolated at the bottom of a page.

You can also use the Conditional End of Page command to keep outlines, tables, and illustrations from being split by page breaks, but for these items the Block Protect command is usually more convenient.

Block Protect

You can protect a block of text from being split by a page break by using the Block Protect feature. Follow these steps to use the Block Protect feature.

Step 1.   Mark the text you want protected by highlighting it with the **Block** (Alt-F4) feature or by dragging the mouse pointer over it, then press **Format** (Shift-F8).

The prompt **Protect block? No (Y**es) appears at the bottom of the screen.

Step 2.   Press **Y (Y**es) to protect the block of text.

Hard Page

When you reach the bottom of a page, WordPerfect inserts a soft page break, displayed as a row of dashes across the screen. The Hard Page (Ctrl-Enter) command, displayed as a row of equal signs across the screen, forces a page break regardless of where you are on the page. You should use the Hard Page command when you want to start a new page for figures and tables or to begin a new chapter. (A hard page break can be deleted by moving the cursor just before the equal signs and then pressing Delete.)

FORCING ODD/EVEN PAGES

In a long document (such as a report, newsletter, brochure, or book) that contains chapters and sections, you may want the first page of every chapter to begin on an odd-numbered page. You may want a particular table or figure to be printed on an even-numbered page. In either of these cases (or similar ones), you can force a particular page to fall on an odd or an even page by following these steps:

Step 1.   Move the cursor to the beginning of the page that you want forced to an odd or even page number.

Step 2.   Press **Format** (Shift-F8), **2 (P**age), and **2** (Force Odd/Even Page).

The prompt **1 O**dd; **2 E**ven: **0** appears on the screen.

Step 3. Press **1** (**O**dd) or **2** (**E**ven) to force the current page to be odd or even.

Step 4. Press **Exit** (F7) to return to your document.

WordPerfect inserts a blank page, if necessary, to make the page number odd or even, depending on which one you specified.

POSITIONING TEXT: ADVANCE

You can position text at almost any location on the screen by pressing Enter until you get to the desired vertical position (as shown by the Ln value on the status line) and pressing Tab or Space Bar until you get to the desired horizontal position (as shown by the Pos value on the status line). This method of positioning text, however, can be cumbersome, and in some cases, impossible.

For example, look carefully at the horizontal rules in Figure 4.6. They are halfway between the headings above and the text below. The following steps demonstrate how to create and accurately position a horizontal line:

Step 1. With a clean document screen, set the desired font typeface and size.

For example, use 12-point Times for this demonstration. Press **Font** (Ctrl-F8), **4** (**B**ase Font), and **N** (**N**ame Search), type the first few characters of the desired font (such as Times), enter the font size (if requested to do so), and press **Exit** (F7).

Step 2. Press **Format** (Shift-F8), **4** (**O**ther), **7** (**U**nderline - Spaces), **Y** (Yes), **Y** (Yes) again, and press **Exit** (F7).

This causes underlining to be *on* for spaces between words and for tabbed regions of the text.

Step 3. Type a boldfaced heading, such as **Demonstration of the Advance Feature**, and then press **Enter** to go down to the next line.

Step 4. Press **Underline** (F8) and **Flush Right** (Alt-F6).

This creates a horizontal rule that spans the entire width of text.

Step 5. Press **End** to move the cursor past the codes Flush Right and Underline, and press **Enter** to go down to the next line.

Step 6. Type the following paragraph of text: `WordPerfect's Ad-` `vance feature allows you to position characters, words,` `phrases, and special marks anywhere on the printed page.`

If you print the page at this point, the rule between the heading and the paragraph looks like Figure 4.9A.

Step 7. Now move the cursor to the left of the underline/flush right codes.

To make sure the cursor is to the left of the underlining, move the cursor up to the horizontal underline and press **Home, Home, Home, Left Arrow**. You are now ready to use WordPerfect's Advance feature to position the horizontal line.

Step 8. Press **Format** (Shift-F8), **4** (**O**ther), and **1** (**A**dvance).

A.

Demonstration of the Advance Feature

WordPerfect's Advance feature allows you to position characters, words, phrases, and special marks anywhere on the printed page.

B.

Demonstration of the Advance Feature

WordPerfect's Advance feature allows you to position characters, words, phrases, and special marks anywhere on the printed page.

Figure 4.9   Demonstration of the Advance feature. A. The horizontal line is created without using Advance Up. B. The horizontal line has been moved up with Advance Up.

The following one-line menu appears at the bottom of the screen: **Advance: 1 U**p; **2 D**own; **3 L**ine; **4 L**eft; **5 R**ight; **6 P**osition: **0**.

> **1 (U**p**)** advances up relative to the current position. The Ln value decreases.

> **2 (D**own**)** advances down relative to the current position. The Ln value increases.

> **3 (L**ine**)** advances to an specified vertical position on the page.

> **4 (L**eft**)** advances left relative to the current position. The Pos value decreases.

> **5 (R**ight**)** advances right relative to the current position. The Pos value increases.

> **6 (P**osition**)** advances to an specified horizontal position on the page.

Note that the commands **1 (U**p**)**, **2 (D**own**)**, **4 (L**eft**)**, and **5 (R**ight**)** invoke moves that change the position *relative* to the current position. The commands **3 (L**ine**)** and **6 (P**osition**)**, on the other hand, set the position to an absolute value.

Step 9. Press **1 (U**p**)**, type 0.12, press **Enter** and then **Exit** (F7).

The horizontal line (produced with Underline and Flush Right) will be printed slightly farther up on the page, as shown in Figure 3.9B.

As another short demonstration, follow these steps to put an x in the middle of an 8.5″ × 11″ page:

Step 1. Press **Format** (Shift-F8), **4 (O**ther**)**, and **1 (A**dvance**)**.

The one-line menu shown above in step 8 appears on the screen.

Step 2. Press **3 (L**ine**)**, type 5.5, and press **Enter**.

This tells WordPerfect that you want to place the next text 5.5 inches from the top of the paper, which is half-way down on an 8.5″ × 11″ page.

Step 3. Press **1 (A**dvance**)**, **6 (P**osition**)**, type 4.25, and press **Enter**.

This tells WordPerfect that you want to place the next text 4.25 inches from the left edge of the paper, which is the midpoint on an 8.5″ × 11″ page.

Step 4. Press **Exit** (F7) to return to the document, and type x.

The x will be printed in the middle of the page. You can see this (without actually printing the page) by pressing Print (Shift-F7) and **6** (**V**iew Document).

You will see other applications of the Advance feature in later chapters.

KERNING

Kerning, an important typesetter's tool, adjusts the spacing between letter pairs. Figure 4.10 shows the letter pair "To" with and without kerning.

Text with kerning is more aesthetically pleasing than text without it, as demonstrated in Figure 4.11. Notice the kerning between the letter pairs "Te," "Aw," "To," and "Yo."

The printer definitions supplied on your original WordPerfect disks allow automatic kerning in your documents. To see how to use kerning in WordPerfect, follow these steps:

Step 1. Move the cursor to the location in your document where you want kerning to begin.

Step 2. Press **Format** (Shift-F8), **4** (**O**ther), and **6** (**P**rinter Functions).

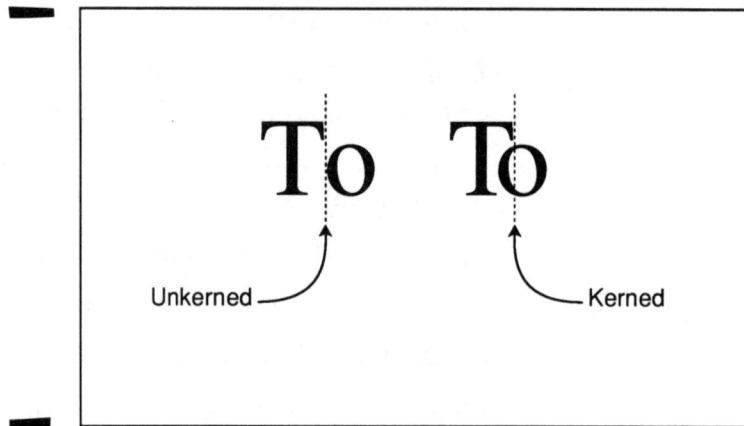

Figure 4.10   Kerning.

Unkerned: Ten Thousand Awards To You

Kerned: Ten Thousand Awards To You

Figure 4.11   The aesthetic appearance of kerned text.

The Format: Printer Functions menu (Figure 4.7) appears on the screen.

Step 3.   Press **1** (**K**erning) and **Y** (Yes).

This turns *on* automatic kerning.

Step 4.   Press **Exit** (F7) to return to your document.

You can turn *off* kerning with the same four steps, but in step 3, press **N** (No) instead of **Y** (Yes).

If you want to define your own kerning table, modify the one shipped by WordPerfect Corporation; or if your font doesn't have a kerning table, use the KERN.TST file and the Printer Definition Program as described in Appendix B, "Using Your Printer."

You also can adjust the letter spacing directly in your document by using WordPerfect's Word Spacing and Letter Spacing features.

SPACING BETWEEN WORDS AND LETTERS

Compare the two logos of the Ocean Breeze Bookstore in Figure 4.12. Both are neat and attractive. But in Figure 14.12B the letters in "Ocean Breeze Bookstore" are closer together than normal and the letters in "QUALITY SERVICE SINCE 1966" are farther apart than normal, creating a pleasing effect.

You can adjust the spacing between words and letters by following these steps:

Step 1.   Move the cursor to the beginning of the text in which you want to adjust the spacing.

Step 2.   Press **Format** (Shift-F8), **4** (**O**ther), and **6** (**P**rinter Functions).

The Format: Printer Functions menu (Figure 4.7) appears on the screen.

Step 3.   Press **3** (Word Spacing).

WordPerfect displays the following one-line menu: **Word Spacing: 1** Normal; **2 O**ptimal; **3 P**ercent of Optimal; **4 S**et Pitch: **2**. The commands have the following effects:

> **1** (**N**ormal) sets the word spacing to the font manufacturer's specifications.

> **2** (**O**ptimal) sets the word spacing to WordPerfect Corporation's specifications.

A.

B.

Figure 4.12   Ocean Breeze Bookstore logo. A. Before adjusting the word and letter spacing. B. After adjusting the word and letter spacing.

3 (**P**ercent of Optimal) sets the spacing scale from 50% to 250%, where 100% is Optimal, 50% is half the optimal spacing, and 250% is 2.5 times the optimal spacing.

4 (**S**et Pitch) sets the spacing scale as measured by the pitch (characters per inch).

Step 4.   Press **3** (**P**ercent of Optimal), type 95 to make the word spacing smaller, and press **Enter**.

This sets the spacing between words to 95% of the optimal, which means that the word spacing will be slightly smaller than usual.

The following one-line menu appears on the screen: **Letter Spacing: 1 N**ormal; **2 O**ptimal; **3 P**ercent of Optimal; **4 S**et Pitch: **2**, where these commands have the same meaning as in Word Spacing, except they refer to spacing between the letters within words.

Step 5.   Press **3** (**P**ercent of Optimal), type 95, and press **Enter.**

You will usually want to set the word spacing and the letter spacing to the same value.

Step 6.   Press **Exit** (F7) to return to your document.

The word and letter spacing in the phrase "Ocean Breeze Bookstore" in Figure 4.12B was set to 95% of optimal. The phrase "QUALITY SERVICE SINCE 1966" was set to 250% of optimal.

If you want only two letters to be closer together (kerned), move the cursor to the first character, follow the six steps above to set the letter spacing to 90% of optimal (for example), move the cursor to the right of the second character, and reset the letter spacing to Optimal.

LEADING (LINE HEIGHT)

Leading (rhymes with *bedding*), another typesetter's tool, is the adjustment of spacing between lines of text. In WordPerfect you can change the spacing with the Advance feature (described above in the section "Positioning Text: Advance"), with the Line Height feature, or with the Leading Adjustment feature.

Figure 4.13, for example, contains two examples of the same bulleted list. In 4.13A, the items in the list are cramped together. You could simply double-space between the items, but then they would be separated by too much space, as if they were unrelated and separate paragraphs. In 4.13B, a small amount of leading between the items gives a pleasing, easy-to-read appearance.

To change the line height for leading, follow these steps:

Step 1.   Move the cursor to the beginning of the line for which you want to increase or decrease the height.

Step 2.   Press **Format** (Shift-F8), **1** (**L**ine), and **4** (Line **H**eight).

The one-line menu **1 A**uto; **2 F**ixed: **0** appears at the bottom of the screen. The default setting is Auto, meaning that the line height is set automatically according to the font size.

Step 3.   Press **2** (**F**ixed), enter the new line height in inches, and press **Exit** (F7).

For example, the line height of the blank lines between the bulleted items in Figure 4.13B is set to 0.08″.

A.

In July of 1982, Ocean Breeze Bookstore inaugurated its Software Division, which manages the acquisition and sale of the following:

- *Computer software*. Home, business and entertainment software for use on the Apple II, Macintosh, and IBM computers.
- *Computer books*. For word processing, spreadsheets, database management, operating systems, programming, and other specialized applications.
- *Computer supplies*. Computer paper, printer ribbons and toner, disks, and miscellaneous items.

The division does not include computer equipment in its inventory.

B.

In July of 1982, Ocean Breeze Bookstore inaugurated its Software Division, which manages the acquisition and sale of the following:

- *Computer software*. Home, business and entertainment software for use on the Apple II, Macintosh, and IBM computers.

- *Computer books*. For word processing, spreadsheets, database management, operating systems, programming, and other specialized applications.

- *Computer supplies*. Computer paper, printer ribbons and toner, disks, and miscellaneous items.

The division does not include computer equipment in its inventory.

Figure 4.13   Demonstration of leading (line height). A. Bulleted list without leading. B. Bulleted list with leading.

Step 4.   Move the cursor to the next line or to the end of a group of lines for which you want the adjusted line height to apply, and repeat steps 2 and 3 to return the line height to Auto.

You can usually guess at the desired adjusted height from the value of the current height, which appears at the prompt after pressing **2** (**Fixed**) in step 3.

The most effective method of changing the leading between paragraphs is with the Leading Adjustment commands. Follow these steps:

Step 1. Move the cursor to the location in your document where you want to change the leading.

Step 2. Press **Format** (Shift-F8), **4** (**O**ther), and **6** (**P**rinter Functions).

The Format: Printer Functions menu (Figure 4.7) appears on the screen.

Step 3. Press **6** (**L**eading Adjustment).

The cursor moves to the right of **Primary-[SRt]**, and waits for you to type a value (usually in inches) for the amount of leading between lines within a paragraph.

Step 4. Just Press **Enter**, since you want the Primary leading to stay at zero.

Step 5. With the cursor to the right of **Secondary-[HRt]**, type the amount of leading you want after each paragraph. For example, type 0.08 and press **Enter** to insert 0.08″ (about one-half line) between paragraphs.

To turn *off* the leading, follow these same steps, except enter zero for both leading adjustment values.

SUMMARY

Formatting text involves the placement of words and letters at the desired location on the page, relative to the paper edges and relative to the positions of other words and letters.

To center text on a line, use the Center (Shift-F6) command. To center text on a page vertically, press **Format** (Shift-F8), **2** (**P**age), and **1** (**C**enter Page (top to bottom)).

You can adjust the tab stop positions and types using **Format** (Shift-F8), **1** (**L**ine), **8** (**T**ab Set) and then setting left, right, center, or decimal align tabs, with or without dot leaders.

WordPerfect allows you to specify any one of four types of justification: Left (aligned left margin, ragged right margin), Center, which centers a phrase between the two margins (ragged on both right and left margins); Right (aligned right margin, ragged left margin); and Full (aligned both right and left margins).

You can also set the word spacing justification limits to improve the appearance of the word and letter spacing in fully justified text. Press **Format** (Shift-F8), **4** (**O**ther), **6** (**P**rinter Functions), and **4** (**W**ord Spacing Justification Limits).

Hyphenation can also improve the appearance of documents, whether the text is justified or not. To turn *on* hyphenation, press **Format** (Shift-F8), **1** (**L**ine), **1** (**H**yphenation), and then press **2** (**A**uto) or **3** (**M**anual). To increase the amount of hyphenation in a document (and decrease the raggedness of the right margin with justification *off* or to decrease the amount of extra spaces between words and letters with justification *on*), press **Format** (Shift-F8), **1** (**L**ine), **2** (**H**yphenation **Z**one), and then type the desired left and right zone locations based upon the percent of the line width.

For documents longer than one page, you have to assure that page breaks don't occur at undesirable locations, such as just after a new heading or just before the last line of a paragraph. WordPerfect provides four features to help you keep text together and avoid inappropriately located page breaks: Conditional End of Page, Block Protect, Widow/Orphan Protection, and Hard Page.

You can also specify that a particular page (such as the beginning of a chapter) is on an odd or even page: press **Format** (Shift-F8), **2** (**P**age), **2** (**F**orce Odd/Even Page), and then press **1** (**O**dd) or **2** (**E**ven).

To position text at specific locations on the page, relative to the top or left edge of the paper or relative to the current text position, use WordPerfect's Advance feature: press **Format** (Shift-F8), **4** (**O**ther), **1** (**A**dvance), and then select the type of advance and the amount of the advance.

WordPerfect also supports the special typesetter's tools of kerning and leading. Turn *on* kerning by pressing **Format** (Shift-F8), **4** (**O**ther), **6** (**P**rinter Functions), **1** (**K**erning), and **Y** (Yes). You can also adjust the spacing between characters with the Word Spacing and Letter Spacing features, accessed by pressing **Format** (Shift-F8), **4** (**O**ther), **6** (**P**rinter Functions), and **3** (**W**ord Spacing). For leading (to add space between lines of text), use the Line Height feature — **Format** (Shift-F8), **1** (**L**ine), **4** (**L**ine **H**eight), and then enter the desired line height in inches; or use the Leading Adjustment feature — Format (Shift-F8), **4** (**O**ther), **6** (**P**rinter Functions), **6** (**L**eading Adjustment, and then enter the amount of leading between lines and between paragraphs.

Chapter 5

Printing Documents

This chapter will explain the following:

- How to ready your printer by means of a printer checklist.

- How to print a document from the screen.

- How to print a document directly from the disk.

- How to print a document from the List Files menu.

- How to change the print options to accommodate special printing cases.

- How to preview a document before printing it.

- How to select nonstandard page sizes, paper types, and page orientation.

PREPARING YOUR PRINTER

Make sure your printer is ready before you try to print. Refer to the printer manual for specific instructions on how to set up and use your printer. In addition, you may want to go through the following checklist before you begin printing.

A Printer Checklist

☐ Is the printer cable firmly attached to your computer on one end and to the printer on the other end?

☐ Is the printer plugged into an electrical outlet and turned on?

☐ Is the On-line or Select (SEL) light on? (Most printers have an On-line, SEL, Print On, or Ready light that must be *on* before you can print. If your printer has an Alert light, it must be *off*.)

☐ Do you have sufficient computer paper, either fanfold (continuous) or single sheets (handfed or sheet-fed)?

☐ Is the paper lined up to begin typing at the top of a page? (Adjust the paper using the "line feed," which moves the paper forward one line at a time, or by the "page (form) feed," which moves the paper forward one full page at a time. You may also need to use the platen knobs on the sides of the printer.)

☐ Is there adequate ribbon, and is the ribbon cartridge positioned properly? Or if you have a laser printer, is the toner cartridge properly installed?

☐ Is the shield in the front of the printer in place? (Most printers won't work until this shield is safely positioned over the print mechanism.)

☐ Is the paper cassette of a laser printer properly installed, with the edges of the paper neatly aligned with the sides of the tray?

☐ If your printer is part of a local area network (LAN), is the network printing system active?

If you have a question about any item in the checklist, consult the printer user's manual or talk to your printer dealer.

SELECTING THE PRINTER

Before printing a document, you must set up (configure) WordPerfect to match your printer; see Appendix B, "Using Your Printer," and the WordPerfect user's manual.

Many printers give you the option of feeding the paper continuously, using fanfold sheets on a tractor feed, or feeding the paper one page at a time (either by hand or with a sheet feeder). You can set up one printer definition for the most frequently used option (for example, continuous feed) and another printer definition (which can actually be the same printer) for the other option (single-sheet feed). Then, when you want to print using the single-sheet feed method, you just change the printer name for that particular job.

PRINTING A DOCUMENT

You can print a document while it is on the screen, or you can print a document directly from the disk.

Printing a Document from the Screen

In order to print a document from the screen, you must first type the document onto the document screen or retrieve the document from the disk. Make sure you have a clear screen and the cursor is located at the left margin of the first line on page 1. Then press **Retrieve** (Shift-F10) and type the filename of the document. A copy of the file will appear on the screen.

Follow these steps to print the document from the screen:

Step 1. Press **Print** (Shift-F7).

The Print and Options menu appears on the screen (see Figure 5.1). The printer listed to the right of **Select Printer** will be the name of your printer. The Print menu includes the following items:

> **1 - Full Document** prints the entire document on the Word-Perfect screen.

```
Print

    1 - Full Document
    2 - Page
    3 - Document on Disk
    4 - Control Printer
    5 - Multiple Pages
    6 - View Document
    7 - Initialize Printer

Options

    S - Select Printer
    B - Binding Offset              0"
    N - Number of Copies            1
    U - Multiple Copies Generated by   WordPerfect
    G - Graphics Quality            Medium
    T - Text Quality                High




Selection: 0
```

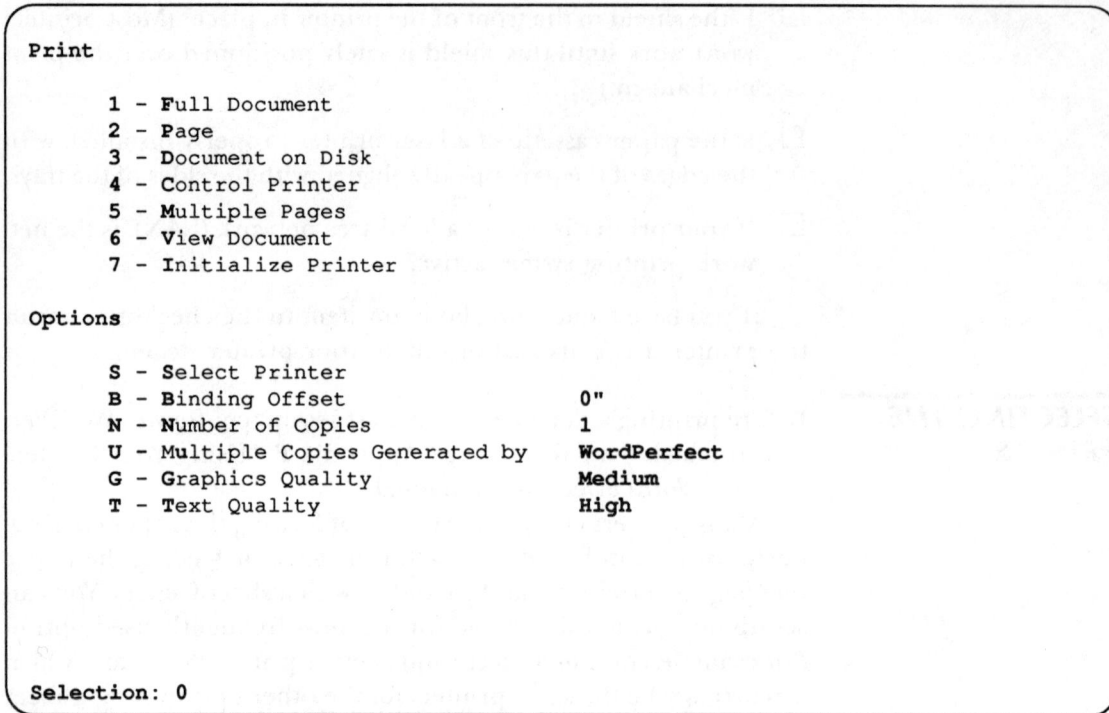

Figure 5.1   The Print and Options menu.

2 - Page prints the current page on the document screen.

3 - Document on Disk prints a document directly from the disk. WordPerfect prompts you for the document filename.

4 - Control Printer allows you to view the status of the current jobs, the list of jobs to be printed, and messages regarding the printer and document. You can also cancel, rush, or stop print jobs and perform other printer control options.

5 - Multiple pages allows you to specify individual pages and page ranges for printing the screen document.

6 - View Document displays a graphic representation of your document as it will appear on the printed page. This is a convenient means of showing text alignment, page numbering, headers, footnotes, font sizes, graphics, etc., prior to printing the document.

7 - **I**nitialize Printer sends initialization codes to your printer to prepare it to receive your document.

The Options menu in Figure 5.1 will be explained later.

Step 2. Press **1** (**F**ull Document) to print the screen document.

You could also press **2** (**P**age), which would print only the page in which the cursor is located.

Printing a Document Directly from the Disk

It isn't necessary to have a document on the screen in order to print it. You can print a document directly from the disk by using the **Print** (Shift-F7) feature or by using the **List** (F5) directory.

Note: If you have saved a document using the Fast Save (unformatted) feature, you must first retrieve the document into WordPerfect and either print it from the screen or save it back to the disk with a normal (formatted) save. Press **Setup** (Shift-F1) and look at item 4, **F**ast Save (unformatted). If **No** appears to the right of the item, then files are saved to the disk in normal (formatted) form and may be printed directly from the disk.

The Print Menu

Follow these steps to print a file directly from the disk using the Print menu:

Step 1. Press **Print** (Shift-F7).

WordPerfect displays the Print menu (Figure 5.1).

Step 2. Press **3** (**D**ocument on Disk).

WordPerfect displays the prompt **Document name:** and waits for you to type a filename (or pathname).

Step 3. Type the filename or complete pathname and press **Enter**.

The prompt **Page(s): (All)** appears at the bottom of the screen. You can press **Enter** to select all pages of the document or specify a range of pages. For example, type 3-4 or 2-19, where the first number is the starting page, the dash stands for the word *to* and the second number is the final page (inclusive). You can also type one or more pages separated by commas, such as 5,8,12 to print pages 5, 8 and 12, or type one number followed by a dash, such as 3- or 14-, to print from the specified page to the end of the document. If you type a dash followed by a number, such as -7 or -18, the document is printed from the beginning of the document to the specified page.

You can also combine the above, for example, 3,7,9-11,16- to print pages 3, 7, 9 through 11, and 16 to the end of the document.

Step 4. Press **4** (Control Printer) to view the current status of the printing.

The Print: Control Printer menu (see Figure 5.2) appears on the screen, with the following options:

> **1 C**ancel Job(s) allows you to cancel one or more jobs in the job queue.
>
> **2 R**ush Job allows you to move a print job to the top of the job queue so that it will be printed next.
>
> **3 D**isplay Jobs allows you to display *all* jobs in the print queue in the event your job queue lists more than the three files displayed on the Control Printer screen at a time.

```
Print: Control Printer

Current Job

Job Number: 1                              Page Number:  None
Status:     Printing                       Current Copy: None
Message:    None
Paper:      Standard 8.5" x 11"
Location:   Continuous feed
Action:     None


Job List

Job Document                Destination        Print Options
 1  Pitch.let               LPT 1



Additional Jobs Not Shown: 0



1 Cancel Job(s); 2 Rush Job; 3 Display Jobs; 4 Go (start printer); 5 Stop: 0
```

Figure 5.2   The Print: Control Printer menu before a print job is selected.

4 Go (start printer) causes the printing to proceed after a printing interruption (because of an error, a requirement for a change in a print wheel, etc.).

5 Stop terminates the current print job.

Step 5. Press **Exit** (F7) to return to the document screen.

PRINTING FROM LIST FILES

To print a document from the List Files menu, follow these steps:

Step 1. Press **List** (F5) and **Enter** to view the files in the current (default) directory.

The top of the screen shows the files and their attributes; the bottom of the screen displays the List Files commands.

Step 2. Press the **Up Arrow**, **Down Arrow**, **Left Arrow**, or **Right Arrow** keys to move the highlight bar to the file you want to print.

Step 3. Press **4** (Print).

The prompt **Page(s): All** is displayed, after which you can press **Enter** to select all pages of the document or specify a range of pages.

Step 4. Press **Enter** to select all pages of the document.

WordPerfect prints the document.

Step 5. Press **Exit** (F7) to return to the WordPerfect screen.

USING PRINT OPTIONS

The Options menu on the Print/Options screen (Figure 5.1) gives five options that allow you to change information about your printer:

A Good Selection: Select Printer

S (Select Printer) allows you to see information about the current printer, to edit the current printer, or to change to a new printer (in case your computer is connected to more than one printer or you want to add a new printer to your computer system).

When you press **S** (Select Printer), WordPerfect displays the Print: Select Printer screen, listing all the currently defined printers. (See Chapter 2, "Using WordPerfect," and Appendix B, "Using Your Printer.") A one-line menu appears at the bottom of the screen: **1** Select; **2 A**dditional Printers; **3 E**dit; **4 C**opy; **5 D**elete; **6 H**elp; **7 U**pdate: **0**. The options have the following meanings:

- **1 S**elect specifies that the highlighted printer (in the list of printers on the screen) is the default; that is, all printing will now be sent to that printer.

- **2 A**dditional Printers selects a new printer from additional printer definitions not shown on the screen (i.e., not previously selected). The additional printer definitions are contained on the WordPerfect printer disks. See Chapter 2, "Using WordPerfect," and Appendix B, "Using Your Printer."

- **3 E**dit evokes the Select Printer: Edit screen that allows you to edit the current setup for the highlighted printer. You can change the name of the printer (although the name of the printer definition file will stay the same), the printer port (usually LPT1:, LPT2:, COM1:, or COM2:), the sheet feeder (if any), the forms (for example, from the continuous form-feed Standard 8.5″ × 11″ to nonstandard manual-feed paper, such as legal-sized paper), the cartridges and fonts (on printers that support additional cartridges or fonts, such as laser printers), the initial font (such as pica to elite or Courier to Times), and the path for downloadable fonts (if you have any and your printer supports them).

- **4 C**opy copies the highlighted printer to another printer definition file. This command is valuable when you want to create a new printer definition file that is similar but not identical to one that is already defined or when you want to use the same printer but with a different set of defaults (initial fonts, paper size, printer port, etc.).

- **5 D**elete erases a printer definition file from the disk and omits the printer name from the list on this screen.

- **6 H**elp provides information about using the highlighted printer, for example, DIP switch settings, downloadable fonts, and features not available with the printer.

- **7 U**pdate reloads the printer definition file (for the highlighted printer) from another disk. Use this command, for example, if you have edited the printer definition file with the WordPerfect printer program PTR.EXE and now want to update the file on your WordPerfect disk.

A Binding Agreement: Binding

B (Binding Offset) — the second item on the Print Options menu — allows a wider margin along the binding edge of the page when the document is printed back-to-back on both sides of a page. This feature shifts the text and graphics to the right on odd-numbered pages and to the left on even-numbered pages to allow for spiral binding, three-hole punch, staples, or other binding. The binding width is usually measured in inches (for example, you could set the binding width to 0.75″).

Number of Copies

N (Number of Copies) specifies how many copies of the document will be printed. If you change this option (for example, to **3**), be sure to change it back after the job has printed unless you want *every* print job to make three copies.

Multiple Copies

M (Multiple Copies Generated by) lets you specify whether your printer or WordPerfect generates multiple copies. Most laser printers, for example, have the ability to generate multiple copies of each page. This is usually much faster than letting WordPerfect generate the multiple pages.

Quality Control: Graphics and Text Quality

Most dot matrix printers and some laser printers support different qualities of text and graphics, for example, a draft mode and a near-letter-quality (NLQ) mode. When you press **G** (Graphics Quality) or **T** (Text Quality), WordPerfect displays the one-line menu **1 D**o **N**ot Print; **2 D**raft; **3 M**edium; **4 H**igh: **0** and allows you to select one of these four options.

CONTROLLING THE PRINTER

WordPerfect provides several printer control options to give you more control over the printing process. From the document window, press **Print** (Shift-F7), **4** (**C**ontrol Printer) to access the Control Printer screen shown in Figure 5.2.

Current Job

The top part of the Control Printer screen displays information about the current print job:

- **Job Number** is the number of the current job being printed (print jobs are numbered consecutively during a WordPerfect session). If no job is currently printing, Job Number displays **None**.

- **Status** reports what is currently happening, for example, **Initializing** (if your laser printer is being initialized), **Printing** (if the job is currently going to the printer), or **End of print job** (if the document has printed and WordPerfect is sending end-of-job printer codes).

- **Message** provides additional information (if any) about the current print job. If all is going well, the message is **None**, but if your printer is not connected, you will see the message **Printer not accepting characters**.

- **Paper** gives the paper size, usually **Standard 8.5″ × 11″**.

- **Location** states the type of paper feed, usually **Continuous Feed** or **Manual Feed**.

- **Action** suggests action that you should take in case of a problem. For example, if the printer is not accepting characters, Action displays **Check cable, make sure printer is ON**.

- **Page Number** gives the current page number being printed or the current page number being read but not printed (if you have specified only one page or a range of pages).

- **Current Copy** displays the current copy being printed. If you have specified the default of only one copy of the document per print job, the current copy is always 1; otherwise, it may be 1, 2, or more, depending on the number of copies you specified and the copy being printed.

Job List

The middle section of the Control Printer screen displays the Job List, a list of the next three print jobs, including their job number (under **Job**), filename (under **Document**), destination (the printer port, usually LPT1: or COM1:), and print options (usually **Continuous** or **Manual**).

Below the job list, the message **Additional Jobs Not Shown** displays the number of print jobs in the job queue that are not shown in the Job List.

Options

The one-line menu **1** Cancel Job(s); **2 R**ush Job; **3 D**isplay Jobs; **4 G**o (start printer); **5 S**top: **0** appears at the bottom of the screen.

1 Cancel Job(s) allows you to cancel any or all of the jobs in the print queue by typing the number of the job to be canceled or typing an asterisk followed by **Y** (Yes) for canceling all of the jobs. After a job has been canceled, the paper in your continuous-feed printer advances automatically to the top of the next page to prepare for the next print job.

2 Rush Job changes the priority of the print jobs, thereby allowing a job to "butt in" ahead of other jobs. You may choose whether or not to interrupt the current print job.

3 Display Jobs displays information on *all* the print jobs in the print queue, not just on the next three displayed under Job List.

4 Go (start printer) gives the printer the command to continue printing from the start of the current print job. This command is usually required to resume printing after an interruption due to the Stop printing command (see below), an error in the printer, the end of a page when the paper location is manual feed, or a request to change the print wheel.

Stop interrupts the printing but does not cancel the job. If you have a continuous form-feed printer, it does not advance the paper to the top of the next page. You'll need to manually set the paper to the top of the next page (if necessary) and then press **4** (**G**o) to continue printing from the start of the current print job.

To exit the Control Printer screen and return to the Print menu, press **Enter** or **0**. To return directly from Control Printer to your document, press **Exit** (F7).

Murphy's Law

Anything that *can* go wrong while printing a document *will* go wrong eventually (if you do enough word processing and desktop publishing). When something does go wrong—you run out of paper or ribbon, the paper gets jammed, the ribbon slips out of position, etc.—don't panic. Just use the features found in the Print: Control Printer menu (Figure 5.2).

For example, pressing **5** (**S**top) from within the Print: Control Printer screen will stop the printer until you signal it to resume printing. After the printer stops, the following warning appears at the bottom of the screen:

WARNING: If you use this option, you will need to initialize your printer before you can continue printing. You will also need to make sure all forms are in their original positions. **Are you sure? (Y/No) No**

Then press **Y** (Yes), make the necessary adjustments to your printer (advance the paper to the top of the page, and so on, as indicated by the printer control message), then press **4** (**G**o) to resume printing. WordPerfect allows you to restart the print job at the beginning of any page you specify.

If you need to cancel a print job and begin again, press **1** (Cancel Job(s)) to cancel the print jobs. Then advance the paper in your printer to the top of the next page and begin the print job again.

Because of Murphy's Law, you should *always save your document to the disk before you print it*. Then if something goes wrong with the printing and causes the computer to "hang," your file is safe on the disk.

VIEWING YOUR DOCUMENT BEFORE PRINTING IT

WordPerfect is not a true WYSIWYG (What-You-See-Is-What-You-Get) program, meaning that the document doesn't appear on the text screen exactly as it appears when you print it. The document screen doesn't display, for example, justification, page numbers, headers, footers, graphics, font styles, or font sizes.

Not to worry. If your computer supports any kind of graphics (CGA, EGA, VGA, Hercules, etc.), you can still view these features with WordPerfect's View Document command.

To preview a document as it will appear when printed, press **Print** (Shift-F7), **6** (View Document), and if you are not viewing the full page, press **3** (Full Page).

The View Document screen displays the following menu at the bottom of the screen: **1 (100%) 2 (200%) 3 (Full Page) 4 (Facing Pages): 3**, where the last number (in this case **3**) indicates the current view.

True What-You-See-Is-What-You-Get

The text in the View Document window is often not legible, but the window is true WYSIWYG: you can see the exact location and format of the text on the page, including justification and the page number centered at the bottom of the page. If the document includes graphics, you will also see the placement of figures, text boxes, and lines.

The Keyboard Commands in View Document

You can use the following keys to scroll through your document or to exit the View Document screen:

- **Right Arrow**, **Left Arrow**, **Up Arrow**, or **Down Arrow** to scroll the screen right, left, up, or down.

- **PgDn** and **PgUp** to see the next or previous page, respectively.

- **Screen Down** (keypad +) or **Screen Up** (keypad −) to see the next or the previous screen of information on the same page.

- **Home, Right Arrow** or **Home, Left Arrow** to go to the right or left edge of the page.

- **GoTo** (Ctrl-Home), **Up Arrow** or **GoTo** (Ctrl-Home), **Down Arrow** to go to the top or bottom of the current page.

- **GoTo** (Ctrl-Home), **Right Arrow** or **GoTo** (Ctrl-Home), **Left Arrow** functions the same as **Home, Right Arrow** or **Home, Left Arrow** (see above).

- **GoTo** (Ctrl-Home), *page number*, **Enter** to go to the specified page number.

- **Cancel** (F1) to return to the Print/Options menu.

- **Exit** (F7) to exit the View Document screen and return to the normal document screen.

SELECTING PAPER SIZE AND PAPER TYPE

To select the paper size and paper type for the current screen document, press **Format** (Shift-F8), **2** (**P**age), and **7** (Paper Size). You'll first see a screen for the type of paper (forms) that you want to print: Envelope (for printing business envelopes with manual feed), Standard (for printing normal 8.5″ x 11″ pages, form feed, portrait orientation), Standard · Wide (for printing normal 11″ x 8.5″ pages, form feed, landscape orientation), and All Others, which allows you to specify any kind of printed page using nonstandard settings.

If you select All Others, WordPerfect displays the Format: Paper Size menu, shown in Figure 5.3. Not all printers support all of these paper sizes. Most printers, in fact, support the Standard 8.5″ × 11″ paper on continuous-feed forms or in paper trays, but all other forms are manual feed. If you are printing to a special form, make the desired selection from the Format: Paper Size menu and see how your printer responds. *Note*: Usually you will have to press **Print** (Shift-F7), **4** (**C**ontrol Printer) to get to the Print: Control Printer menu (Figure 5.2), and press **4** (**G**o) to start the printing.

```
Format: Paper Size

     1 - Standard              (8.5" x 11")

     2 - Standard Landscape    (11" x 8.5")

     3 - Legal                 (8.5" x 14")

     4 - Legal Landscape       (14" x 8.5")

     5 - Envelope              (9.5" x 4")

     6 - Half Sheet            (5.5" x 8.5")

     7 - US Government         (8" x 11")

     8 - A4                    (210mm x 297mm)

     9 - A4 Landscape          (297mm x 210mm)

     0 - Other


Selection: 1
```

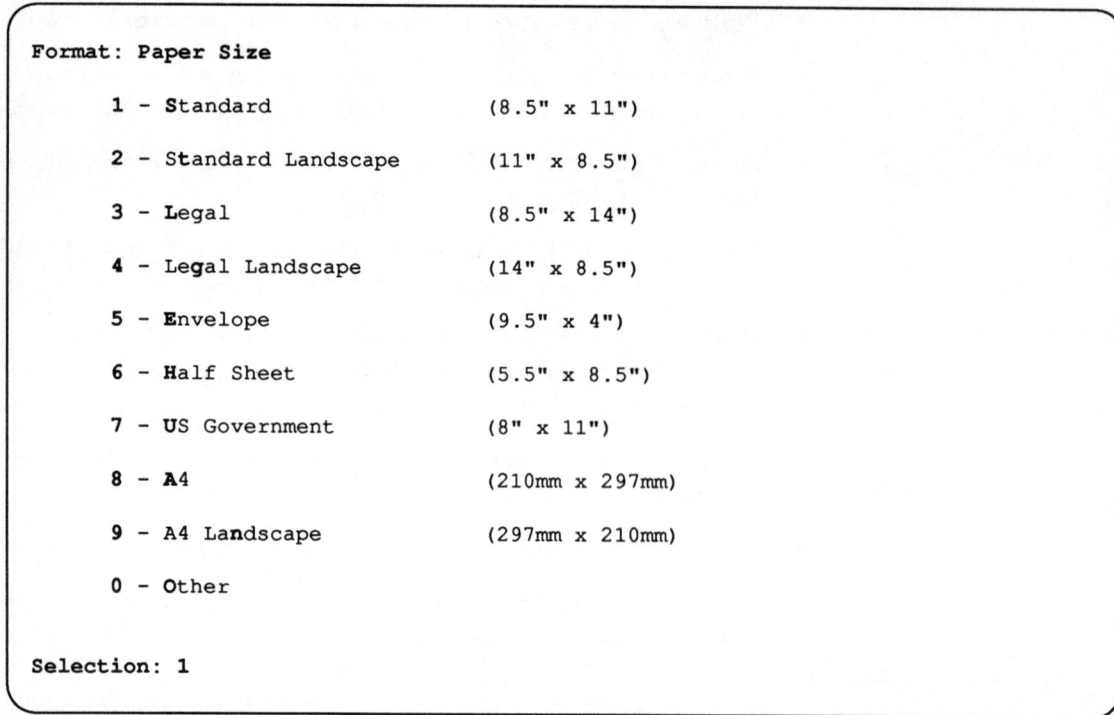

Figure 5.3   The Format: Paper Size menu.

After you make a selection from the Format: Paper Size menu (Figure 5.3), WordPerfect will automatically evoke the Format: Paper Type menu shown in Figure 5.4. Use this menu to select one of the common paper types. If you have a printer with multiple paper-feed bins, the printer may automatically select the proper bin (provided the printer definition file has been configured appropriately). If you have a standard printer, you should select either **1** (**S**tandard) for continuous-feed printing or one of the other types for manual-feed printing.

You can change the paper size and type at the beginning of any new page in your document so that part of the document can be printed, for example, on Standard 8.5″ × 11″ continuous-feed paper and part on Landscape (sideways) 11″ × 8.5″ manual-feed paper (for a wide table or chart).

```
Format: Paper Type

       1 - Standard

       2 - Bond

       3 - Letterhead

       4 - Labels

       5 - Envelope

       6 - Transparency

       7 - Cardstock

       8 - Other




Selection: 1
```

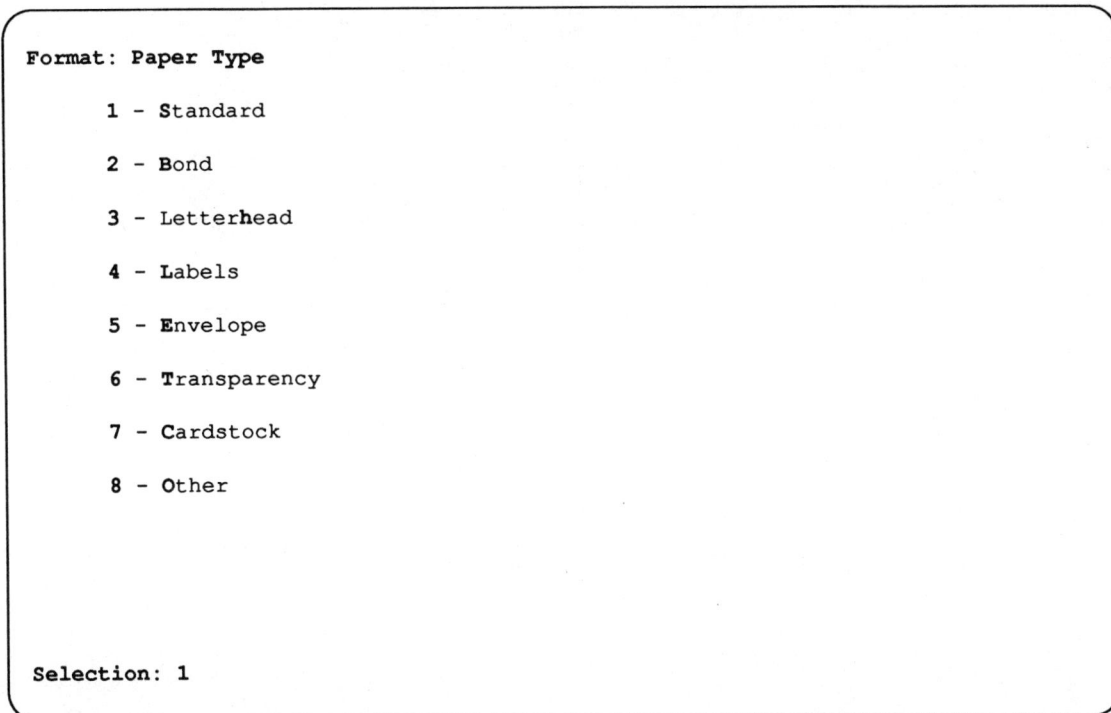

Figure 5.4   The Format: Paper Type menu.

SUMMARY

Make sure your printer is ready before attempting to print a document. You can print a document while it is on the screen, or you can print a document directly from the disk. WordPerfect allows you to change the established print options to accommodate special cases, such as printing on special stationery or printing more than one copy of a document. The Print: Control Printer menu allows you to cancel or temporarily stop a printing job at any time. Remember to always save your document to the disk before you print it.

To preview how a document will look when you print it — including graphics, headers, footers, text spacing, and so on — press **Print** (Shift-F7), **6** (View Document). WordPerfect provides various keyboard commands that help you move through the document and view the document in various ways.

To select a special paper size or paper type, press **Format** (Shift-F8), **2** (**Page**), **8** (**Paper Size/Type**), then make your selections.

Chapter 6

Generating Columns

Your home or company newsletter may never be able to compete with the *Washington Post* or the *Los Angeles Times*. But with WordPerfect, you will be able to create—almost automatically—attractive text columns that will impress your boss, co-workers, and friends.

In this chapter, you will learn how to do the following:

- Use two types of columns—newspaper (snaking) columns and parallel (script) columns.

- Edit text within these columns.

- Manage special column formatting needs.

- Solve specific problems encountered in using columns.

SETTING UP NEWSPAPER COLUMNS

Making newspaper-type columns requires five steps:

Step 1. With the cursor positioned where you want the text columns to begin, define the text columns (i.e., specify the number of columns per page, the amount of space between the columns, etc.).

Step 2. Turn *on* column mode.

Step 3. If necessary, adjust the tab stops for proper paragraph indentation within each column, and, if desired, turn *on* hyphenation and/or justification.

Step 4. Type the text in the columns.

Step 5. Turn *off* column mode.

That's all there is to it. These five steps appear in greater detail in the next few sections of this chapter.

Typing a Newsletter

You should follow these same five steps while typing an issue of the *Ocean Breeze Banner* (shown in Figure 6.1). The base font in the newsletter is 11-point Palatino, but you may use any typeface and point size between 10 and 12 that you wish. (If you want to install additional fonts in WordPerfect before typing this newsletter, see Chapter 10, "Installing Fonts.")

Ocean Breeze Banner

San Diego, California, February 1989

Published by Ocean Breeze Bookstore   Volume 5 Number 3

Autograph Signing

Ocean Breeze Bookstore is pleased to announce an autograph signing party to be held February 8, 1989, to honor local author Grace Fuller. A former member of the Southern California Civic Ballet, Ms. Fuller will be on hand to autograph her new book, *Dance, Ballerina, Dance*, published by Turner Press and currently a national best seller.

Children's Story Hour

Take advantage of Children's Story Hour, every Friday from 2:00 to 3:00 p.m. at the Central City Public Library. This month Stella Torrey will read children's fairy tales. Parents attending the story hour with their children will receive a coupon worth 10% off the price of any children's book at Ocean Breeze Bookstore.

Summer Reading Contest for Children

Ocean Breeze Bookstore, Double Decker Ice Cream Store, and several school districts within the San Diego area are sponsoring a Summer Reading Contest. Elementary School students who set and reach summer reading goals will receive a free ice cream cone from Double Decker and are eligible to participate in a drawing for over $400 in books, software, and school supplies at Ocean Breeze Bookstore. The drawing is August 10, 1989. Information concerning the Summer Reading Contest and entry blanks are available at your local elementary school or at Ocean Breeze Bookstore.

Home Delivery

Do you need that special birthday book but don't have time to go to the store and pick it up? Are you anxious to start reading the latest best seller but don't have transportation to the bookstore? Do you want a book title but don't know where to find it?

If the answer to any of these questions is *yes*, then the new Ocean Breeze Bookstore Home Delivery Service is for you!

Just call our toll-free number 1-800-BOOKBUY and give us the title (and if possible the author and publisher) of the book you want. A representative from our store will make a free delivery to your home. You will be billed for the book later.

Figure 6.1 An issue of *Ocean Breeze Banner*, demonstrating text columns.

Before you begin, you may want to prepare the newsletter masthead. Otherwise, go directly to the steps for making newspaper columns. Follow these steps to prepare the newsletter masthead:

Step 1. Clear the WordPerfect screen by typing **Exit** (F7) and answering the questions that follow. Be sure to answer **N** (No) when asked if you want to exit WordPerfect.

Step 2. Increase the size of the top margin by pressing **Enter** twice.

Step 3. Set the typeface size to extra large by pressing **Font** (Ctrl-F8), **1** (Size), **7** (Ext Large).

Step 4. Select the features for the newsletter title by pressing **Center** (Shift-F6), **Bold** (F6), **Font** (Ctrl-F8), **2** (Appearance), and **4** (Italc), and type the title Ocean Breeze Bookstore. Press **End** to move the cursor past the **[italc]**, **[bold]**, and **[ext large]** codes, and press **Enter** twice to double-space.

If your printer doesn't support large, italicized typefaces, WordPerfect will ignore the codes.

Step 5. Center the subheading by pressing **Center** (Shift-F6), type San Diego, California, February 1989, and press **Enter** twice to double-space.

Step 6. Set the underline to appear in spaces and tabs by pressing the following: **Format** (Shift-F8), **4** (Other), **7** (Underline), **Y** (Yes), **Y** (Yes), **Enter** (to return to the Format menu), **Enter** (to return to the document).

Step 7. Create a horizontal line by pressing **Underline** (F8), **Flush Right** (Alt-F6), **Right Arrow** (to move past the flush right code), **Enter** (to go to the next line), and **Enter** (to double-space after underline).

Step 8. Type the line Published by Ocean Breeze Bookstore, press **Flush Right** (Alt-F6), type Volume 5 Number 3, **Enter**, and make another horizontal line by pressing **Underline** (F8), **Flush Right** (Alt-F6), **Right Arrow**, and **Enter**, as you did before. Press **Enter** again to double space after the horizontal rule.

You are now ready to start the five steps in making newspaper columns. (If you want to use different typefaces for the newsletter and have the printer support them, use the procedures discussed in Chapter 11, "Using Fonts.")

Follow the five steps below for making newspaper columns:

Step 1. Position the cursor where you want the columns to start, then define the columns by first pressing **Columns/Table** (Alt-F7). (If you prepared the *Ocean Breeze Banner* masthead as instructed above, you should press **Enter** to space between the heading lines and where you want the columns to start.)

The one-line menu appears:
1 Columns; **2** Tables; **3 M**ath: **0**. Press **1**, (**C**olumns) and **3** (**D**efine) to select the column definition. WordPerfect displays the Text Column Definition screen shown in Figure 6.2.

1 · Type specifies the type of columns (newspaper, parallel, or parallel with block protect).

```
Text Column Definition

    1 - Type                                    Newspaper

    2 - Number of Columns                       2

    3 - Distance Between Columns

    4 - Margins

    Column    Left     Right    Column    Left     Right
      1:      1"       4"         13:
      2:      4.5"     7.5"       14:
      3:                          15:
      4:                          16:
      5:                          17:
      6:                          18:
      7:                          19:
      8:                          20:
      9:                          21:
     10:                          22:
     11:                          23:
     12:                          24:

  Selection: 0
```

Figure 6.2. The Text Column Definition screen, used to create text columns.

2 · Number of Columns specifies the number of columns on a page.

3 · Distance Between Columns specifies the distance (usually in inches) between each column. How the distance is measured depends upon the default unit of measure (inch, centimeter, point, or letter space).

4 · Margins specifies the right and left margins of each of the columns.

The default column type is Newspaper (also called snaked columns), so you do not need to change option 1. Now press **2** (Number of Columns), **3** (to specify three columns), and **Enter.** Press **3** (Distance Between Columns) (0.5 automatically appears to specify one-half inch between columns); then press **Enter.** WordPerfect automatically sets the column margins based upon the page margins and the number of columns you specified.

    If you wanted to change one or more of the margins, you would select **4** (**M**argins), press **Enter** to move the cursor to the desired margin, and retype the margin value. Since the margins are okay as given, write down the values of the margins (you will need them later) and press **Enter** once to return to the one-line Columns menu. WordPerfect inserts the column definition code into your text.

Step 2.   With the one-line Columns menu still on the screen, press **1** (**O**n) to turn *on* column mode.

From this point in the text to the end of the document or until you turn column mode *off,* WordPerfect will put any text you type into the columns indicated by the current column definition.

Step 3.   Adjust the tab setting so that paragraph indentations fit the columns, then turn *on* justification and hyphenation.

In our example, we want tab stops at one-third inch from the beginning (left margin) of each column. Therefore, press **Format** (Shift-F8), **1** (**L**ine), **8** (**T**ab Set), **Clear to EOL** (Ctrl-End), **0**, **Enter**, 0.33, **Enter**, 2.33 (the left margin of the second column), **Enter**, 2.66, **Enter**, 4.66 (the left margin of the third column), **Enter**, 5.00, **Enter**, **Exit** (F7) (to exit the Tab Set menu), **Enter** (to return to the Format menu), and **Enter** (to return to the document).

    Then press **Format** (Shift-F8), **1** (**L**ine), **1** (**H**yphenation), and **Y** (**Y**es). (See Chapter 4, "Formatting Documents," for more information on hyphenation.) Now, as you type the text of the newsletter, Word-Perfect will pause when a word is a candidate for hyphenation, at which point you should press **Right Arrow** or **Left Arrow** to position the hyphen between syllables, and press **Esc**. If you don't want the word hyphenated, press **Cancel** (F1). Make sure justification is *on* by pressing **3** (**J**ustification), **4** (**F**ull), **Enter** (to return to the Format menu), and **Enter** (to return to the document screen).

Step 4. Type the text of the newsletter.

Each heading is in large type—evoked by pressing **Font** (Ctrl-F8), **1** (**S**ize), **5** (**L**arge)—bold (F6) and centered (Shift-F6). Notice that as the text reaches the bottom of the page in the first column, the cursor automatically jumps up to the top of the second column.

Step 5. When you have completed typing the text of the newsletter, press **Columns/Table** (Alt-F7), **1** (**C**olumns), and **2** (**O**ff) to turn *off* column mode.

WordPerfect inserts a soft page break ([SPg] code) and moves the cursor to the left edge of the page.

Making the Column Lengths Even

As you can see, the last column of the newsletter does not extend to the bottom of the page, and therefore the three columns are not even at the bottom. In other cases when you type a newsletter, the last page may contain only one or two columns. If you want all pages to have three columns of equal length, you should estimate how long the columns should be, calculate the distance from the bottom of the page to the bottom of the columns, and reset the bottom margin to that value. You can calculate this value (if you are good at math), or you can find the correct bottom margin by trial and error. For example, in Figure 20.1 (where the font is 11-point Palatino), we moved the cursor to the top of the page (by pressing **Home**, **Home**, **Home**, **Up Arrow**) and set the bottom margin to 3″ by pressing **Format** (Shift-F8), **2** (**P**age), **3** (**M**argins), **Enter** (to keep the top margin at 1″), **3**, **Enter** (to set the bottom margin to 3″), and **Enter** twice to return to the document. You may also want to insert extra hard returns [HRt] to adjust the line spacing between text and headings to improve the appearance of the newsletter.

If your newsletter columns are *not* justified, you can also adjust the column lengths by inserting a page break where you want one column to end and the subsequent text to move to the next column. Just move the cursor to the desired location and press Hard Page (Ctrl-Enter).

Displaying One Column at a Time

When you get ready to edit your newsletter, you may find that cursor movement is very sluggish with three columns on the screen. You can increase the screen update speed by displaying only one column on the screen at a time. Press **Setup** (Shift-F1), **2** (**Display**), **6** (**Edit-Screen Options, 7** (**Side-by-side Columns Display**), **N** (**No**), and **Enter** three times to return to your document. WordPerfect will print the columns side by side but will display only one column on the monitor, significantly increasing the speed of the screen rewrite. If you have a relatively fast computer (such as an IBM AT or PS/2 Model 70), you can keep columns displayed side by side without significant loss of cursor speed.

Moving Between Columns

The most important cursor movement command to learn in editing columns is **Go To** (Ctrl-Home). Press **Go To-Right Arrow** to move from the current column to the right adjacent column, and **Go To-Left Arrow** to move to the left adjacent column. Press **Go To-Home, Left/Right Arrow** to move to the far left or far right of the adjacent column.

Mixing Columns with Regular Text

You may want to make a newsletter in which part of the page is in columns and part is in regular (single-column) text. You can do this by turning *on* column mode when you want multiple columns and turning *off* column mode when you want regular text. In the middle of a column, press **Hard Page** (Ctrl-Enter) to force a new column. This does *not* force a page break (as you would expect) unless the cursor is in the last (right-most) column. By setting and resetting the column definition and using the **Hard Page** command, you can have, for example, regular text on part of the page, double columns on another part of the page, and triple columns on still another part of the page.

SETTING UP PARALLEL COLUMNS

In addition to supporting newspaper columns, WordPerfect also supports "script" columns, called *parallel columns*. These columns are the kind you would use in writing a script, with the name of a character in one column and the line spoken by the character in another column. The names and the spoken lines are of unequal length but still must be grouped together. An example of this type of document is shown in Figure 6.3, a description of recently acquired books at Ocean Breeze Bookstore, set in 11-point Palatino.

If you want to create the title for this document, follow the steps listed for creating the newsletter masthead given at the beginning of this chapter. Then space between the title and table headings. Set the tabs for the table headings; then type the headings, following these steps:

Step 1.   Set the tabs to 0″, + 1.75″, and + 3.5″.

Step 2.   Type the headings (Title, Author, and Description) with a tab between each word.

Step 3.   Turn *off* justification.

The cursor should now be at the location where you want the columns to begin. Now follow the five steps required to set up columns:

Step 1.   Define the columns by pressing **Columns/Table** (Alt-F7), **1** (**C**olumns), **3** (**D**efine), **1** (**T**ype), **2** (**P**arallel, to specify parallel columns this time), **2** (**N**umber of Columns), **3** (to specify that you want three columns), **Enter**, **3** (**D**istance Between Columns), type 0.25 (to specify one-fourth inch between columns), and press **Enter**. Then press **4** (**M**argins) and set the following margins (by typing each number and pressing **Enter**):

Column 1:	1	2.5
Column 2:	3	4.5
Column 3:	5	7.5

Step 2.   Press **Enter** and **1** (**O**n) to turn columns *on*.

Step 3.   We do *not* want justification, hyphenation, or tab stops in this particular example, so we will skip step 3 and go to step 4.

Step 4.   Type the column text by entering the name of the first book (Computers on Parade) in italics in the first column and then press **Hard Page** (Ctrl-Enter).

The Hard Page forces the cursor to go to the top of the next column. After typing the author's name (Rowland Compton), press **Hard Page**

Book Descriptions

The following is a description of recent arrivals at the Ocean Breeze Bookstore.

Title	Author	Description
Computers on Parade	Rowland Compton	This is a combination tutorial and buyer's guide dealing with all popular brands of personal computers for home and business.
Encyclopedia of Computers	Noah Ahl and Chip Hacking	This huge volume includes descriptions and definitions of all aspects of micro-, mini-, and mainframe computers.
How to Pray	Neil Downey and Theo Goodsell	For the religious and nonreligious alike, this book is a collection of twelve interesting essays and five amazing anecdotes on prayer, written by well known evangelists, scientists, and ordinary people.
How to Play Master Chess	Chester Knight	A complete guide to tournament chess, written by a popular United States Chess Federation Certified Tournament Director. Includes opening, middle game, and end game tactics and strategy.

Figure 6.3   Book descriptions, demonstrating parallel ("script") columns.

again to force the cursor to the third column. Finally, after typing the description of the book, press **Hard Page** once more to force the cursor back to the first column and down to the next item. Each group (consisting of a book title, author, and description) always stays in parallel columns. If you had selected Parallel Columns with Block Protect, each set of items would have stayed together on the same page regardless of where the real page breaks fell. Since you have selected Parallel Columns without Block Protect, a long description, for example, of one of the books could span two (or more) pages.

Step 5.   Turn *off* column mode by pressing **Columns/Table** (Alt-F7) and **3** (**C**olumn On/Off).

SUMMARY

Newspaper columns can make your company newsletter more at- tractive and easier to read. Parallel (or "script") columns are valua- ble for making tables of information and scripts of plays and other productions. To use WordPerfect's column feature, follow five steps: (1) Position the cursor where you want the columns to start, then define the columns by pressing **Columns/Table** (Alt-F7), **1** (**C**olumns), and **3** (**D**efinition). (2) Turn *on* column mode by pressing **1** (**On**). (3) Adjust the tab setting—so that paragraph indentations fit the columns—and, if desired, turn *on* justification and hyphenation. (4) Type the text of the newsletter. And (5) turn *off* column mode by press- ing **Columns/Table** (Alt-F7), **1** (**C**olumns), and **2** (**Off**).

Chapter 7

Drawing Lines and Boxes

Drawing lines and boxes is a fundamental operation of desktop publishing. Lines separate parts of text, direct the reader to key points on the page, create special effects, provide guides for filling in blank forms, and make page layout more aesthetically pleasing. Boxes have essentially the same function as straight lines but also serve to highlight text (such as titles, sidebars, and summaries), to create checklists, and to make square "bullets" (for bulleted lists).

This chapter will cover the following topics:

- How to use WordPerfect's Underline (F8) command to draw horizontal lines.

- How to use WordPerfect's Graphics (Alt-F9) command to draw horizontal and vertical lines of different widths and gray shading.

- How to use WordPerfect's Table (Alt-F7) feature to draw lines and boxes.

- How to draw boxes of different shades of gray, with or without text. (Chapter 9, "Displaying Graphics," will discuss boxes used for graphics.)

- How to create text boxes — for sidebars, pull quotes, summaries, and emphasized text.

- How to position lines and boxes accurately on the printed page.

- How to use boxes for special purposes: check boxes, bullets, white-on-black text, and so forth.

USING UNDERLINE TO DRAW A LINE

Drawing a horizontal line with WordPerfect's Underline (F8) feature is fast and simple. This method, however, has disadvantages compared to drawing a horizontal line with the Graphics (Alt-F9) feature, because underlining lacks flexibility in positioning the line and in changing the line width or the gray shading.

To draw a horizontal line using the Underline method, follow these steps:

Step 1.   At the beginning of the document or just before using the Underline feature, press **Format** (Shift-F8), **4** (**O**ther), **7** (Underline), **Y** (Yes), **Y** (Yes), and **Exit** (F7).

This causes spaces and tabs to be underlined when underlining is *on*.

Step 2.   Move the cursor to the position (as indicated by the **Ln** value at the bottom of the screen) where you want the horizontal line.

You can either press **Enter** until the cursor has the desired **Ln** value or use the Advance feature: press **Format** (Shift-F8), **4** (**O**ther), and **1** (**A**dvance), then enter the new cursor position (see "Positioning Text: Advance" in Chapter 4, "Formatting Documents"). Note that the **Ln** value indicates the location of the upper left corner of the character at the cursor.

Step 3. Press **Underline** (F8) to begin underlining.

Step 4. Press **Space Bar**, **Tab**, or **Flush Right** (Alt-F6) to create the underlining.

USING GRAPHICS TO DRAW HORIZONTAL LINES

Using WordPerfect's Graphics command to draw horizontal lines is also fast and simple, and provides the added features of varying line widths and gray shading.

To draw a horizontal line using Graphics (Alt-F9), follow these steps:

Step 1. Move the cursor to the position (as indicated by **Ln** at the bottom of the screen) where you want the horizontal line.

You can either press **Enter** until the cursor has the desired **Ln** value or use the Advance feature: press **Format** (Shift-F8), **4** (**O**ther), and **1** (**A**dvance), then enter the new cursor position (see "Positioning Text: Advance" in Chapter 4, "Formatting Documents").

Step 2. Press **Graphics** (Alt-F9), **5** (**L**ine), and **1** (**H**orizontal Line).

WordPerfect displays the Graphics: Horizontal Line menu (Figure 7.1, explained below.).

Step 3. Select the desired features (Horizontal Position, Vertical Position, Length of Line, Width of Line, and Gray Shading) from the Graphics: Horizontal Line menu (Figure 7.1).

Note that the position refers to the location on the page of the upper left corner of the line or box.

Setting the Horizontal Position

To set the horizontal (left and right) position of the line on the page, press **1** (**H**orizontal Position) from within the Graphics: Horizontal Line menu. WordPerfect then displays the one-line menu: **Horizontal Pos: 1** Left **2** Right **3** Center; **4** Full **5** Set position: **0**. The following is an explanation of each of these options:

- **1** (**L**eft) positions the line against the left margin.

```
Graphics: Horizontal Line

    1 - Horizontal Position          Left & Right

    2 - Vertical Position            Baseline

    3 - Length of Line

    4 - Width of Line                0.01"

    5 - Gray Shading (% of black)    100%













    Selection: 0
```

Figure 7.1 The Graphics: Horizontal Line menu.

The left margin has the default value of 1″, so if you haven't changed the margin settings, the left tip of the line begins at position 1″.

- **2 (Right)** positions the line against the right margin.

  The right margin has the default value of 1″, so if you haven't changed the margin settings, the right tip of the line begins at position 7.5″ on an 8.5″ × 11″ page.

- **3 (Center)** centers the line between the left and right margins.

- **4 (Full)** draws the line from the left margin to the right margin.

  With options **1** through **3** you have to specify the length of the line, but with option **4** the length is automatically set by the values of the left and right margins.

- **5 (Set position)** allows you to specify the distance from the left margin of the page to the left edge of the horizontal line.

Setting the Vertical Position

To set the vertical position (distance from the top of the page), press **2** (Vertical Position) from the Graphics: Horizontal Line menu. Word-Perfect then displays the one-line menu: **Vertical Position: 1 B**aseline; **2 S**et Position: **0**. Press **1** (**B**aseline) to draw the line at the baseline of the text. Press **2** (**S**et Position) to set the vertical position in inches from the top of the page.

Specifying the Length of the Line

Press **3** (Length of Line) from the Graphics: Horizontal Line menu (Figure 7.1) to specify the desired length of the horizontal line. After pressing **3** (**L**ength of Line), type the length (in inches or other specified unit of measure) and press **Enter**. If the horizontal position is set at Full, you can't specify the line length, since it is automatically set by the width of the text.

Examples of several line lengths are shown in Figure 7.2.

Setting the Width of the Line

The *width* of the line means the *thickness* of the line. Press **4** (Width of Line) from within the Graphics: Horizontal Line menu to set the line width. Figure 7.3 gives a sample of several line widths.

Using Gray Shading

You can also set the gray shading (also called *gray scale*) of a line by pressing **5** (**G**ray Shading) and entering a number from 0 (white) to 100 (black). Figure 7.4 shows various gray shadings of horizontal lines.

DRAWING VERTICAL LINES

Drawing vertical lines uses the same steps as drawing horizontal lines but has some additional flexibility.

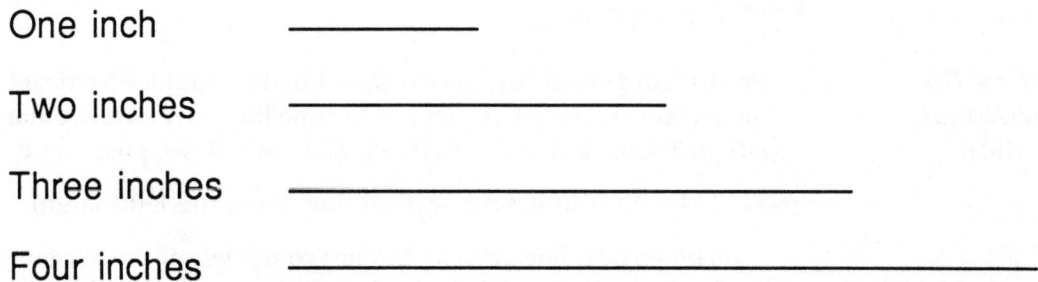

One inch ────────

Two inches ──────────

Three inches ────────────

Four inches ──────────────────

Figure 7.2 Sample line lengths.

Width 0.01″ ─────────────────

Width 0.02″ ─────────────────

Width 0.05″ ━━━━━━━━━━━━━━━━━

Width 0.1″ ■■■■■■■■■■■■■■■■■

Width 0.5″ ████████████████

Figure 7.3   Sample line widths.

To draw a vertical line, follow these steps:

Step 1.   Press **Graphics** (Alt-F9), **5** (Line), and **2** (Vertical Line).

WordPerfect displays the Graphics: Vertical Line menu (Figure 7.5, explained further on). Note that you don't need to move the cursor to the location of the vertical line, since the Vertical Line menu allows you to select both the horizontal and the vertical positions of the line.

Step 2.   Select the desired features (Horizontal Position, Vertical Position, Length of Line, Width of Line, and Gray Shading) from the Graphics: Vertical Line menu (Figure 7.5).

You can use the Vertical Line feature with the cursor anywhere on the page and draw a vertical line at that position or anywhere else on the page.

Setting the Horizontal Position

Press **1** (Horizontal Position) from within the Graphics: Vertical Line menu. WordPerfect then displays the one-line menu: **Horizontal Position: 1 L**eft; **2 R**ight; **3 B**etween Columns; **4 S**et position: **0**.

- **1** (Left) positions the vertical line along the left margin.

The vertical line actually lies just to the left of the left margin, as shown in Figure 7.6.

100%	
90%	
80%	
70%	
60%	
50%	
40%	
30%	
20%	
10%	
5%	
2%	

Figure 7.4 Sample line gray shadings.

- **2 (R**ight) positions the line along the right margin.

  The vertical line actually lies just to the right of the right margin, as shown in Figure 7.6.

- **3 (B**etween Columns) draws the line between columns when column mode is *on*.

- **4 (S**et position) allows you to specify the location of the vertical line relative to the left margin of the page.

Setting the Vertical Position

When you press **2** (Vertical Position) from the Graphics: Vertical Line menu, WordPerfect displays the following one-line menu: **Vertical Position: 1 F**ull Page; **2 T**op; **3 C**enter; **4 B**ottom; **5 S**et position: **0**. The following explains each of these options:

- **1 (F**ull Page) produces a line that spans from the top margin to the bottom margin.

  If you choose this option, you can't specify the line length, since it depends on the settings of the top and bottom margins.

- **2 (T**op) positions the line against the top margin of the page.

- **3 (C**enter) centers the line vertically on the page.

```
Graphics: Vertical Line

        1 - Horizontal Position          Left Margin

        2 - Vertical Position            Full Page

        3 - Length of Line

        4 - Width of Line                0.01"

        5 - Gray Shading (% of black)    100%













        Selection: 0
```

Figure 7.5   The Graphics: Vertical Line menu.

- **4** (**B**ottom) positions the line against the bottom margin of the page.

- **5** (**S**et position) allows you to specify a vertical position relative to the top margin of the page.

Specifying the Length of the Line

Press **3** (Length of Line) from the Graphics: Vertical Line menu (Figure 7.5) to specify the desired length of the vertical line. After pressing **3** (Length of Line), type the length (in inches, if those are your units of measure) and press **Enter**. If the vertical position is set at Full Page, you can't specify the length of the line, since Word-Perfect will automatically calculate the length according to the margins.

Setting the Width of the Line

You can set the line *width* (or line *thickness*) by pressing **4** (Width of Line) from within the Graphics: Vertical Line menu. See Figure 7.3 for various widths of lines.

The lines to the right and left of this paragraph demonstrate that choosing Left Margin or Right Margin from the Horizontal Position option of the Graphics: Vertical menu draws the lines *outside* the margins, not *on* the margins. This prevents the line from covering text located within the margins.

Figure 7.6 Vertical Lines positioned for the left and right margins. The vertical lines actually appear outside the margins to avoid covering text within the margins.

Using Gray Shading

You can set the gray shading of a vertical line by pressing **5** (**G**ray Shading) and entering a number from 0 (white) to 100 (black). Figure 7.4 shows various gray shadings of lines.

EDITING LINES

With WordPerfect 5.1, you can edit horizontal or vertical lines. Just follow these steps:

Step 1.   Move the cursor to the right of the WordPerfect code for the line that you want to edit.

Step 2.   Press **Graphics** (Alt-F9), **5** (**L**ine), **3** (**H**orizontal) or **4** (**V**ertical).

The Graphics: Horizontal Line menu (Figure 7.1) or the Graphics: Vertical Line menu (Figure 7.5) appears.

Step 3.   Change the settings for the line.

You can now modify the position, length, width, or gray shading of the line.

Step 4.   Press **Exit** (F7) to return to the document screen.

USING TABLES TO DRAW LINES AND BOXES

The WordPerfect Tables feature is a powerful tool for creating lines and boxes, not just for creating data tables (see Chapter 13, "Typing Tables and Equations"). For example, if you want to draw a box around a paragraph, you can use a text box as explained below, but you can also use the Tables feature by following these steps:

Step 1.   With the cursor at the location where you want a box around a paragraph, press **Columns/Table** (Alt-F7).

The one-line menu, **1 C**olumns; **2 T**ables; **3 M**ath: **0**, appears on the status line.

Step 2.   Press **2** (Tables).

WordPerfect displays the menu **Tables: 1 C**reate; **2 E**dit: **0.**

Step 3.   Press **1** (Create).

Step 4.   At the prompt **Number of Columns,** enter **1.**

Since you want a single box, you should specify only one column in your table.

Step 5.   At the prompt **Number of Rows,** enter **1.**

A box with double lines on all sides appears on the screen. You can press **Exit** (F7) now if you want the box with double lines, or you can continue with the next step if you want a box with single lines.

Step 6.   Press **3** (Lines), **7** (All), and **2** (Single) to set all lines of the box to single.

You could set any side of the box to any type of line you want, or to no line at all. By selecting the proper location and type of lines, you can draw horizontal or vertical lines, as well as boxes, within the text of your document.

Step 7.   After the box has the desired appearance, press **Exit** (F7).

Step 8.   Type the paragraph.

As the number of lines in the paragraph grows, the box grows with it.

Using the Tables feature to create lines and boxes has several advantages over the **Graphics** (Alt-F9) methods:

- The boxes and lines are visible on the text screen. You don't have to go into View Document to see what the boxes and lines look like.

- The boxes and lines expand or contract as you add or delete text from within the box.

- The boxes and lines are easy to edit.

- For boxes and lines associated with text, Tables are easier to manipulate than graphics boxes and lines.

Using the Tables feature also has some disadvantages:

- You can't set the table at an absolute location on the page. The boxes move relative to the text.

- You can't insert graphics into the boxes.

You'll see more details on using Tables in Chapter 13, "Typing Tables and Equations." In the next section, you'll see how to draw boxes in the normal way, using the WordPerfect **Graphics** (Alt-F9) features.

DRAWING BOXES

A *box*, as used in WordPerfect, is a graphics unit. The box may contain a figure or text, or it may be empty. The edges of the box may be single lines, double lines, or no lines at all.

Chapter 9, "Displaying Graphics," will cover how to use boxes with charts, diagrams, digitized photographs, line drawings, or any other kind of artwork. This chapter will focus on empty boxes (used, for example, to make check boxes and bullets) and boxes containing text.

General Principles of WordPerfect Boxes

- All graphics (figures, tables, and text boxes) are contained in a graphics box. A box may be empty, may contain a graphics image, or may contain text, but it may not contain graphics and text at the same time (although boxes may overlap in order to superimpose text on graphics images).

- All the types of graphics (figures, tables, and text boxes) are accessed through the Graphics (Alt-F9) key, which evokes the one-line menu **1** **F**igure; **2** **T**able Box; **3** **T**ext **B**ox; **4** User-defined Box; **5** **L**ine; **6** **E**quation: **0**, allowing you to create, edit, renumber, or specify options for any box type.

- A graphics box may be one of four types: figure, table, text, and user-defined. WordPerfect does not, however, differentiate between the functions of these four types. For example, each chapter in this book treats all side matter (text, graphics, charts, diagrams) as figures, and therefore we use only Graphics (Alt-F9), **1** (**F**igure) to insert side matter. In our technical papers, however, we number figures (usually graphics images) and tables (usually text) separately and therefore would choose **1** (**F**igure) for the figures and **2** (**T**able Box) for the tables.

- WordPerfect numbers all graphics boxes consecutively and independently according to the type of box. If you insert, delete, or change the order of a particular type of box (for example, a figure), WordPerfect automatically renumbers the figures consecutively, but it doesn't change the order or numbering of the tables, text boxes, or user-defined boxes.

- You may treat the options for each type of graphics box independently. The specific attributes of the boxes include the following: the border style (type and size of lines around the box, if any), the outside border space (the area left blank between the document text and the box border), the inside border space (the area left blank between the figure inside the box and the box border), the numbering method, the caption number style and position, the minimum offset from the beginning of the paragraph, and the gray shading.

- The location of a box is marked by the position on the page of the upper left corner of the box. The horizontal position is measured from the left edge of the page; the vertical position is measured from the top of the page.

Specifying the Graphics Box Options

Each type of graphics box (figure, table, text, user-defined) has a default set of characteristics. To change the defaults, follow these steps:

Step 1. Move the cursor to the location in the text where you want a box.

This step is not always necessary; for some types of boxes you can specify the horizontal and vertical positions of the box on the page.

Step 2. Press **Graphics** (Alt-F9).

The following one-line menu appears on the screen: **1** Figure; **2** Table Box; **3** Text Box; **4** User-defined Box; **5** Line; **6** Equation: **0**. We have already discussed option **5** (**Line**).

Step 3. Press a number or mnemonic letter corresponding to the box you want to make.

All four types of boxes function exactly the same, but we suggest that you use **3** (Text **B**ox) to create a text box and **4** (User-defined Box) to create an empty box. WordPerfect now displays the one-line menu (for example): **1** Create; **2** Edit; **3** New Number; **4** Options: **0**.

Step 4. Press **4** (Options).

The Options: Text Box menu appears on the screen (see Figure 7.7 and explanation below).

Step 5. Set the options according to the specific needs of your document.

Step 6.   Press **Exit** (F7) after you have specified the options.

The cursor returns to the document screen.

Changing the graphics box options is, of course, optional. You can use the default characteristics of a box, change them once at the first of your document, or change them many times throughout the document. You may even wish to set new options for each box you create.

The Options: Text Box Menu

Figure 7.7 shows the Options: Text Box menu. It is similar to the Options menus for figures, tables, and user-defined boxes.

- **1** (**B**order Style) evokes the one-line menu: **1** None; **2** Single; **3** Double; **4** Dashed; **5** Dotted; **6** Thick; **7** Extra Thick: **0** for setting the type of border line on the left, right, top, and bottom. See Figure 7.8 for examples of border styles.

- **2** (**O**utside Border Space) specifies the amount of space between the border of the box and any text that wraps around it.

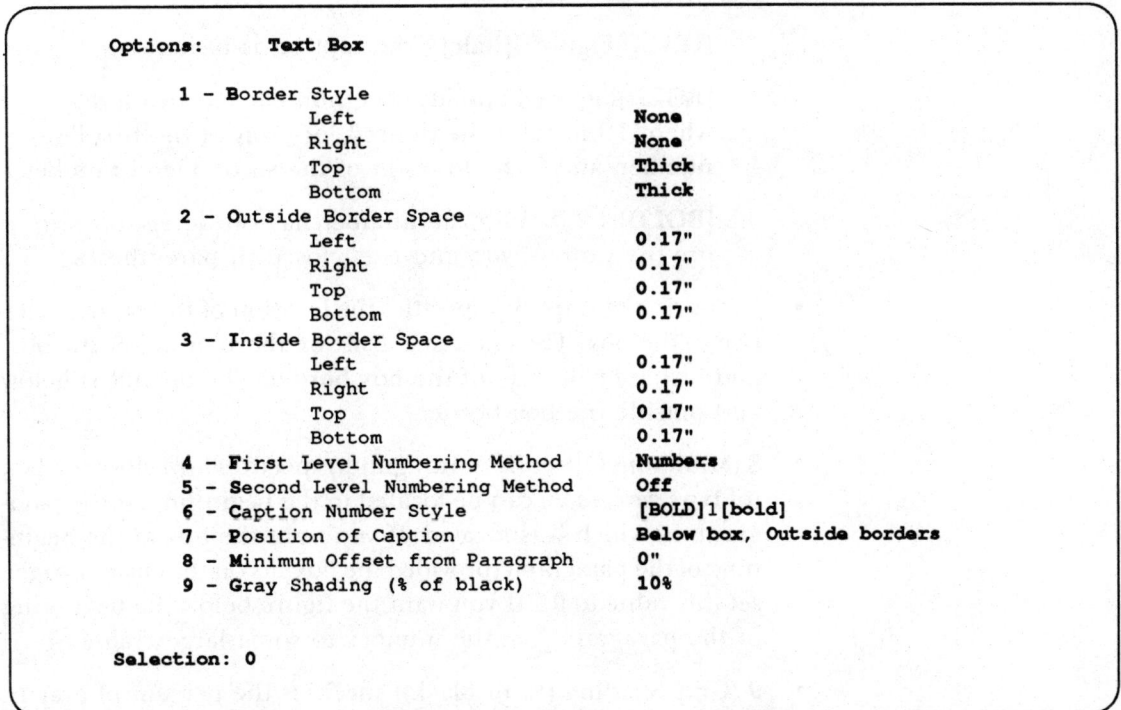

```
Options:      Text Box

     1 - Border Style
              Left                          None
              Right                         None
              Top                           Thick
              Bottom                        Thick
     2 - Outside Border Space
              Left                          0.17"
              Right                         0.17"
              Top                           0.17"
              Bottom                        0.17"
     3 - Inside Border Space
              Left                          0.17"
              Right                         0.17"
              Top                           0.17"
              Bottom                        0.17"
     4 - First Level Numbering Method       Numbers
     5 - Second Level Numbering Method      Off
     6 - Caption Number Style               [BOLD]1[bold]
     7 - Position of Caption                Below box, Outside borders
     8 - Minimum Offset from Paragraph      0"
     9 - Gray Shading (% of black)          10%


     Selection: 0
```

Figure 7.7 The Options: Text Box menu.

- **3** (**I**nside Border Space) specifies the amount of space between the border of the box and any text or graphics within the box.

- **4** (**F**irst Level Numbering Method) evokes the one-line menu **1** Off; **2** Numbers; **3** Letters; **4** Roman Numerals: **0**, allowing you to turn *off* figure numbering or to specify the numbering type: numbers (1, 2, 3, . . .), letters (A, B, C, . . .), and roman numerals (I, II, III, . . .). When numbering is *on*, WordPerfect includes the figure number with the figure box in your text.

- **5** (**S**econd Level Numbering Method) evokes the same one-line menu as the **F**irst Level Numbering Method item. If you specify a second-level numbering method (other than *off*), WordPerfect will automatically number the figures as 1.1, 1.2, 1.3, etc., rather than 1, 2, 3, etc. To go to the next first-level number, use the New Number option described above.

- **6** (**C**aption Number Style) specifies how you want the figures numbered in the caption (if caption is *on*). The default format is **[BOLD]**1**[bold]** for text boxes, but you can choose almost any desired format, such as:

  [ITALC]Figure 1**[italc]** (The caption is in italics.)

  [BOLD]Figure 1.2**[bold]** (The number has two levels, where 1 indicates the desired location of the first-level number, and 2 the location of the second-level number.

  [BOLD](1.2)**[bold]** (The number has two levels, doesn't use the word *Figure,* and is enclosed in parentheses.)

- **7** (**P**osition of Caption) specifies the location of the caption relative to the box. The choices consist of above or below the box, and inside or outside of the box border. The default is below and outside the box border.

- **8** (**M**inimum Offset from Paragraph) specifies how close the box (of type *paragraph*) can be located to the beginning of the paragraph in which it is located. If you want the box at the beginning of the paragraph (provided the box fits on the current page), set this value to 0″. If you want the figure below the beginning of the paragraph, set the number to some larger value.

- **9** (**G**ray Shading (% of black)) specifies the percent of gray in the figure box. 0% is white; 100% is black. See Figure 7.8 for several examples of gray shading.

Default text box;
thick line top and
bottom; 10% gray
shading.

Thick lines;
50% gray shading.

Thin single lines;
0% gray shading.

Extra thick lines;
80% gray shading.

Double lines;
5% gray shading.

Mixed border types;
0% gray shading.

Dashed lines;
20% gray shading.

Thin single lines;
100% gray shading.

Dotted lines;
0% gray shading.

No border lines;
2% gray shading.

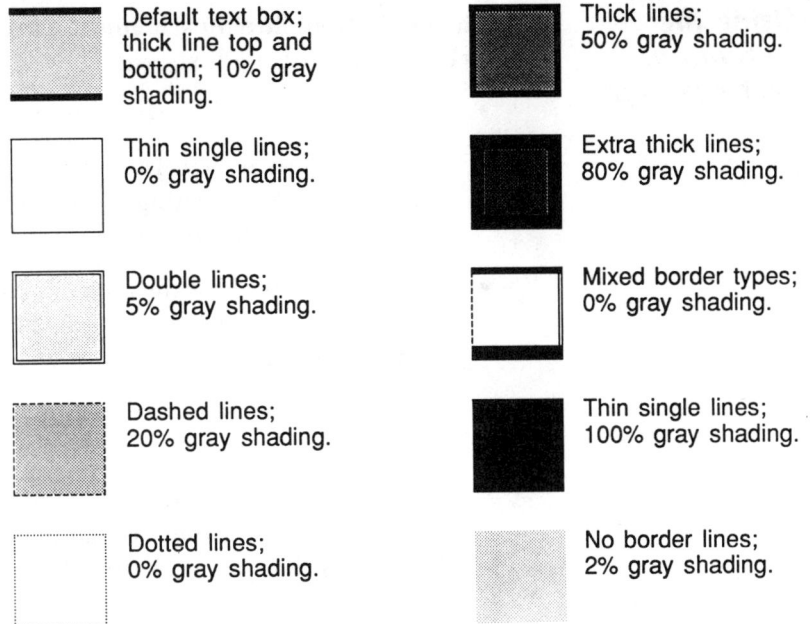

Figure 7.8 Sample border styles and gray shading of boxes.

Creating a Box

To create a box, follow these steps (we will use the example of a text box, but the same basic steps apply to all four types of boxes):

Step 1. Press **Graphics** (Alt-F9), press **3** (Text **B**ox), and **1** (**C**reate).

The Definition: Text Box menu appears on the screen (see Figure 7.9).

Step 2. Make the desired selections from the Definition: Text Box menu.

The menu allows you to load graphics, DOS text, or a WordPerfect file into the box, create a caption, designate the type of text box (Paragraph, Page, or Character, as explained later), set the vertical and horizontal positions, specify the size of the box, indicate whether you want text to wrap around the box, and edit the information (graphics or text) in the box. You can also enter text into the box through the **8** (**E**dit) command. Remember that the location of the box is the position on the page of the upper left corner of the box.

Step 3. Press **Exit** (F7) or **Enter** to return to the document screen.

An outline of the figure appears (in part or in whole) on the text screen. To see how the text box will appear on the printed page, press **Print** (Shift-F7), **6** (View Document).

***Using the
Definition:
Text Box Menu***

The Definition: Text Box menu (Figure 7.9) allows you to specify characteristics of the text box:

- **1** (**F**ilename) loads a text or graphics file into the box.

  The text file may be a DOS (ASCII) text file or a WordPerfect file. Chapter 8 ("Creating Graphics") and Chapter 9 ("Display-ing Graphics") discuss how to use boxes with graphics.

- **2** (**C**ontents) specifies the type of material contained within the box. You can select **1** (**G**raphics), **2** (**G**raphics on **D**isk), **3** (**T**ext), or **4** (**E**quation).

- **3** (**C**aption) specifies the contents (but not the location or box number) of the box caption.

  The location is defined in the Options: Text Box menu (Figure 7.7), and the box number is automatically determined by Word-Perfect (unless you explicitly change the box number).

```
Definition: Text Box

     1 - Filename

     2 - Contents               Text

     3 - Caption

     4 - Anchor Type            Paragraph

     5 - Vertical Position      0"

     6 - Horizontal Position    Right

     7 - Size                   3.25" wide x 0.62" (high)

     8 - Wrap Text Around Box    Yes

     9 - Edit



     Selection: 0
```

Figure 7.9 The Definition: Text Box menu.

- **4** (Anchor Type) sets the type of box: Paragraph, Page, or Character.

  The Paragraph type, as the name implies, is associated with the paragraph in which the box was created. The box always stays with the paragraph unless the paragraph begins near the bottom of the screen and the box can't fit at the bottom, in which case the box moves to the next page.

  The Page type places the box at a specified location on the page that is independent of where the actual box code occurs in the document or what text surrounds the box.

  The Character type behaves as a single character in a line of text. If the character box has a height greater than the normal line height, WordPerfect increases the line height to accommodate the box.

- **5** (Vertical Position) sets the vertical position relative to the paragraph, page, or line (depending on the type).

- **6** (Horizontal Position) sets the horizontal position on the page.

  For example, you can specify the left margin, right margin, or center for a paragraph type box, or specify the exact offset (in 0.01-inch increments) from the left edge of the page.

- **7** (Size) indicates the size (width and height) of the box.

  WordPerfect automatically expands or compresses your graphics image to fit the size that you specify.

- **8** (Wrap Text Around Box) specifies whether text lines should wrap around the box or print across the box.

- **9** (Edit) allows you to edit text or add new text within the text box.

  You can use most of WordPerfect's editing and formatting features while editing the box contents.

USING TEXT BOXES IN YOUR PUBLICATIONS

You can use WordPerfect text boxes in published material in the following ways (depending upon the capabilities of your printer):

- To accent titles, summaries, warnings, or mathematical equations.

- To create sidebars (ancillary notes) and pull quotes (a short quote from the main text, usually set in enlarged type).

- To make reversed type (white characters on a dark background, also called *dropout* or *surprinted* text). This feature is supported by PostScript printers but not by Hewlett-Packard-compatible printers.

- To create rotated text. (Some printers don't support this feature.)

- To insert an enlarged character, such as the initial letter of an article or chapter.

- To make check boxes.

- To display square bullets (for bulleted lists).

Figure 7.10 is a one-page document that uses several of these types of boxes.

Printing White on Black

PostScript printers support reversed type (white on black), but Hewlett-Packard-compatible printers do not. If your printer can't print white on black, create the title for Figure 7.10 using normal black-on-white text. To create the title "Customer Assurance Plan" in reversed type (white on black), follow these steps:

Step 1. Press **Graphics** (Alt-F9), **3** (Text **B**ox), **4** (**O**ptions).

The Options: Text Box menu (Figure 7.7) appears.

Step 2. Press **1** (**B**order Style) and **1** (**N**one) four times to set the border to None.

Step 3. Press **9** (**G**ray Shading), type 100, press **Enter** to make an black-filled box, and press **Exit** (F7) to return to the document screen.

Step 4. Press **Graphics** (Alt-F9), **3** (Text **B**ox), and **1** (**C**reate).

The Definition: Text Box menu (Figure 7.9) appears.

Step 5. Press **4** (**A**nchor **T**ype), **2** (**P**age), **Enter** (to accept 0 pages to skip), **5** (**V**ertical Position), **2** (**T**op), **6** (**H**orizontal Position), **1** (**M**argins), **3** (**C**enter), **7** (**S**ize), **1** (Set **W**idth/Auto Height), type 6.16, press **Enter**, and **9** (**E**dit).

These commands define the attributes of the text box and display the text box edit screen.

Customer Assurance Plan

Ocean Breeze Bookstore

Ocean Breeze Bookstore is committed to customer satisfaction. We pledge to you the following:

☐ *An unconditional 90-day guarantee on all merchandise sold in our store.* If you find that the item you purchased is defective or unsatisfactory in any way, return it for full refund.

☐ *Knowledgeable sales personnel.* Our employees are avid readers who know books. We stay informed of the latest in the book world.

☐ *Friendly employees.* Ocean Breeze Bookstore wants to help you in your entertainment and educational reading.

☐ *Wide selection of books and software.* We have the largest showcase of books in the San Diego area. Our software packages include all the most popular computer programs in the industry.

In addition to the above guarantees, we also provide the following community programs to assist our customers and to encourage reading among the children of our community:

☐ *Children's Story Time* at the Central City Public Library. This popular program encourages reading and library use during the summer. Stella Torrey, a noted author of children's fairy tales, is a frequent guest.

Our employees are avid readers who know books.

☐ *The Children's Reading Contest* is also held each summer. Co-sponsored by the Ocean Breeze Bookstore, the Double Decker Ice Cream Store, and several school districts in the San Diego metropolitan area, the program promotes summer reading by offering prizes to children who set and achieve reading goals.

Figure 7.10 Customer Assurance Plan, demonstrating boxes and lines.

Step 6. Press **Font** (Ctrl-F8), **5** (Print Color), **2** (White), and **Enter.**

This makes the text white, to produce a white-on-black phrase.

Step 7. Press **Font** (Ctrl-F8), **4** (Base Font), and select 12-point Helvetica; then press **Font** (Ctrl-F8), **1** (Size), and **7** (Ext Large).

Step 8. Type Customer Assurance Plan, and press **Exit** (F7) twice.

Step 9. Press **Exit** (F7) again to return to your document.

You can use this same technique to produce white on gray, light gray on dark gray, or any text color on any other background color (if your printer supports color).

Here are two hints to help you create reversed type:

- Make sure the text isn't too big to fit in the text box. If the text is too big, it simply won't print. Make sure your box dimensions are large enough.

- While preparing the document, use 0% gray shading so that View Document will show how the document looks. Then use 100% gray shading (black) in the final printed version.

Rotating the Text

To create rotated text in your document (PostScript printers only), follow these steps:

Step 1. Press **Graphics** (Alt-F9), **3** (Text **B**ox) (or any of the other box types), and **4** (**O**ptions).

Step 2. Set the desired options for the box, then press **Exit** (F7) to return to your document.

Step 3. Press **Graphics** (Alt-F9), **3** (Text **B**ox) (or some other box type), and **1** (**C**reate).

Step 4. Set the type, positions, and size of the box.

Step 5. Press **9** (**E**dit), type the desired text, and use any desired WordPerfect formatting command.

Step 6. Anytime while editing the box text, press **Graphics** (Alt-F9).

WordPerfect displays the one-line menu: **Rotate Text: 1** 0°; **2** 90°; **3** 180°; **4** 270°: **0.** Figure 7.11 shows how WordPerfect defines text rotations.

Step 7. Select the desired rotation by pressing **1** (0°), **2** (90°), **3** (180°), or **4** (270°).

Step 8. Press **Exit** (F7) to exit the text box editor and return to the Definition: Text Box menu.

Step 9. If necessary, change the position and dimensions of the text box.

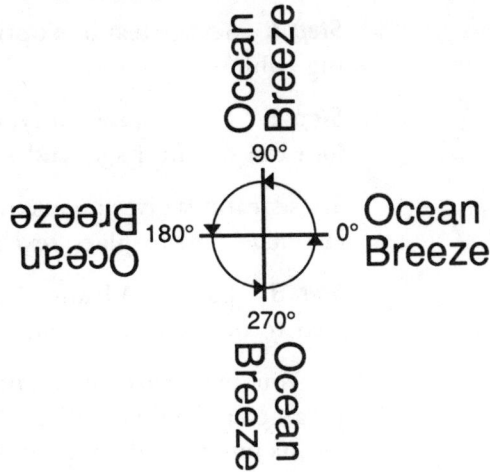

Figure 7.11 Text Rotation. To rotate text, press **Graphics** (Alt-F9) while editing the text in a text box.

If you set the text rotation to 90° or 270° the text may no longer fit properly within the dimensions of the box, since *only the text within the box rotates, not the box itself.* Regardless of the text rotation, WordPerfect uses the upper left corner of the box to define the box position on the page.

Creating Check Boxes and Square Bullets

To create a check box or bullet (like the small open square bullets in Figure 7.10), follow these two general steps:

Step 1. Set the text box options for thin, single-line borders to make check boxes or for no border at all to make bullets, and then set the desired gray shading.

For check boxes, use 0% gray shading; for bullets use any value from 0% to 100%.

Step 2. Create the text box as type Character and set the size to approximately 0.15″ × 0.15″.

If you are going to insert several check boxes or bullets into the document, put the commands for these two steps in a style (see Chapter 14, "Using Styles") or in a macro (see Chapter 15, "Using Macros").

Making an Enlarged Initial Letter

Follow these steps to make an enlarged initial letter like the "O" in Ocean Breeze Bookstore at the beginning of the body of the document in Figure 7.10:

Step 1. Set the text box options to no border and to 0% gray shading (white).

Step 2. Create a box of type Page, position the box at the desired location on the page, and select Wrap Text Around Box to *No.*

These features give you maximum flexibility to position the enlarged character and to place text around it.

Step 3. Use the Advance feature as necessary to position the text next to or around the enlarged letter.

You may have to spend some time adjusting the text box parameters and using View Document to see how the enlarged letter fits into your document. The procedure can be tedious the first time, but after gaining experience, you can create enlarged letters quite easily.

Creating a Pull Quote

Follow these general steps to create the pull quote (the shaded box containing "Our employees are avid readers who know books") in Figure 7.10:

Step 1. Set the text box options.

In this example, press **Graphics** (Alt-F9), **3** (Text **B**ox), and **4** (**Op**tions) to access the Options menu (Figure 7.7), then set the top and bottom borders to Thick, the left and right borders to None, and the gray shading to 40%.

Step 2. Create the text box.

In this example, use type Page, set the vertical position to Center, specify a horizontal position of about 3.4″ (from the left edge of the paper), set a width (with auto height) of about 2.2″, and leave the Wrap Text to *yes.*

Step 3. Type the text in the box.

From within the Definition: Text Box menu (Figure 7.9), press **9** (**E**dit), set the desired font typeface, size, and appearance, and type Our employees are avid readers who know books.

SUMMARY

Drawing lines and boxes in desktop published material allows you to create special effects, direct the reader's attention, make rules, create white-on-black text, rotate text, insert check boxes, create bullets, produce sidebars, and insert pull quotes.

You can draw horizontal lines using the Underline feature or the Graphics Horizontal Line feature of WordPerfect. When drawing horizontal or vertical lines from the Graphics menu, you can specify the horizontal and vertical positions, determine the line length, set the line width, and designate the gray shading.

For some applications, you can use the Tables feature to create boxes and lines.

WordPerfect provides power and flexibility in creating text boxes. You can specify the top, bottom, left, and right border styles, designate the gray shading of the box, include text or leave the box blank, and position the box anywhere on the page.

Chapter 8

Creating Graphics

USING THIRD-PARTY SOFTWARE AND HARDWARE
  Graphics Software
  Scanners
  Mouse Input Devices

USING BITMAP IMAGES AND LINE DRAWINGS
  Bitmap Graphics
  Line Graphics

PREPARING A FIGURE WITH LOTUS 1-2-3
  Creating the Lotus 1-2-3 Worksheet
  Creating the Lotus Bar Chart

USING A SCANNER

USING CLIP ART

USING THE GRAB UTILITY
  GRAB Startup Options

SUMMARY

The purpose of graphics is to make printed material more reada-ble, more easily understood, or more interesting. WordPerfect's graphics feature, therefore, is ideal for producing readable, under-standable, and interesting documents.

WordPerfect graphics involves more than just pictures. It includes all types of artwork: lines, text boxes, and graphic images. The previ-ous chapter dealt with lines and boxes. This chapter deals with how to create graphic images that can be incorporated into a WordPer-fect document. The next chapter will explain how to insert the im-ages into a document.

In this chapter you will learn the following:

- How to use third-party (non-WordPerfect) software and hardware for creating graphics.

- How to create the two types of graphic images: *bit-mapped* (or *paint*) images and *line* (or *draw*) images.

- How to use Lotus 1-2-3 to create charts and graphs for use in WordPerfect.

- How to use a scanner to create digitized photographs for use in WordPerfect.

- How to use clip art with WordPerfect.

- How to use WordPerfect's GRAB utility to save graphics screens in a WordPerfect graphics file.

Again we stress that this chapter deals only with creating graphics. Chapter 9, "Displaying Graphics," will demonstrate how to insert the graphics into a WordPerfect document.

USING THIRD-PARTY SOFTWARE AND HARDWARE

WordPerfect contains a graphics editor, but its function is limited to scaling, cropping, rotating, and inverting the image. You can't ac-tually edit dots and lines on the image itself. You must create all figures, therefore, using WordPerfect's graphics program, DrawPer-fect, or third-party (non-WordPerfect) software and hardware.

Graphics Software

The third-party graphics programs supported by WordPerfect are listed in Figure 8.1. WordPerfect can directly read the files produced by some of the programs—for example, PC Paintbrush and Lotus 1-2-3—but can't read files produced by other software—for exam-ple, Harvard Graphics—unless the graphics are saved (exported) in a special format.

Graphics Program	Direct Support?	Export File Format
Adobe Illustrator	□	EPS
AutoCAD	■	DXF, HPGL
Boeing Graph	□	IMG
CCS Designer	□	HPGL
ChartMaster	□	HPGL
CIES (Compuscan)	□	TIFF
DFI Handy Scanner	□	IMG, TIFF
DiagramMaster	□	HPGL
Diagraph	□	HPGL
Dr. Halo II	■	DHP
Energraphics	□	IMG, TIFF
Freelance Plus	□	CGM
GEM Paint	■	IMG, TIFF
GEM SCAN	■	IMG, TIFF
Generic CAS	□	HPGL
Graph-in-the-Box	□	HPGL
Graphwriter	□	CGM
Harvard Graphics	□	HPGL, CGM, EPS
HP Graphics Gallery	□	TIFF, PCX
HP Scanning Gallery	□	TIFF, PCX
IBM CADAM, CATIA, CBDS, GDDM, GPG	□	HPGL
Lotus 1-2-3	■	PIC
MacPaint	■	PNTG
Microsoft Chart	□	HPGL
PC Paintbrush Plus	■	PPIC
PC Paintbrush	■	PCX
PicturePack	■	WPG, CGM, PCX
PlanPerfect	□	CGM
Professional Plan	■	
Quattro	□	PIC, EPS
SignMaster	□	HPGL
SlideWrite Plus	□	HPGL, TIFF, PCX
SuperCalc 4	□	PIC
Symphony	■	PIC
Versacad	□	HPGL
VP Planner	□	PIC
Windows Paint	■	MSP
Words & Figures	□	PIC

Figure 8.1 Graphics programs that can produce WordPerfect-readable files. The solid boxes indicate direct support; the open boxes indicate indirect support through exported files. CGM = Computer Graphics Metafile; DHP = Dr. Halo PIC format; DXF = AutoCAD format; EPS = Encapsulated Postscript; HPGL = Hewlett-Packard Graphics Language Plotter File; IMG = GEM Paint format; MSP = Microsoft Windows Paint format; PCX = PC Paintbrush format; PIC = Lotus 1-2-3 format; PNTG MacPaint format; PPIC = PC Paint Plus format; TIFF = Tagged Image File Format; WPG = WordPerfect Graphics.

You will see examples of how to produce compatible graphics files with PC Paintbrush, Harvard Graphics, Lotus 1-2-3, and the DFI Handy Scanner later in this chapter.

See Appendix D, "Directory of Products," for a list of selected graphics software packages.

Scanners

Besides the normal computer hardware used in desktop publishing (computer, monitor, keyboard, mouse, and printer), you may also use a scanner (digitizer) to produce computerized images. Graphics scanners are devices that transfer a photograph, line drawing, or other artwork from paper to a digitized electronic image. Optical character recognition (OCR) scanners are devices that convert text from a printed page into a computer text file. This book uses the word *scanner* or *digitizer* to refer to a graphics scanner and the abbreviation *OCR* to refer to an optical character recognition scanner. (Some scanners can perform both graphics and OCR functions.)

Both handheld scanners and desktop scanners are available commercially. Handheld scanners are portable and inexpensive ($200 to $400) but produce pictures with relatively low resolution. Desktop scanners are large and expensive ($1000 to $10,000) but produce pictures quickly, with high resolution, and with multiple gray shades. Appendix D, "Directory of Products," gives a list of selected scanners and their manufacturers.

You will see how to use a scanner in a later section of this chapter.

Mouse Input Devices

Most graphics software and scanners support or require mouse input devices. If you are serious about producing graphics, buy a mouse. A list of selected suppliers is listed in Appendix D, "Directory of Products."

USING BITMAP IMAGES AND LINE DRAWINGS

Graphics software produces one of two types of pictures:

- *Bitmap graphics.*

- *Line graphics.*

Bitmap graphics, also called *paint* images, are created by varying the colors of small dots (called picture elements, or *pixels*) on the screen. The simplest bitmap images have only two colors — black and white, with pixels being either *on* or *off*. On the other extreme, sophisticated bitmap images may have up to 256 colors.

Line graphics, also called *draw* or *vector* graphics, are created by defining the paths of objects (lines, circles, boxes, etc.).

Bitmap graphics have the following advantages:

- Bitmap graphics software is generally less expensive than line graphics software.

- Bitmap graphics offer greater flexibility for making detailed changes. You can either turn *on* and *off* one pixel at a time or fill regions with color or gray shading. Line graphics software doesn't support editing individual pixels.

- Freehand drawing with bitmap graphics is generally easier than freehand drawing with line graphics. Some line graphics software, in fact, doesn't support freehand line drawing.

Line (vector) graphics have the following advantages:

- Line graphics software produces smoother lines and curves in the printed output (see Figure 8.2A) than those produced by bitmap images (Figure 8.2B), and the resulting output has a much more professional look.

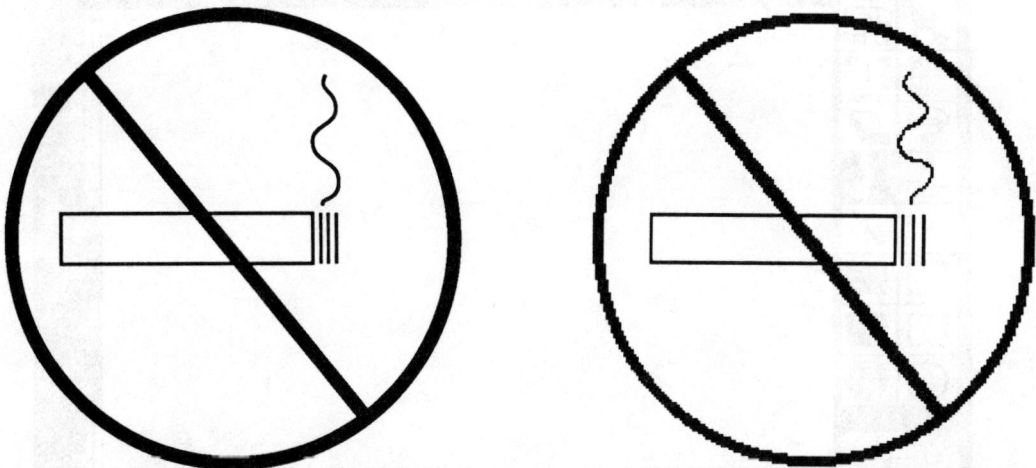

Figure 8.2   Sample figure using (A) line graphics and (B) bitmap graphics. Notice that the lines and curves in the line graphic are smooth, while those in the bitmap graphic are jagged.

- Editing lines and shapes is much easier with line graphics. You just have to "grab" the object and move it, elongate it, shrink it, rotate it, or change its fill pattern. Bitmap graphics doesn't support these editing features.

- Line-graphics software usually has built-in objects for making professional graphs, diagrams, charts, and figures that are ideally suited for business, education, and science.

We suggest that you obtain and use both types of software. Some figures lend themselves better to bitmap images and other figures better to line drawings. Consult your computer dealer or graphics software manufacturers for information on the type of graphics produced by a particular software package.

Bitmap Graphics

The graphics edit screen of a bitmap graphics program will look something like Figure 8.3. You use the mouse and the software tools (the icons that appear along the left edge of the screen) to create and edit a bitmap picture.

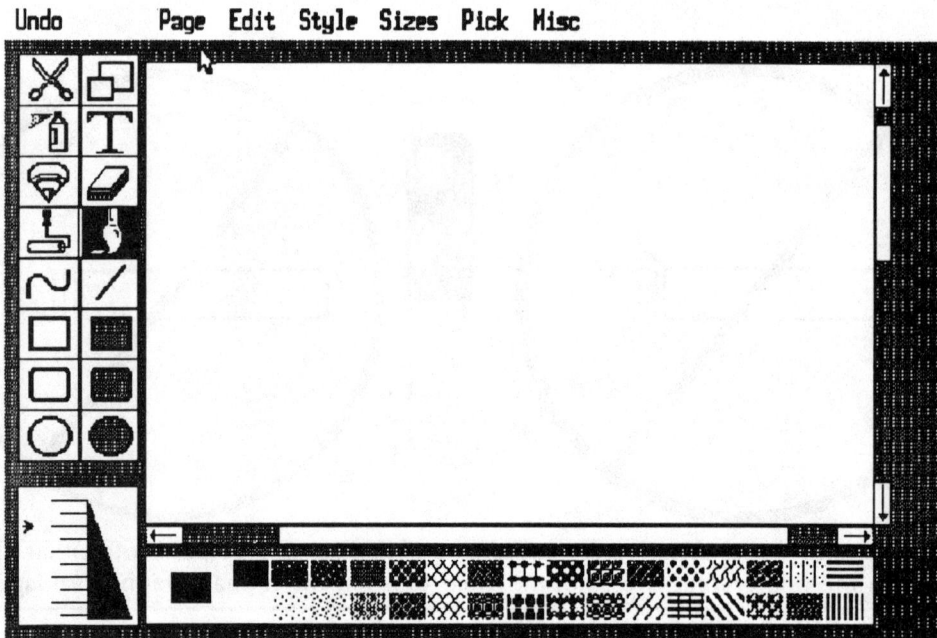

Figure 8.3   PC Paintbrush graphics edit screen.

The software tools usually include scissors for cutting and moving sections of the image, a spray can for coloring parts of the picture, a text tool for inserting alphanumeric symbols, a paint roller for filling enclosed regions of the figure with color patterns or gray shades, a brush for painting lines and shapes, a curved line tool for creating smooth curved lines, a straight line tool for drawing straight lines, and box and circle tools for drawing open or filled boxes and ellipses.

Figure 8.4 shows a graphics picture drawn using PC Paintbrush, a bitmap graphics program.

Line Graphics

Line graphics software includes many of the same tools used in bitmap graphics programs. In addition, the lines and shapes created in a line graphics program can be edited as objects. Thus you can change the length of a line, the size of a box, the shape of an ellipse, or the fill pattern of an object. On the other hand, you can't change individual pixels.

Figure 8.4 A graphics picture drawn with the paint (bitmap) program PC Paintbrush.

Figure 8.5 shows a graphics picture created using Harvard Graphics, a line graphics program. If you compare this figure with Figure 8.4, you can see the major difference between bitmap graphics and line graphics: the curved lines in the line graphic are smoother than those in the bitmap graphic.

PREPARING A FIGURE WITH LOTUS 1-2-3

The popular electronic spreadsheet program Lotus 1-2-3 (from Lotus Development Corporation) saves graphics files in a .PIC format, which WordPerfect can read directly.

We assume in the following discussion that you know how to use Lotus 1-2-3.

Creating the Lotus 1-2-3 Worksheet

Figures 8.6 shows a worksheet for estimating the monthly profits of the Home Delivery Program at Ocean Breeze Bookstore. This Lotus template demonstrates one valuable application of an electronic spreadsheet: you can change the number of books (the estimated monthly sales), the average retail cost of the books (based upon expected purchases and prices of hardback and softback titles), and

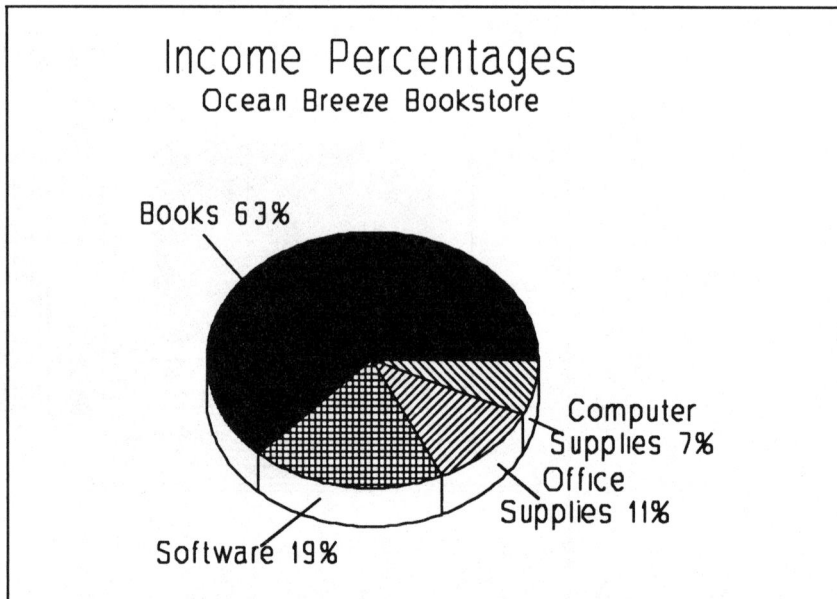

Figure 8.5 A graphics picture drawn with the draw (line) graphics program Harvard Graphics.

```
PROJECTED MONTHLY PROFITS
BOOK HOME DELIVERY
------------------------------------------
Number of Books:        700
     Ave Retail:      19.70
   Expense/Book:      13.91
    Profit/Book:       5.79
                   ----------
Monthly Profit:      4054.00
                   ==========
------------------------------------------
Expense              Cost      Total
Item (Average)    per book      Cost
------------------------------------------
Book, wholesale      11.15   7805.00
Postage, orders       0.17    119.00
Delivery Cost         0.92    644.00
Receipt Forms         0.04     28.00
------------------------------------------
           TOTAL:    12.28   8596.00

------------------------------------------
Fixed              Amount      Cost
Expense         per month  per book
------------------------------------------
Advertising        200.00      0.29
Salaries           578.00      0.83
Automobile         147.00      0.21
Office Expenses    215.00      0.31
------------------------------------------
           TOTAL: 1140.00      1.63
```

Figure 8.6   Projected Profits of Book Home Delivery, a Lotus 1-2-3 worksheet.

the estimated item expenses and fixed expenses, then let the spreadsheet automatically calculate the overall expense per book and the expected monthly profit. Use Lotus 1-2-3 and Figures 8.6 and 8.7 to create the worksheet. When you are done, save the worksheet under the name PROFIT (and Lotus will add the filename extension .WKS). Do not exit Lotus 1-2-3.

Creating the Lotus Bar Chart

With the worksheet in Figure 8.6 still on the Lotus 1-2-3 screen, you can make bar charts or line graphs of any set of data you want. For example, press the Lotus command / and choose **Graphics** to get

```
A1:  'PROJECTED MONTHLY PROFITS        A18:  'Receipt Forms
A2:  'BOOK HOME DELIVERY               B18:  (F2) 0.04
A3:  \-                               C18:  (F2) +$B$4*B18
B3:  \-                               A19:  \-
C3:  \-                               B19:  \-
A4:  "Number of Books:                C19:  \-
B4:  700                              A20:  (F2) "TOTAL:
A5:  "Ave Retail:                     B20:  (F2) @SUM(B15..B18)
B5:  (F2) 19.7                        C20:  (F2) @SUM(C15..C18)
A6:  "Expense/Book:                   A22:  \-
B6:  (F2) +B20+C31                    B22:  \-
A7:  Profit/Book                      C22:  \-
B7:  (F2) +B5-B6                      A23:  'Fixed
B8:  \-                               B23:  "Amount
A9:  "Monthly Profit:                 C23:  "Cost
B9:  (F2) +B7*B4                      A24:  'Expenses
B10: \=                               B24:  'per month
A11: \-                               C24:  "per book
B11: \-                               A25:  \-
C11: \-                               B25:  \-
A12: 'Expense                         C25:  \-
B12: "Cost                            A26:  'Advertising
C12: "Total                           B26:  (F2) 200
A13: 'Item (Average)                  C26:  (F2) +B26/$B$4
B13: 'per book                        A27:  'Salaries
C13: "Cost                            B27:  (F2) 578
A14: \-                               C27:  (F2) +B27/$B$4
B14: \-                               A28:  'Automobile
C14: \-                               B28:  (F2) 147
A15: 'Book, wholesale                 C28:  (F2) +B28/$B$4
B15: (F2) 11.15                       A29:  'Office Expenses
C15: (F2) +$B$4*B15                   B29:  (F2) 215
A16: 'Postage, orders                 C29:  (F2) +B29/$B$4
B16: (F2) 0.17                        A30:  \-
C16: (F2) +$B$4*B16                   B30:  \-
A17: 'Delivery Cost                   C30:  \-
B17: (F2) 0.92                        A31:  "TOTAL:
C17: (F2) +$B$4*B17                   B31:  (F2) @SUM(B26..B29)
                                      C31:  (F2) @SUM(C26..C29)
```

Figure 8.7   The cell contents of the Lotus 1-2-3 worksheet shown in Figure 8.6.

into the graphics menu; then set graph **Type** to **Bar**, the **X** coordinates to cells **A26 . . . A29**, and the **A** coordinates to **C26 . . . C29**. Then select **View** to see the figure, and finally select **Save** to save the figure using the filename BARCHART (Lotus automatically appends .PIC). The figure is now ready for loading into WordPerfect (see Figure 8.8).

USING A SCANNER

You can use a scanner (digitizer) for creating disk files from photographs and from other printed material. For example, Figure 8.9 shows a scanned image (at 100 DPI, a relatively low resolution) of a photograph of the authors' youngest daughter. This figure was scanned and edited using the DFI Hand Scanner (from Diamond Flower Electric Instrument Company) and the accompanying program called SCAN.

USING CLIP ART

Many software companies sell *clip art*, computer images drawn by professional artists. Using clip art has the following advantages:

- Clip art is easy to use. You don't have to be an artist to include graphics in your publications.

- Clip art is high-quality, since it is created by professional artists.

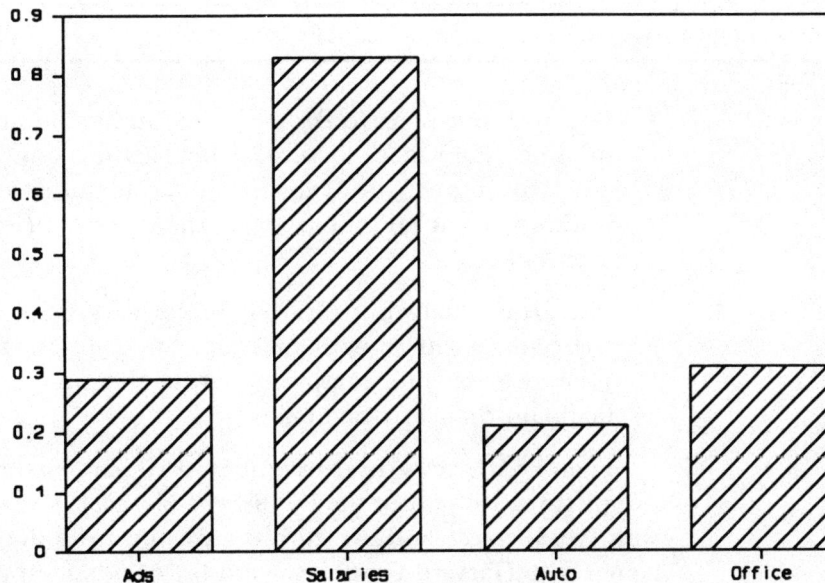

Figure 8.8 A Lotus 1-2-3 figure of the cost per book for advertisements, salaries, automobile (deliveries), office expenses.

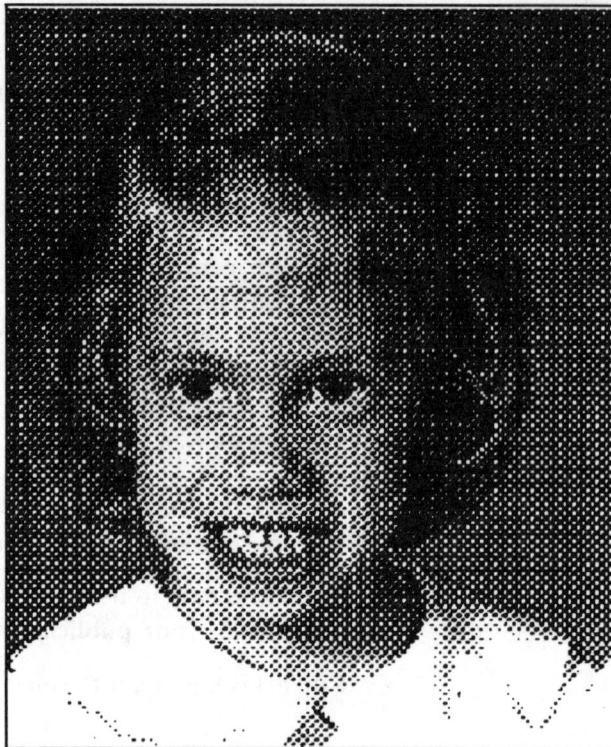

Figure 8.9   A scanned image at a resolution of 100 DPI.

- Clip art is inexpensive. For example, you can buy about 200 pictures of a Publisher's PicturePak (Marketing Graphics Incorporated) for under $100. If you had to create the art yourself, even working fast at minimum wages, the labor cost would be well over $400.

- Clip art is usually line (draw) graphics, and therefore WordPerfect prints it with smooth lines (compare Figures 8.2A and 8.2B). When you expand, compress, or rotate the line drawings, they maintain their artistic quality.

Figure 8.10 shows three examples of clip-art pictures. The first two pictures are part of the Publisher's PicturePak that is bundled with WordPerfect, and the third is a picture from the clip art that comes with Harvard Graphics. For a list of other suppliers of clip art, see Appendix D, "Directory of Products."

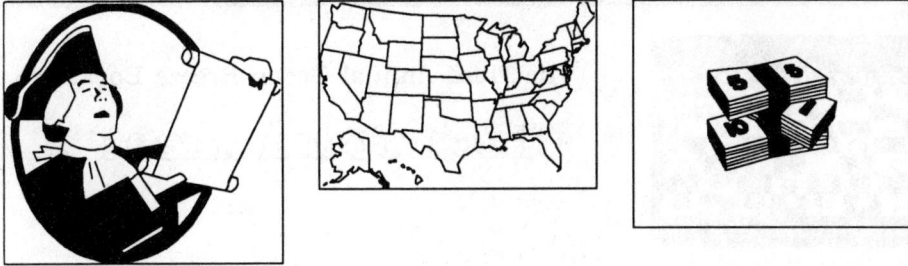

Figure 8.10   Examples of clip art. The first two pictures are from the Publisher's PicturePak and the third is from Harvard Graphics.

If the clip art is in .WPG (WordPerfect Graphics) format or one of the compatible formats shown in Figure 8.1, you can use the art directly. Otherwise, you have to load the art into a graphics program that can read the clip-art file format and then save it in a WordPerfect-compatible format. For example, WordPerfect can't read the Harvard Graphics clip-art directly; therefore you have to load the art into Harvard Graphics and save it back to the disk as a .EPS or .HPGL file.

USING THE GRAB UTILITY

If your graphics software can't produce a file format compatible with WordPerfect, you can use WordPerfect's GRAB utility to capture a graphics screen and save it to the disk.

For example, suppose you have to prepare the advertisement for the Ocean Breeze Bookstore annual chess tournament and want a picture of a chess board (see Figure 8.11). To capture a picture from almost any graphics software using GRAB, follow these steps:

Step 1.   Exit WordPerfect (if necessary) and get into the directory C:\WP51 (or whatever directory contains the WordPerfect program GRAB.COM.

Step 2.   Type grab /h and press **Enter**.

The /h is the *help* command and causes GRAB to display information about using the program, but does not install the program. You should carefully read the information.

Step 3.   Type grab and press **Enter** to install the program in memory.

A message informing you that GRAB was successfully installed appears on the screen. GRAB is a so-called TSR (terminate-and-stay

The Third Annual Ocean Breeze Bookstore

Chess Tournament

DATES: February 8 to March 15, 1989

PARTICIPATION: Open

FORMAT: 5 round Swiss System, one game per week.
Rated by the United States Chess Federation.

TIME CONTROL: 40/2 & 20/1

ENTRY FEE: $15 in advance; $20 after February 8, 1989.

PRIZES: Trophies and gift certificates for first three places overall, and for top two under 2000, under 1800, under 1500, under 1200, and unrated.

DIRECTOR: Charles Chaney, USCF Senior Tournament Director

Registration forms are available at all Ocean Breeze Bookstore Offices.

Figure 8.11   Advertisement for the Ocean Breeze Bookstore chess tournament, demonstrating how to use WordPerfect's GRAB utility.

resident) program since it now stays resident in memory while you run other programs.

Step 4. Run your computer chess program.

Almost any graphics-oriented program will work, but for our purposes we have chosen the chess program.

Step 5. Play through several moves until the board is in the desired setup.

Step 6. Press **Alt-Shift-F9** to activate GRAB.

You will hear a low-pitched buzz if the screen is in text mode or if the screen capture is impossible to complete for some other reason. Otherwise, you will hear a two-tone sound (low pitch to high pitch) indicating that GRAB is active and ready to capture a picture. GRAB also displays a box that borders the capture image. You can move the box, change its size, etc., with the following keyboard commands:

> **Up Arrow, Right Arrow, Down Arrow, Left Arrow** keys move the box (but do not change its size).
>
> **Shift**-*arrow keys* change the size of the box.
>
> **Ins** toggles between course and fine increments in moving or resizing the box.
>
> **Esc** aborts the GRAB program and returns you to your chess game.

Step 7. Use the arrow keys and **Shift**-arrow keys to surround the image you want to capture.

Step 8. Press **Enter** to capture the image.

GRAB produces a two-tone sound (high pitch to low pitch) indicating that the image has been captured.

GRAB saves the image in the default directory under the name GRAB.WPG. If you capture more images, the second filename is GRAB1.WPG, the third is GRAB2.WPG, etc.

Having saved the image as a .WPG file, you can directly load the file into a WordPerfect document using the Graphics (Alt-F9) commands described in the next chapter.

GRAB Startup Options

The WordPerfect GRAB utility supports several startup options (so-called *switches*):

- /D=*pathname* specifies the directory where GRAB.WPG, GRAB1.WPG, etc., will be saved.

- /H displays the help screens for using GRAB.

- /R removes GRAB from memory.

- /I ignores the DOS-busy flag. This is required in order for GRAB to run with some applications software.

- /M forces the GRAB.WPG files to be monochrome bitmaps.

- /S installs the additional command (when GRAB is active) **Space Bar,** which enables you to toggle between move mode and size mode. The arrow keys (without modifiers) are used in both modes.

- /K causes the cutout box size from the previous image capture to be similar each time GRAB is activated.

For example, typing the command (at the DOS prompt) grab /d=c:\wp51 /s installs the image-capture utility, specifies that the captured images will be saved in the directory C:\WP51, and installs the Space Bar command.

SUMMARY

To include graphics in your publications, you must create the graphics (outside of WordPerfect) using graphics software, a scanner, or clip art.

WordPerfect supports two types of graphics: bitmap (paint) graphics and line (draw) graphics. An example of a program that creates bitmap graphics is PC Paintbrush (bundled with the Microsoft Mouse). An example of a program that creates line graphics is Harvard Graphics. WordPerfect directly supports .PIC files from Lotus 1-2-3.

Using high-quality clip art in your publications is easy and inexpensive.

If you want to use a picture from a graphics program that doesn't save pictures in any WordPerfect-compatible format, use the WordPerfect GRAB utility.

In the next chapter ("Displaying Graphics") you will see how to use these various types of graphics in your own publications.

Chapter 9

Displaying Graphics

Once you have created or obtained a figure, chart, diagram, digitized photograph, or clip art (as explained in the previous chapter, "Creating Graphics"), you are ready to insert the graphics file into your WordPerfect document. In this chapter you will learn the following:

- How to specify the general features of a graphics box, including border style, outside and inside border space, figure numbering and captions, and gray shading.

- How to retrieve a figure into a graphics box, insert the caption, position the figure on the page, and specify the figure size.

- How to edit graphics within a WordPerfect graphics box: scaling (expanding and compressing) the figure within the graphics box, moving the figure within the box, and rotating and inverting the figure.

- How to print the figure (within a document) in draft, medium, or high quality.

GENERAL PRINCIPLES OF WORDPERFECT GRAPHICS

The following points will help you better understand WordPerfect's graphics capabilities:

- All graphics (figures, tables, and text boxes) are contained within a graphics box. The box may not contain both a figure and text at the same time (although boxes may overlap in order to superimpose text on graphics images).

- All of these types of graphics (figures, tables, and text boxes) are accessed through the Graphics (Alt-F9) key, which evokes the one-line menu **1** Figure; **2** Table Box; **3** Text Box; **4** User-defined Box; **5** Line; **6** Equation: **0**, allowing you to create, edit, renumber, or specify options for any graphics type.

- The graphics box may be one of four types: figure, table, text, and used-defined. WordPerfect does not, however, specify the *function* of a figure, table, text box, or user-defined box. For example, each chapter in this book treats all side matter (text, graphics, charts, diagrams) as figures, and therefore we use only Graphics (Alt-F9), **1** (Figure) to insert side matter. In our technical papers, however, we number figures (usually graphics images) and tables (usually text) separately and therefore would choose **1** (Figure) for the figures and **2** (Table) for the tables.

- WordPerfect numbers all graphics boxes consecutively and independently according to the type of box. If you insert, delete, or change the order of a particular type of box (for example, a figure), WordPerfect automatically renumbers the figures consecutively, but it doesn't change the order or numbering of the tables, text boxes, or user-defined boxes.

- You may treat the options for each type of graphics box independently. The specific attributes of the boxes include the following: the border style (type and size of lines around the box, if any), the outside border space (the area left blank between the document text and the box border), the inside border space (the area left blank between the figure inside the box and the box border), the numbering method, the caption number style and position, the minimum offset from the beginning of the paragraph, and the gray shading.

The Key to WordPerfect Graphics

The key—literally and figuratively—to WordPerfect graphics is the Graphics (Alt-F9) key, which produces the one-line menu **1** Figure; **2** Table Box; **3** Text Box; **4** User-defined Box; **5** Line; **6** Equation: **0**. The following is a description of these options:

- **1** Figure allows you to create, edit, renumber, or specify options for document figures.

- **2** Table Box allows you to create, edit, renumber, or specify options for document tables.

- **3** Text Box allows you to create, edit, renumber, or specify options for text boxes.

- **4** User-defined Box allows you to create, edit, renumber, or specify options for user-defined boxes.

- **5** Line allows you to draw horizontal or vertical straight lines (of specified widths, lengths, locations, and gray shades).

- **6** Equation allows you to create mathematical, statistical, and scientific equations.

Remember, from WordPerfect's point of view, the box options are identical except that they are numbered and defined independently. For a discussion of creating text boxes, see Chapter 7, "Drawing Lines and Boxes."

INSERTING GRAPHICS INTO A DOCUMENT

Usually, a figure includes some type of graphics image – a digitized photo, line drawing, or artwork. The general steps required to incorporate a figure into a WordPerfect document are as follows (we will give *specific* steps for creating graphics figures later):

Step 1. Create the original figure outside of WordPerfect.

Although WordPerfect can resize, scale, rotate, or invert a figure, it cannot create images or modify the lines, colors, or dots in graphics. Therefore, you must create the graphics outside of WordPerfect. See Chapter 8, "Creating Graphics," for details.

Step 2. If necessary, save or convert the figure produced in step 1 to a WordPerfect compatible file format.

WordPerfect directly supports many popular graphics file formats, which means you can load certain files (i.e., PIC files from Lotus 1-2-3, PCX files from PC Paintbrush, PPIC files from PC Paint Plus, DHP files from Dr. Halo II, IMG files from GEM Paint and GEM SCAN, DXF files from AutoCAD, and MSP files from Windows Paint) directly into WordPerfect and skip this step in the procedure. Other graphics file formats (such as HPGL files from Harvard Graphics, PIC files from Quattro, SuperCalc 4, and VP Planner) must be saved in a special format. Check Figure 8.1 (of the previous chapter) to determine if WordPerfect directly supports your graphics program. If your graphics program doesn't support any of the file formats listed in Figure 8.1, you should use the WordPerfect GRAB utility (also described in the previous chapter).

Step 3. Specify the options for the box that will contain the graphics.

Press **Graphics** (Alt-F9), **1** (**Figure**), **4** (**Options**) to access the Options: Figure menu (Figure 9.1) to specify the attributes of the box. We will discuss these options in the next section.

Step 4. Enter the filename of the figure you created in step 1 (or saved to the disk in step 2).

Press **Graphics** (Alt-F9), **1** (**Figure**), **1** (**Create**) (to access the Definition: Figure menu, Figure 9.2), **1** (**Filename**), and then type the name of the graphics file (or press **List** (F5) and retrieve a file from the List Files screen). We will perform these operations and discuss the

```
Options:        Figure

         1 - Border Style
                 Left                       Single
                 Right                      Single
                 Top                        Single
                 Bottom                     Single
         2 - Outside Border Space
                 Left                       0.16"
                 Right                      0.16"
                 Top                        0.16"
                 Bottom                     0.16"
         3 - Inside Border Space
                 Left                       0"
                 Right                      0"
                 Top                        0"
                 Bottom                     0"
         4 - First Level Numbering Method   Numbers
         5 - Second Level Numbering Method  Off
         6 - Caption Number Style           [BOLD]Figure 1[bold]
         7 - Position of Caption            Below box, Outside borders
         8 - Minimum Offset from Paragraph  0"
         9 - Gray Shading (% of black)      0%

    Selection: 0
```

Figure 9.1   The Options: Figure menu.

Definition: Figure menu later in this chapter. WordPerfect will load the graphics file into your document, converting it to the .WPG format.

Step 5.   Specify other features of the figure: caption, type (paragraph, page, or character), vertical and horizontal positions on the page, and size.

This also is done in the Definition: Figure menu (Figure 9.2).

Step 6.   If desired, edit the figure.

Within the Edit Graphics screen (accessed from the Definition: Figure menu), you can move, scale (shrink or expand in one or both directions), rotate, or invert the figure.

USING THE OPTIONS MENU

The Options: Figure menu (Figure 9.1) contains the following Options:

```
Definition: Figure

    1 - Filename

    2 - Contents              Empty

    3 - Caption

    4 - Anchor Type           Paragraph

    5 - Vertical Position     0"

    6 - Horizontal Position   Right

    7 - Size                  3.25" wide x 3.37" (high)

    8 - Wrap Text Around Box  Yes

    9 - Edit




Selection: 0
```

Figure 9.2   The Definition: Figure menu.

- **1** - **B**order Style evokes the one-line menu **1 None**; **2 Single**; **3 Double**; **4 Dashed**; **5 Dotted**; **6 Thick**; **7 Extra Thick: 0** for setting the type of border line on the left, right, top, and bottom. See Figure 9.3 for examples of border styles.

- **2** - **O**utside Border Space specifies the amount of space between the border of the box and any text that wraps around it.

- **3** - Inside Border Space specifies the amount of space between the border of the box and any text or graphics within the box.

- **4** - First Level Numbering Method evokes the one-line menu **1 Off**; **2 Numbers**; **3 Letters**; **4 R**oman Numerals: **0**, allowing you to turn *off* figure numbering or to specify the numbering type: numbers (1, 2, 3, . . .), letters (A, B, C, . . .), and roman numerals (I, II, III, . . .). When numbering is *on*, WordPerfect includes the figure number with the figure box in your text.

- **5** - Second Level Numbering Method evokes the same one-line menu as the First Level Numbering Method item. If you specify a second-level numbering method (other than *off*), WordPerfect will automatically number the figures as 1.1, 1.2, 1.3, etc., rather than 1, 2, 3, etc. To go to the next first-level number, use the New Number option described above.

- **6 - C**aption Number Style specifies how you want the figures numbered in the caption (if caption is *on*). The default format is **[BOLD]**Figure 1**[bold]**, but you can choose almost any desired format, such as:

    [ITALC]Figure 1**[italc]** (The caption is in italics.)

    [BOLD]Figure 1.2**[bold]** (The number has two levels, where 1 indicates the desired location of the first-level number, and 2 the location of the second-level number.

Thin single-line border (default)

Thick-line border

Double-line border.

Extra-thick-line border

Dashed-line border

No border

Dotted-line border

Mixed-line border

Figure 9.3   Examples of border styles for figure boxes.

[**BOLD**](1.2)[**bold**] (The number has two levels, doesn't use the word *Figure*, and is enclosed in parentheses.)

- **7 · P**osition of Caption specifies the location of the caption relative to the graphics box. The choices consist of below or above the box, and inside or outside of the box border. The default is below and outside the grapics box border.

- **8 · M**inimum Offset from Paragraph specifies how close the graphics box (of type *paragraph*) can be located to the beginning of the paragraph in which it is located. If you want the graphics at the beginning of the paragraph (provided the figure fits on the current page), set this value to 0 ″. If you want the figure below the beginning of the paragraph, set the number to some larger value.

- **9 · G**ray Shading (% of black) specifies the percent of gray in the figure box. 0% is white; 100% is black. See Figure 9.4 for examples of 10% and 60% gray shading.

These options stay in effect for all subsequent figures or until you change the options.

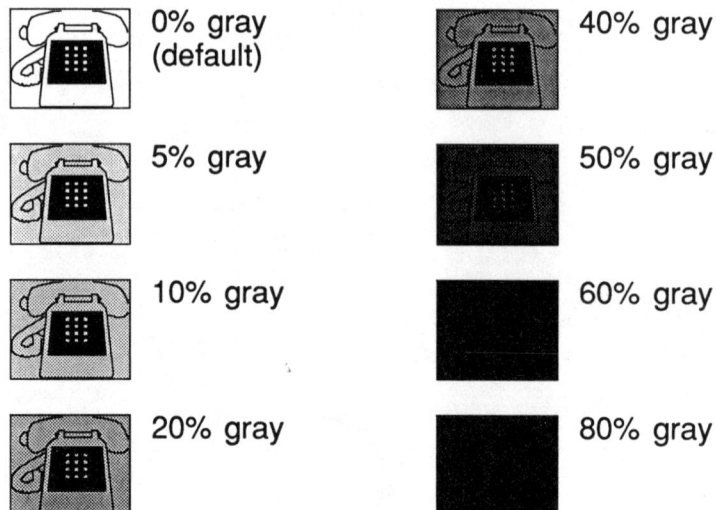

Figure 9.4   Examples of gray shading in figure boxes.

USING THE DEFINITION MENU

To insert a figure into your document, press **Graphics** (Alt-F9) and **1** (Figure) (or use one of the other graphics boxes). WordPerfect displays the Definition: Figure menu, shown in Figure 9.2. The following is an explanation of the options:

- **1 - F**ilename loads a text or graphics file into the figure box.

- **2 - C**ontents yields the one-line menu **Contents: 1 G**raphics; **2** Graphics on **D**isk; **3 T**ext; **4 E**quation: **0,** allowing you to specify the type of contents for the graphics box. For option **1** (**G**raphics), WordPerfect loads the image into the document and makes it a permanent part of the figure. For option **2** (Graphics on **D**isk), WordPerfect records the filename of a graphics image on disk but doesn't actually load the image into the figure. This reduces the size of the document file but requires that the graphics file be available on disk whenever you print the document. For option **3** (**T**ext), WordPerfect marks that the figure contains text and then uses a text edit box when you select **9** (**E**dit) from the Definition: Figure menu. For option **4** (**E**quation), WordPerfect marks that the figure contains an equation and then uses the equation editor when you select **9** (**E**dit) from the Definition: Figure menu.

- **3 - C**aption specifies the contents (but not the location or figure number) of the figure caption.

  The location is defined in the Options: Figure menu (Figure 9.1), and the figure number is automatically determined by Word-Perfect (unless you explicitly change the figure number).

- **4 - T**ype sets the type of figure: Paragraph, Page, or Character.

  The Paragraph type, as the name implies, is associated with the paragraph in which the figure was created. The figure always stays with the paragraph unless the paragraph begins near the bottom of the screen and the figure can't fit at the bottom, in which case the figure moves to the next page.

  The Page type places the figure at a specified location on the page that is independent of where the actual figure code occurs in the document or what text surrounds the figure.

  The Character type behaves as a single character in a line of text; text lines above or below the one containing the figure are on separate lines (i.e., you can have only one line of text to the left or right of a character type figure). Only character type figures are allowed in footnotes and endnotes.

- **5** · **V**ertical Position sets the vertical position relative to the paragraph, page, or line (depending on the type).

- **6** · **H**orizontal Position sets the horizontal position on the page. For example, you can specify the left margin, right margin, or center for a paragraph type figure, or specify the exact offset (in 0.01-inch increments) from the left edge of the page.

- **7** · **S**ize indicates the size (width and height) of the figure.

  WordPerfect automatically expands or compresses your graphics image to fit the size that you specify.

- **8** · **W**rap Text Around Box specifies whether text lines should wrap around the figure or print across the figure.

- **9** · **E**dit allows you to edit (expand, compress, scale, rotate, invert) the graphics image.

EDITING GRAPHICS

When you press **9** (**E**dit) from the Definition: Figure menu (Figure 9.2), you can view and edit your figure on the graphics edit screen, shown in Figure 9.5.

In certain circumstances, you might want to edit a graphics image in WordPerfect: The figure may not be positioned in the graphics box exactly as you want, the graphics image may be too small or too large for the box, the image may be too tall and narrow (or too short and wide) for the box, or the image may need to be inverted or rotated. To perform any of these editing operations on the graphics image, follow these steps:

Step 1.   From the WordPerfect document screen, press **Graphics** (Alt-F9) and **1** (**F**igure).

Step 2.   Press **1** (**C**reate), **1** (**F**ilename), and retrieve the graphics file; or press **2** (**E**dit), **1** (or any other figure number), and **Enter** (to select that figure number for editing).

For example, you may wish to retrieve the figure BOOK.WPG that comes with your WordPerfect software. The Definition: Figure menu (Figure 9.2) appears on the screen.

Arrow keys Move; PgUp/Dn Scale; +/- Rotate; Ins % Change; GoTo Reset
1 Move; 2 Scale; 3 Rotate; 4 Invert On; 5 Black & White: 0   (10%)

Figure 9.5   The Edit Graphics screen.

Step 3. Press **8** (**E**dit) to access the Edit Graphics screen (Figure 9.5).

The Edit Graphics screen requires a graphics adaptor and a compatible monitor. The top line of the screen displays a list of the main keyboard commands: **Arrow keys** Move; PgUp/Dn Scale; +/− Rotate; Ins % Change; GoTo Reset. The bottom line of the screen displays a one-line menu: **1 M**ove; **2 S**cale; **3 R**otate; **4** Invert On; **5** Black & White: **0**. Not all of these options are available with all types of graphics images. For example, you cannot rotate bitmap graphics, but you can rotate line (vector) graphics.

Step 4. Press **Up Arrow, Right Arrow, Down Arrow,** and **Left Arrow** to see how these keys affect the location of the figure within the graphics box.

Note that you can crop the figure by moving part of it past the inside margin of the graphics box. Figure 9.6 gives sample locations of the clip-art image BOOK.WPG within the same-sized figure box. After experimenting for a few moments, use the arrows to center the figure in the box.

Image positioned near
the center of the box
Scale: x = 80, y = 80

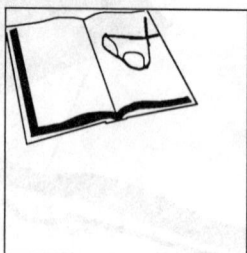

Image positioned in
the upper left corner

Image positioned in
the upper right corner

Image positioned below
the bottom of the box

Figure 9.6   Positioning the image within the figure box.

Step 5.   Press **PgUp** or **PgDn** to expand or compress the graphics image.

Pressing **PgUp** increases the horizontal (X) and vertical (Y) scales and makes the image larger; pressing **PgDn** decreases the horizontal (X) and vertical (Y) scales and makes the image smaller. Figure 9.7 gives several examples of sizing and scaling the image within the

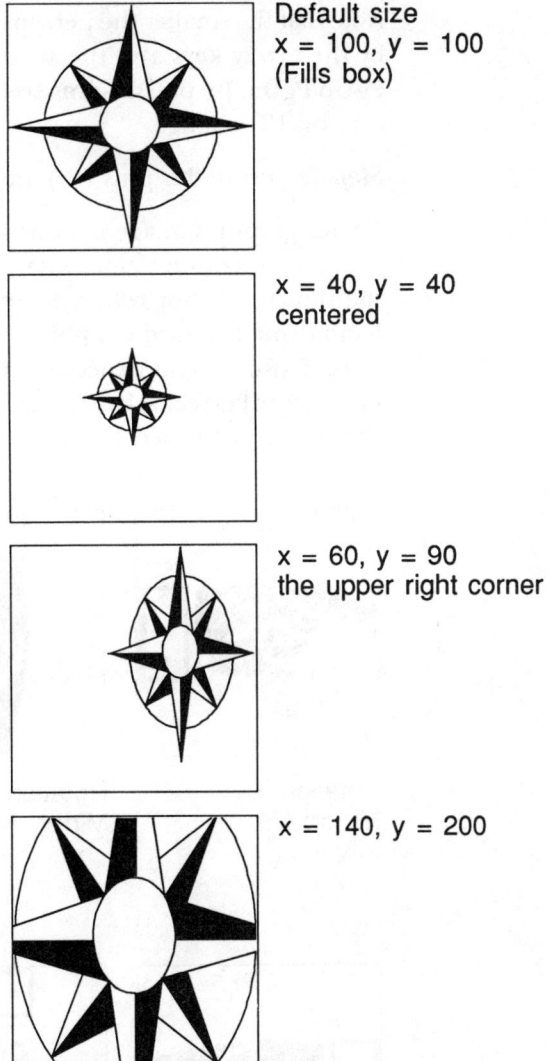

Default size
x = 100, y = 100
(Fills box)

x = 40, y = 40
centered

x = 60, y = 90
the upper right corner

x = 140, y = 200

Figure 9.7 Sizing and scaling the image within the figure box. The X value is the scale in the horizontal direction; the Y value is the scale in the vertical direction.

same figure box. After experimenting with these keys, enlarge the figure so that the image barely fits in the graphics box.

Step 6.   Press **Ins** to decrease the percent change value displayed in the lower right corner of the screen, and then repeat steps 4 and 5.

Note that the smaller the percent change, the smaller the move caused by the arrow keys and the smaller the scale change caused by the **PgUp/PgDn**. By pressing **Ins** several times, you can select 25%, 10%, 5%, or 1% change.

Step 7. Press the plus (+) and minus (−) keys.

If your graphics image is a line drawing, the figure will rotate clockwise (+) or counter-clockwise (−). If you have a bit-mapped image, the figure will not rotate. Figure 9.8 shows examples of a pointer hand (from Harvard Graphics) in various rotation values. When you press **3** (**R**otate) and specify a rotation value (or keep the current one), WordPerfect asks **Mirror Image? No** (**Yes**). If you press **Y** (**Yes**), the image is flipped horizontally, as shown in Figure 9.8.

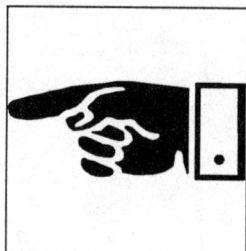

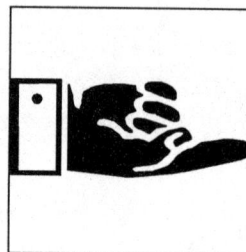

Rotation: 0
Mirror: No

Rotation: 90
Mirror: No

Rotation: 180
Mirror: No

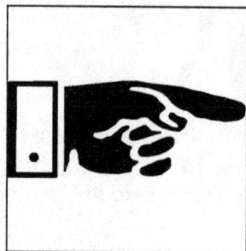
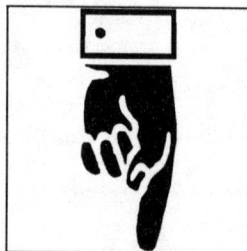

Rotation: 0
Mirror: Yes

Rotation: 90
Mirror: Yes

Rotation: 325
Mirror: Yes

Figure 9.8 Several rotations of an image within a figure box. The rotate options also allow you to produce the mirror image of the figure.

Step 8. Press **GoTo** (Ctrl-Home) to reset the image to the original settings.

Step 9. Press **1** (Move), and at the prompt **Horizontal:**, enter 0.5 and at the prompt **Vertical:**, enter -0.5

The move command allows you to position the image relative to the edge of the figure. The horizontal value is the distance (in inches) from the *left edge* of the graphics box; positive (plus) horizontal values move the image right, and negative (–) values move the image left. The vertical value is the distance (in inches) from the *bottom* of the graphics box; positive vertical values move the image up, and negative values move the image down.

Step 10. Press **2** (Scale), and at the prompt **X:**, enter 120 and at the prompt **Y:**, enter 160.

The effect of the X and Y scales values is shown in Figure 9.7 above.

Step 11. Press **4** (Invert On).

The invert command changes white pixels (picture elements or dots) to black and changes black pixels to white. This usually shows up on the screen but, for some images, has no effect when you print the figure. You'll just have to experiment to see the effects on your graphics images. Figure 9.9 shows a normal and an inverted figure. If you later decide not to invert the picture, press **4** (Invert Off) from the Graphics Edit menu.

Step 12. Press **Exit** (F7) twice to return to your document.

Normal Image   Inverted Image

Figure 9.9   A normal image and the same image inverted.

Saving and Printing the Figure

To save and then print the figure, follow these steps:

Step 1. Press **Save** (F10) and enter `fig.dem`.

WordPerfect saves the document to the disk under the filename FIG.DEM (for *figure, demo*).

Step 2. Press **Print** (Shift-F7) to access the Print and Options menus.

Step 3. Check in the Options menu (in the bottom half of the screen) to make sure the correct printer is selected. If not, press **S** (Select Printer) and choose a new printer (see Chapter 2, "Using WordPerfect," and Appendix B, "Using Your Printer").

Step 4. To change the quality of the graphics, press **G** (Graphics Quality), and then **2** (**D**raft), **3** (**M**edium), or **4** (**H**igh).

Because documents with graphics print very slowly and use up printer ink or toner, you should set the graphics quality to the lowest possible setting until you have polished your document. When you are ready to print the final version, select high-quality graphics. Be aware that your printer may not support all of the above WordPerfect features.

Step 5. Press **1** (Full Document) to print the document.

SUMMARY

In this chapter you have learned some of the general features of WordPerfect graphics, including how to specify the general features of a graphics box using the Options: Figure menu, how to retrieve a figure into a graphics box and to specify parameters about the box from the Definition: Figure menu, how to edit graphics within a WordPerfect graphics box (scaling, moving, rotating, and inverting the figure), and how to print the figure.

Chapter 10

Installing Fonts

All printers have at least one resident font. A letter-quality (impact) printer, for example, has just one font at a time—on a daisy wheel or thimble—currently installed. Modern dot matrix printers usually have six to ten fonts—for generating pica and elite in draft mode, pica and elite in near-letter-quality mode, compressed type, expanded type, and so forth.

Laser printers have anywhere from three to a hundred built-in fonts. For example, the popular Hewlett-Packard LaserJet Series II comes standard with six built-in fonts; the Hewlett-Packard Laser-Jet 2000 has 34 built-in fonts; the Apple LaserWriter IInt and IIntx have 35 built-in fonts; and the C. Itoh LIPS II has a whopping 92 built-in fonts.

Moreover, laser printers support cartridges and soft fonts that expand the number of available typefaces. A *cartridge* is a device that inserts into a port on the printer and increases the number of type-faces available to the printer. A *soft font* is a typeface generated with software that the computer system can transfer (*download*) from a disk into printer memory (see Figure 10.1). There, the printer can use the soft font as if it were one of its built-in fonts.

This chapter deals with using cartridges and soft fonts with your laser printer. Specifically, you will learn the following:

• How to purchase soft fonts.

• How to choose desirable soft fonts.

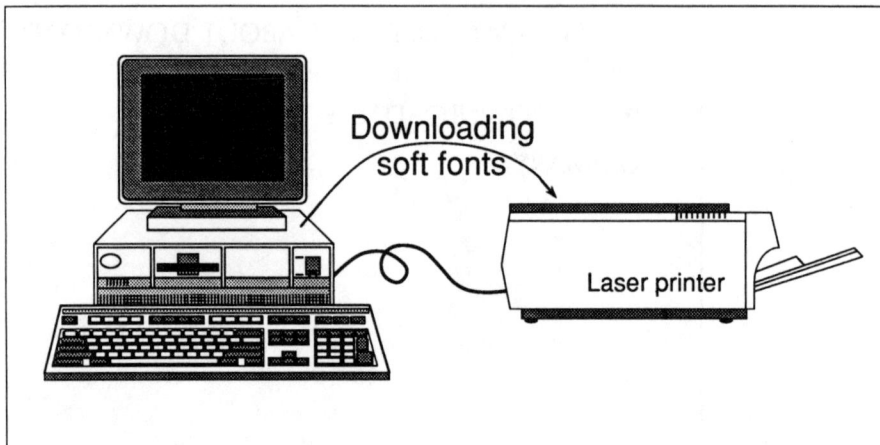

Figure 10.1   Downloading soft fonts.

- How to install fonts in WordPerfect for automatic downloading into your laser printer.

- How to use downloadable fonts.

The next chapter ("Using Fonts") will describe how to change fonts within a WordPerfect document and how to manage font typefaces, font sizes, attributes, colors, and gray shades.

PURCHASING SOFT FONTS

If your printer already has a variety of built-in fonts, buying additional soft fonts may be a luxury. But if your printer furnishes a limited selection of fonts, buying soft fonts is an absolute necessity for desktop publishing.

What You Need

To use additional fonts with WordPerfect, you need the following (Figure 10.2):

- *An installation kit.* This is a program, supplied on a disk by the font manufacturer, that configures WordPerfect for using the soft fonts. The installation kit is sometimes called a *font manager.*

- *The soft font(s).* These are files, supplied on a disk, that contain the definitions of the typefaces.

- *A compatible laser printer.* Some fonts work with only the Hewlett-Packard LaserJet and compatible printers; some fonts work only with PostScript printers.

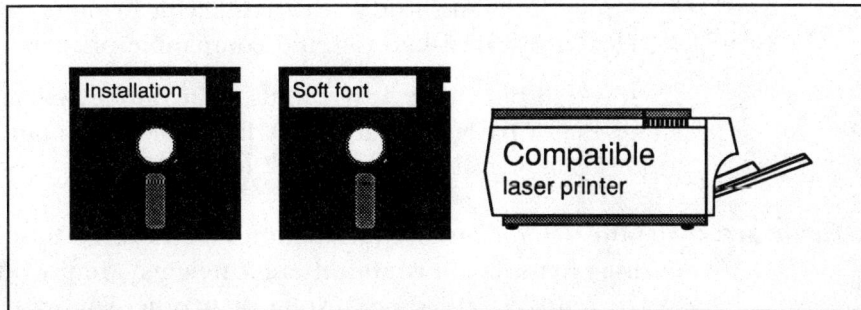

Figure 10.2 The three requirements for using soft fonts: the installation program, the soft fonts, and a compatible printer.

You can't buy soft fonts, therefore, from just anyone. You must buy fonts from a company that sells an installation kit for using their fonts with WordPerfect and provides fonts compatible with your printer.

Adobe Type Libraries

Probably the most famous supplier of downloadable fonts is Adobe Systems Incorporated. Adobe lists a wide selection of fonts in its excellent *Font & Function* catalog, which not only lists the fonts by name and example but gives short histories and uses of each typeface.

The advantages of Adobe Type Libraries are the following:

- Adobe fonts work well with PostScript printers, such as the Apple LaserWriter.

- WordPerfect supports several Adobe Fonts with PostScript printers, including the typefaces Optima, ITC Garamond, Helvetica, ITC Korinna, Goudy Old Style, Aachen Bold, University Roman, Revue, and Freestyle Script. You just have to order a supplementary disk; call WordPerfect Corporation at (801) 225-5000. The cost is $10 for shipping and handling.

- Installation and use of Adobe fonts is fast and simple.

- Adobe offers a wide variety of attractive, effective typefaces.

The disadvantages of the Adobe Type Libraries are the following:

- Adobe fonts are expensive. Most libraries contain only one typeface with bold and italic variations.

- Adobe fonts work only with PostScript printers, *not* with the Hewlett-Packard LaserJet and compatible printers.

If you wish to order Adobe fonts, write Adobe Systems Incorporated, 1585 Charleston Road, P.O. Box 7900, Mountain View, CA 94039-7900, or call 1-800-833-6687 (toll free).

Bitstream Fontware

The Bitstream Fontware installation kit and three Bitstream fonts (or nine fonts, if you count different weights) are provided almost free to WordPerfect owners. If you wish to order Fontware, call WordPerfect Product Support at 1-800-222-9409 (toll free). Have available the registration number of your WordPerfect 5.0 (or later version) and your charge card. You will have to pay only a $10 shipping and handling fee.

The advantages of Bitstream Fontware are the following:

- The installation kit is free with the soft fonts.

- The soft fonts from Bitstream include Times (called Dutch by Bitstream) and Helvetica (called Swiss by Bitstream) — two extremely popular, excellent-looking typefaces. You also get Charter typeface, an attractive and versatile font. See Figure 10.3. If you have only modest desktop publishing requirements, you could do 80 to 100 percent of your desktop publishing with just these three typefaces.

- Bitstream produces a wide selection of handsome, exciting, formal, casual, traditional, and modern fonts.

- The Fontware installation kit works with almost any laser printers. You can install the soft fonts to support the Hewlett-Packard LaserJet, the Apple LaserWriter, and most other printers. The Bitstream fonts also work with other popular software, such as PC PageMaker, Ventura Publisher, and PC Excel.

The disadvantage of the Bitstream Fontware is the price of additional fonts. To purchase additional fonts or for further information, write Bitstream Inc., Athenaeum House, 215 First Street, Cambridge, MA 02142 (617-497-7512).

Glyphix Fonts

A company that produces inexpensive fonts is Swfte International, maker of Glyphix fonts. Swfte sells a Font Manager (installation kit) and set of typefaces at very reasonable prices.

> Bitstream Charter Roman
> Swiss (Helvetica)
> Dutch (Times Roman)

Figure 10.3. The three soft fonts of Bitstream Fontware that WordPerfect provides for a nominal fee.

The disadvantage of Glyphix fonts is that they are designed for the Hewlett-Packard LaserJet and do not work with PostScript printers.

For more information, write Swfte International, P. O. Box 219, Rockland, DE 19732 (302-429-8434).

SoftCraft LaserFonts

SoftCraft produces several software applications for installing, managing, and producing soft fonts for use with WordPerfect and the HP LaserJet II. The SoftCraft Font Editor allows you to create or modify your own soft fonts. Font Effects modifies font characters with special effects such as shadows, outlines, contours, and so forth.

For information, write SoftCraft, 16 N. Carroll Street, Suite 500, Madison, WI 53703 (608-257-3300).

Other Soft Fonts

As desktop publishing with WordPerfect becomes more popular, more companies will produce installation kits and soft fonts for WordPerfect. Look for advertisements and reviews in the magazines listed in Appendix C, "Additional Reading."

CHOOSING SOFT FONTS

If you feel you need additional fonts but aren't sure which typefaces to buy, here is a list to get you started (the typefaces are listed in order of importance):

1. A strong, traditional font with serifs for the main text of letters, reports, books, and other common documents. (*Serifs* are small

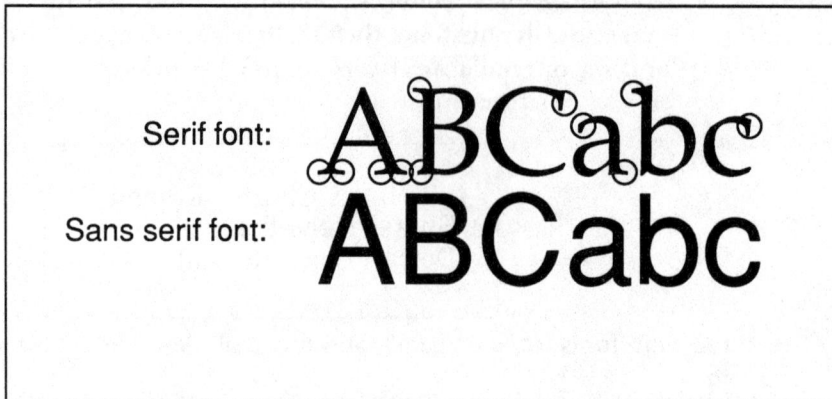

Serif font: ABCabc

Sans serif font: ABCabc

Figure 10.4   A serif font (Palatino) and a sans serif font (Helvetica). The serifs are circled.

embellishments at the ends of the character line strokes; see Figure 10.4.) Fonts in this category are New Century Schoolbook, Palatino, Garamond, Bookman, and Bitstream Charter. These typefaces are attractive, traditional, and legible. They also support special effects such as bold, outline, italics, outline, and shadow.

2. A traditional sans serif font (*sans* = without) for titles, headings, and legends. The fonts in this category include Helvetica (or Bitstream Swiss), Optima, and Univers.

3. A narrow, traditional serif font for type set in newspaper-type columns. The main font in this category is Times Roman (or Bitstream Dutch), but Garamond may also serve well in this category.

4. A calligraphic font for certificates, invitations, advertisements, and other specialty documents. Examples include ITC Zapf Chancery and University Roman.

5. An icon or symbols font for accents and special symbols. Zapf Dingbats is a good choice here.

This list is summarized in Figure 10.5. The selections and order on the list are, of course, a matter of personal taste. Use your own judgment and experience to select the fonts you think are best for your publishing needs. After acquiring fonts in these five categories, add to your font inventory as time, money, and needs permit. See Chapter 11, "Using Fonts," and consult the catalogs of typeface suppliers listed in Appendix D, "Directory of Products."

INSTALLING SOFT FONTS

Instructions for installing soft fonts for WordPerfect differ from one supplier to the next, but the general steps are the same. For details on how to install a specific soft font in WordPerfect, carefully read the manufacturer's instruction manual.

Running the Installation Program

The general steps for installing soft fonts are as follows:

Step 1. Make backup copies of your installation disk(s) and your font disks(s).

Step 2. Copy the soft font files into the directory that contains WordPerfect.

Some installation programs may do this automatically, in which case it isn't a separate step.

What Soft Fonts to Buy

1. Strong, traditional, serif font

New Century Schoolbook—excellent for the main body of text in letters, reports, and books.

2. Traditional sans serif font

Helvetica (called Swiss by Bitstream)—ideal for titles, headings, and captions.

3. Narrow, traditional serif font

Times Roman (called Dutch by Bitstream)—designed for narrow columns of newspapers, brochures, and newsletters.

4. Calligraphic font

Zapf Chancery Medium Light Italic—perfect for certificates, invitations, and announcements.

5. Icon or symbols font

Zapf Dingbats:

❖○✷✳✳✱✳✴✳✳✱●○■□□□◻▲▼◆◇►❙❙❙
✿✝✞✜✛✦✧☆★✩○★★★★★☆✪✱✲✳✴✵✶✷✸✹✺
☞✌➳➺➽✓✐✔✗✘☓☒✖✗☎☓✗➼╋➥✑✉✄✎☂☞☜
✴✶✻❝➀✝✚✿✝☜✿❞

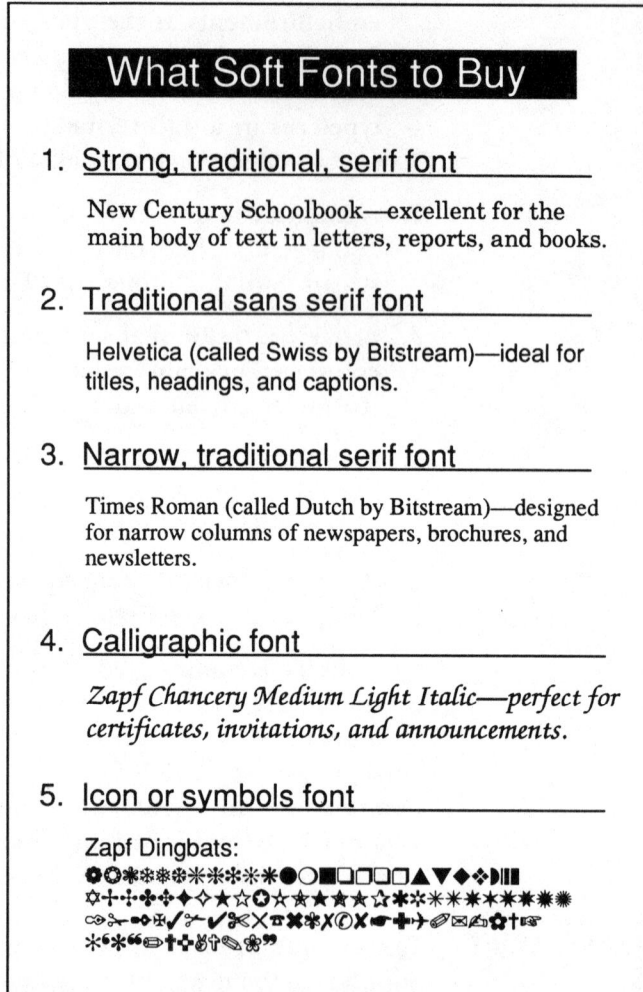

Figure 10.5 Selecting soft fonts. You should purchase at least one font in each of the five categories. The example given under each item in the list is only one of many possible typefaces.

Step 3. Execute the installation program.

For example, Adobe's installation program is called INSTALL and Bitstream's installation program is named FONTWARE, so you simply change the default disk and directory to the location of IN-STALL.EXE or FONTWARE.EXE, and enter `install` or `fontware`.

Step 4. Follow the directions given on the computer monitor and in the user's manual for using the installation program.

These steps are generally easy to follow and self-explanatory. We were able to install Adobe and Bitstream fonts almost without looking at the user's manual.

Installing Additional Fonts

Once you have used the installation program to set up WordPerfect with the soft fonts, you can add new soft fonts by repeating the installation program with the disk that contains the new font.

Problems with Installation

Typical problems encountered while installing soft fonts (and their possible solutions) are given below:

- The installation program appears to "hang" (that is, do nothing).

  Be patient. Installing and configuring soft fonts from Bitstream can be very slow. Adobe Type Libraries, on the other hand, install very rapidly, so if the system appears to hang it probably has encountered a problem. You may have to reboot the system and start the process again. If you can't solve a problem, call the manufacturer's customer support line.

- The disk runs out of space.

  Soft fonts obviously take up disk space. Bitstream Charter, for example, requires about 55 Kb (kilobytes) of disk space. This isn't a large amount, but the occupied region can quickly fill up if you have many fonts. The solution is to remove unused files from your disk or limit the number of fonts you choose.

- The installation program can't locate the soft font that you request.

  You specify the location (disk drive and directory) on which the soft font is located. New fonts should generally be on a floppy disk in drive A or drive B.

  After you successfully install the font(s) in WordPerfect, you are ready to create a WordPerfect document using the new fonts.

ADVISING WORDPERFECT ABOUT DOWNLOADABLE FONTS

Before you can use a newly installed downloadable font, you must tell WordPerfect the location (on your hard drive) of the file containing the font description. Follow these steps to set up WordPerfect to use the soft font:

Step 1.   From within WordPerfect, press **Print** (Shift-F7) to access the Print/Options menu, press **S** (Select Printer) to display the Print: Select Printer menu, press the **Up Arrow** or **Down Arrow** keys to highlight the printer for which you have installed the soft font, and press **3** (**E**dit).

WordPerfect displays the Select Printer: Edit menu, shown in Figure 10.6.

Step 2.   Press **6** (Path for **D**ownloadable Fonts), type the path for the soft font file, and press **Enter**.

For example, enter `c:\wp51` if you have installed the soft fonts in the WP51 directory on drive C, or enter `c:\psfonts` if you have installed Adobe PostScript fonts.

Step 3.   Press **4** (Cartridges and Fonts) and, if requested to do so, insert the printer disk in drive A and press **Enter**.

```
Select Printer: Edit

         Filename                    PAKXP109.PRS

    1 - Name                         Panasonic KX-P1092i

    2 - Port                         LPT1:

    3 - Sheet Feeder                 None

    4 - Forms

    5 - Cartridges and Fonts

    6 - Initial Font                 Pica 10 pitch

    7 - Path for Downloadable
          Fonts and Printer
          Command Files


    Selection: 0
```

Figure 10.6   The Select Printer: Edit menu.

The Select Printer: Cartridges and Fonts menu appears on the screen. The **Font Category** lists the type of font: cartridge, print wheel, or downloadable font. The **Resource** is the computer or printer part that uses the font: *memory* is the resource for a downloadable font and a printer cartridge *port* is the resource for a cartridge. The **Quantity Number** is the number of slots available to cartridges (usually 1) or the amount of memory available for downloadable fonts. The memory available for downloadable (soft) fonts is set to the normal factory specifications. If you buy extra memory with your printer or add more memory, you should increase the Quantity Number.

Step 4. Move the highlight bar to the desired font category and press **1** (Select Fonts).

If you have properly installed a downloadable font, *downloadable font* should be listed as a font category, so select that category. WordPerfect now displays a list of available fonts or cartridges.

Step 5. Move the cursor to a font that you want to use with your printer, then press * (Present When Print Job Begins) or press + (Can be Loaded (Unloaded) During Print Job).

Repeat this step for as many fonts as you want to use. Fonts marked *Present When Print Job Begins* (with *) are downloaded when the printer initializes at the beginning of a print job or whenever you select the Initialize Printer Option from the Print menu. The font stays resident in the printer until another soft font replaces it in another print job or until you turn *off* the printer. Fonts marked *Can be Loaded (Unloaded) During Print Job* (with +) are downloaded only if and when they are needed in the document being printed and are replaced by other soft fonts required during the print job. In general, you should mark fonts used frequently in a document with * and fonts used rarely with +. If you make a mistake in marking a font, press the * or + again to unmark it. The fonts you mark will appear (along with the built-in fonts) in the Base Font menu described in the next section. Don't mark fonts with both * and +.

Step 6. After marking the desired soft fonts, press **Exit** (F7) four times to return to your document.

Your soft fonts are now ready to use in your document.

USING DOWNLOADABLE FONTS

To change from the current font to any other built-in or download-able font, follow these steps:

Step 1.   From the main document screen, press **Font** (Ctrl-F8) and **4** (Base Font).

WordPerfect displays the Base Font menu, which contains not only the built-in fonts but also the downloadable fonts.

Step 2.   Highlight the desired font and press **1** (Select).

Step 3.   If necessary, type the desired font size and press **Enter.**

WordPerfect inserts the font change code into your document. When you print the document, WordPerfect automatically down-loads the soft font from the disk into the printer.

SUMMARY

Downloadable fonts (also called *soft fonts*) allow you to select and use fonts that aren't normally available to your printer. Several manufacturers market soft fonts that support WordPerfect with popu-lar laser printers (see Appendix D, "Directory of Products").

Installing soft fonts requires an installation program, the soft fonts, and a compatible laser printer.

As a minimum, you should choose five fonts: (1) a strong, tradi-tional serif font, such as New Century Schoolbook; (2) a traditional sans serif font, such as Helvetica; (3) a narrow, traditional serif font, such as Times Roman; (4) a calligraphic font, such as Zapf Chan-cery; and (5) an icon or symbols font, such as Zapf Dingbats.

To use downloadable fonts, you must install the fonts using the installation program, specify the path for WordPerfect to find the font files on the disk, indicate which fonts you want downloadable, and then use the fonts as you would a built-in font. WordPerfect au-tomatically downloads the soft fonts as they are needed.

Chapter 11

Using Fonts

"Each typeface, like a human face, has a subtle character all its own. Depending on which face you choose, the same word can have many different shades of meaning. And since you must have type in order to have words, why not make sure those words are presented in the most elegant, or the most powerful, or softest way possible?" So says Roger Blank, former director of editorial art at *The New York Times* (quoted in *Fonts & Function*, The Adobe Type Catalog, Spring 1988). Selecting the proper typeface (along with other principles of design) enables you to create and hold your readers' interest and to present a written message effectively.

The main purpose of this chapter is to help you utilize various fonts (typefaces) so that you can select the right face for your publications. Specifically, you will learn how to:

- Select different fonts (typefaces) within your document.

- Change the size of the font.

- Select the appearances (bold, underline, double underline, italics, outline, shadow, etc.) of the font.

- Change the color or gray shading of the font.

- Understand the principles of design in selecting typefaces.

MANAGING FONTS

A *typeface* is a family of type that has an overall, unified design. A *font* is a complete set of typeface characters of the same size. Font sizes are generally measured in *points*, and one point equals about 1/72 of an inch (i.e., 72-point type is one inch high). The font height is measured from the top of the ascenders to the bottom of the descenders (that is, from the cap line to the descender line), as shown in Figure 11.1. Font sizes are also measured in *pitch*; pitch 10 means 10 characters per inch (pica) and pitch 12 means 12 characters per inch (elite). Technically, 10-point Courier is the same typeface as 12-point Courier, although they are different fonts. Current desktop publishing jargon, however, often uses the terms *font* and *typeface* interchangeably.

All typefaces can be categorized as either *serif* or *sans serif*. Serifs are small embellishments at the ends of the character line strokes (see Figure 10.4 in the previous chapter). Examples of sans serif fonts are Helvetica and Avant Garde; examples of serif fonts are Times, Palatino, and Bookman. See Figure 11.2 for sample fonts.

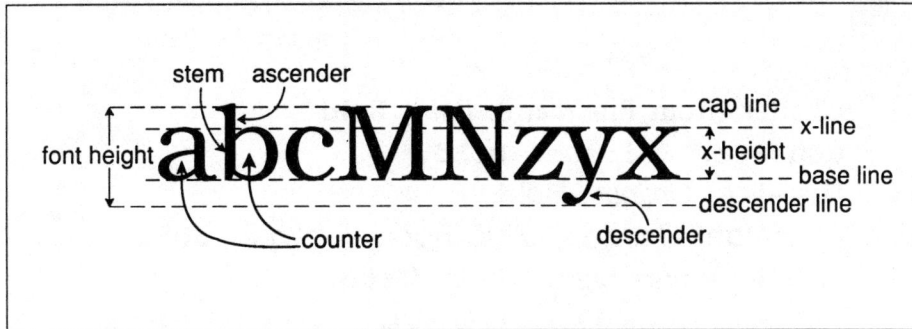

Figure 11.1 The parts of a typeface.

Using Fonts (Typefaces)

Figure 11.2 shows several popular fonts (typefaces) in their unmodified form, in italics (called *oblique* in some typefaces), and in bold (called *demi* in some typefaces).

- *Courier* has the appearance of the type created by a standard typewriter. Most letter-quality impact printers (with daisy wheels or thimbles) and dot matrix printers support this typeface.

- *Charter* is part of the Bitstream Fontware that is free to WordPerfect owners (see Chapter 10, "Installing Fonts"). It is a solid font specifically designed for desktop publishing. Its heavy serifs show up well on 300 DPI (dots-per-inch) laser printers. Its versatility and traditional look make it useful for the main body of text of letters, reports, manuals, newsletters, and other standard publications.

- *Helvetica* is the most popular sans serif typeface. Most publishers prefer a serif typeface (such as Palatino or Times Roman) in the main text of a book but use Helvetica in titles and headings.

- *ITC Avant Garde Gothic Book*, another sans serif typeface, provides a distinctive modern look to documents. It is an excellent font for use in advertisements and announcements where you want a look that is classy but clean. (ITC stands for International Typeface Corporation, which licenses the proprietary version of many typefaces.)

- *ITC Bookman*, as the name implies, is designed for book printing. It is strong and legible, excellent for the wide text columns found in most books. It has many of the same uses as, but is less conservative than, New Century Schoolbook or Times Roman.

Charter (from Bitstream), *Italic*, **Bold**
Courier, *Oblique*, **Bold.**
Helvetica, *Oblique*, **Bold**.
ITC Avant Garde Gothic Book, *Oblique*, **Bold**.
ITC Bookman Light, *Italic*, **Demi.**
*ITC Zapf Chancery Medium Italic, **Bold***
New Century Schoolbook, *Italic*, **Bold**.
Palatino, *Italic*, **Bold**.
Times Roman, *Italic*, **Bold**.

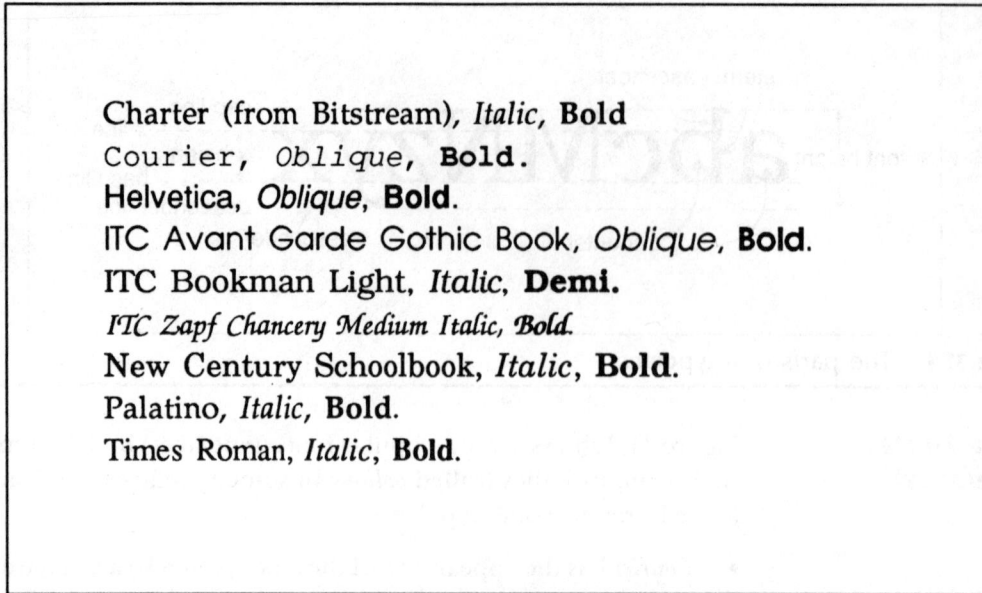

Figure 11.2   Examples of fonts. All of these examples are 12-point in size, with a 16-point line height.

- *ITC Zapf Chancery* presents a graceful calligraphic look, and is usually used for wedding announcements, certificates, and other special printed matter.

- *New Century Schoolbook* is a solid, extremely legible font that would serve well as the main typeface in almost any document, including a letter, essay, report, newsletter, or manual. For wide blocks of text, New Century Schoolbook is preferred over the narrower Times Roman (see below).

- *Palatino* is a combination of modern and classical styles. It is attractive and legible, an excellent choice for user's manuals and long reports.

- *Times Roman* was developed in 1931 for the London *Times* to save space and provide legibility for newsprint columns. It is a good typeface for newsletters when you want a traditional and elegant look.

To become acquainted with a particular typeface, you should print several paragraphs in that typeface and then look for that typeface in professionally printed documents. With time and experience, you will see how font typefaces affect printed messages.

Changing the Font (Typeface)

WordPerfect's **Font** (Ctrl-F8) command allows you to specify the typeface, font size, appearance, and color of the type in your document. Be aware, however, that the appearance of your final printed document depends upon the capabilities of your printer. For example, our dot matrix Panasonic KX-P1092i printer is limited to 11 different base fonts (typefaces and sizes), while our Apple LaserWriter allows 34 typefaces and an infinite number of type sizes. Neither printer supports colored text, although the LaserWriter allows gray shaded text.

To change the font in your WordPerfect document, follow these steps:

Step 1. Move the cursor to the position where you want the font change to occur.

This may be anywhere in your document—at the beginning of the document, at the beginning of a page, in the middle of a paragraph, or even in the middle of a word.

Step 2. Press **Font** (Ctrl-F8) to select the Font menu.

WordPerfect displays the menu **1** Size; **2** Appearance; **3** Normal; **4** Base Font; **5** Print Color: **0**.

Step 3. Press **4** (Base Font).

WordPerfect displays a list of the fonts available on the current printer. Figure 11.3 shows a list of fonts displayed in a Base Font menu. Each printer has its own list of fonts, so your list will probably be different from the one in Figure 11.3. If you want to change the printer for the current document, you should now press **Exit** (F7), **Print** (Shift-F7), **S** (Select Printer), choose the desired printer, and then repeat this step.

Step 4. Press **Up Arrow** or **Down Arrow** to move the highlight bar to the desired font.

You could also press **N** (Name search) and then type the first few characters of the name of the desired font to move the highlight bar, and then press **Enter**.

```
Base Font

  Century Schoolbook 10pt (SA)
* Courier 10 pitch (PC-8)
  Courier 10 pitch (Roman-8)
  Courier Bold 10 pitch (PC-8)
  Courier Bold 10 pitch (Roman-8)
  Helv 10pt (AC)
  Letter Gothic 12pt 12 pitch (DA)
  Line Draw 10 pitch (DA)
  Line Printer 16.66 pitch (PC-8)
  Line Printer 16.66 pitch (Roman-8)
  Prestige Elite 10pt 12 pitch (EA)
  Solid Line Draw 10 pitch
  Solid Line Draw 12 pitch
  Tms Rmn 10pt (AC)




  1 Select; N Name search: 1
```

Figure 11.3   A list of fonts displayed in the Base Font menu. Your printer may provide a different list.

Step 5.   With the desired font highlighted, press **1** (**Select**).

If the selected font (typeface) supports different font sizes (which is usually the case with PostScript printers), WordPerfect then prompts **Point size:** and waits for you to type the point size.

Step 6.   If asked to do so, type the point size of the selected font and press **Enter**.

WordPerfect allows any point value (depending upon the printer), although any size below 2-point is illegible and any size above 800-point fits only one character per page.

The selected base font is the main text typeface from this location in your document until you change the base font or until the end of the document.

Setting the Initial Font (Typeface)

If your printer supports more than one font (typeface), you may select an initial (or default) base font to begin all documents using that printer. The default on the original WordPerfect printer definition is usually Courier.

To set the initial font, do the following: From anywhere in your WordPerfect document, press **Print** (Shift-F7), **S** (Select Printer), **Down Arrow** (several times, if necessary, to highlight the desired printer), **6** (Initial Font), and then follow steps 4 through 6 above to select the desired initial font.

CHANGING FONT SIZE

To change the font size of the base font, follow the steps above for changing the base font (typeface) and either select a larger or smaller font or type a larger or smaller point size. Figure 11.4 demonstrates various point sizes for the Helvetica typeface.

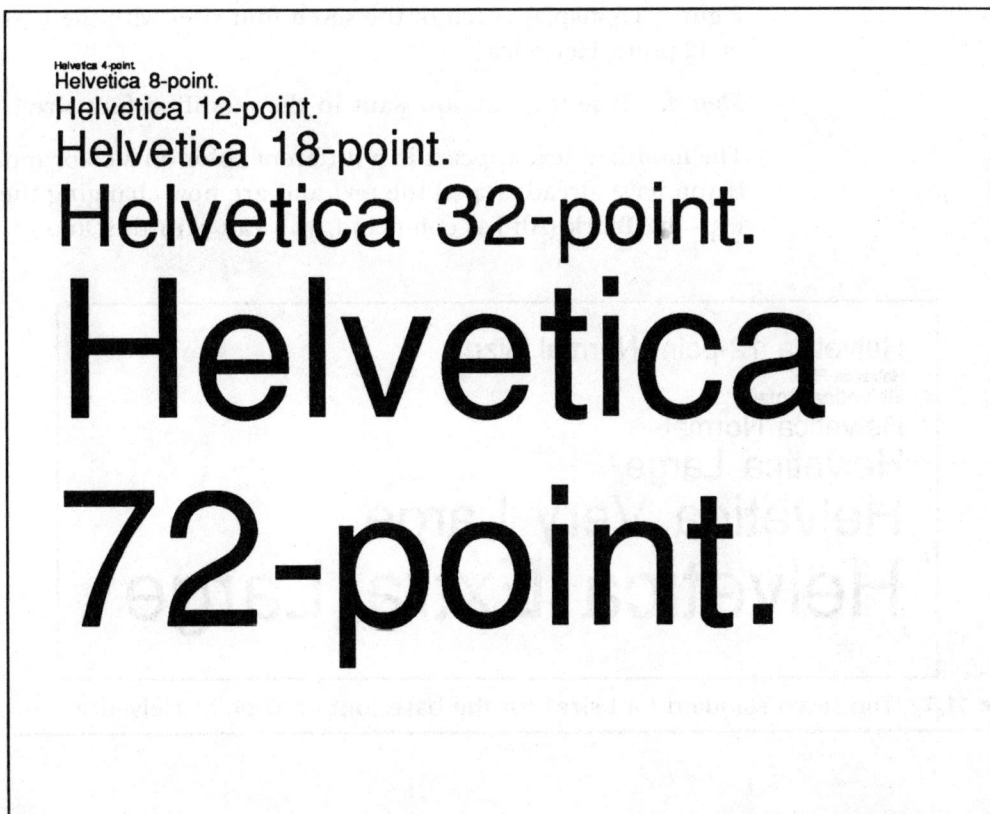

Helvetica 4-point
Helvetica 8-point.
Helvetica 12-point.
Helvetica 18-point.

Helvetica 32-point.

Helvetica 72-point.

Figure 11.4 Helvetica typeface in various font sizes. The line height was kept on *automatic*.

But you can temporarily change the font size in a more efficient manner by following these steps:

Step 1.   Move the cursor to the location in your document where you want larger or smaller characters.

If you have already typed the characters, highlight (block) them using the **Block** (Alt-F4) command before proceeding to the next step.

Step 2.   Press **Font** (Ctrl-F8) and **1** (Size).

WordPerfect displays the following menu on the status line:
1 Suprscpt; **2** Subscpt; **3** Fine; **4** Small; **5** Large; **6** Vry Large; **7** Ext Large: **0**.

Step 3.   Press a number **1** through **7** (or the corresponding letter) to select the desired font size.

Figure 11.5 displays each of the seven font sizes with the base font of 12-point Helvetica.

Step 4.   Type the text you want in the modified font size.

The modified text appears in a different color on a color monitor. If you have already typed the text and are now changing the font with the **Block** (Alt-F4) command, you can skip this step.

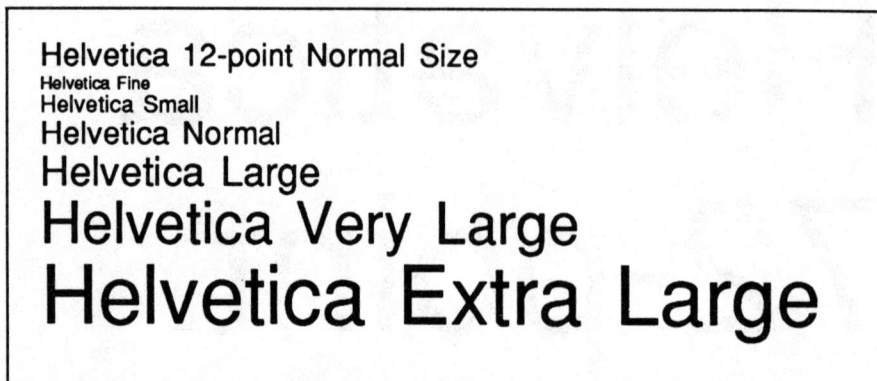

Helvetica 12-point Normal Size
Helvetica Fine
Helvetica Small
Helvetica Normal
Helvetica Large
Helvetica Very Large
Helvetica Extra Large

Figure 11.5   The seven standard font sizes for the base font of 12-point Helvetica.

Step 5. To return to the base font size, press **Right Arrow** to move past the font size code, or press **Font** (Ctrl-F8) and **3** (Normal).

Changing from the base font size to a new font size works just like changing from normal typeface to boldfaced or underlined typeface. WordPerfect inserts a code at the beginning of the modified text to turn *on* the new feature and at the end of the modified text to turn *off* the feature. When you select the feature by pressing **Bold** or **Underline** or by invoking **Font** (Ctrl-F8) and **1** (Size), WordPerfect inserts *both* the beginning and the ending codes into the text. You can turn *off* the feature either by invoking the command again or by simply moving the cursor past the ending code with the **Right Arrow**.

As a rule of thumb, the smallest font size (Fine) is about one-half the height of the base font, and the largest font size (Extra Large) is about twice the height of the base font. Superscripts and subscripts are the same size as Fine.

We again stress that although WordPerfect supports these various font sizes, your printer may not. The best way to see if your printer can output the size Very Large, for example, is to try it: Press **Font** (Ctrl-F8), **1** (Size), and **6** (Vry Large), type some text (The quick brown fox jumps over the lazy dog.), and print the document.

SELECTING FONT APPEARANCES

Once you know how to change the font size, selecting different font appearances (bold, underline, double underline, italic, outline, shadow, small caps, redline, and strikeout) is simple:

Step 1. Move the cursor to the location in your document where you want a different font appearance.

If you have already typed the characters, highlight (block) them using the **Block** (Alt-F4) command before proceeding to the next step.

Step 2. Press **Font** (Ctrl-F8) and **2** (Appearance).

WordPerfect displays the following menu on the status line:
1 Bold **2** Undrln **3** Dbl Und **4** Italc **5** Outln **6** Shadw **7** Sm Cap **8** Redln **9** Stkout: **0**

Step 3. Press a number **1** through **9** (or the corresponding letter) to select the desired font appearance.

Figure 11.6 displays each of the nine font appearances with the base font of 18-point Times Roman. Not all of these appearances are supported by all printers.

Step 4. Type the text you want in the modified font appearance.

The modified text appears in a different color on a color monitor. If you are changing the font color of a block of text (using the **Block** command), you may skip this step.

Step 5. To return to the unmodified base font, press **Right Arrow** to move past the font appearance code, or press **Font** (Ctrl-F8) and **3** (Normal).

Selecting **Bold** (F6) or **Underline** (F8) is usually easier than pressing **Font** (Ctrl-F8) and **1** (**B**old) or **2** (**U**ndrln) from the Font Appearance menu but produces the identical results.

You can mix font sizes and appearances in the same text (if your printer supports it). For example, you could have a phrase that is bold, double underlined, and very large, all at the same time. Figure 11.7, for example, shows mixed appearances.

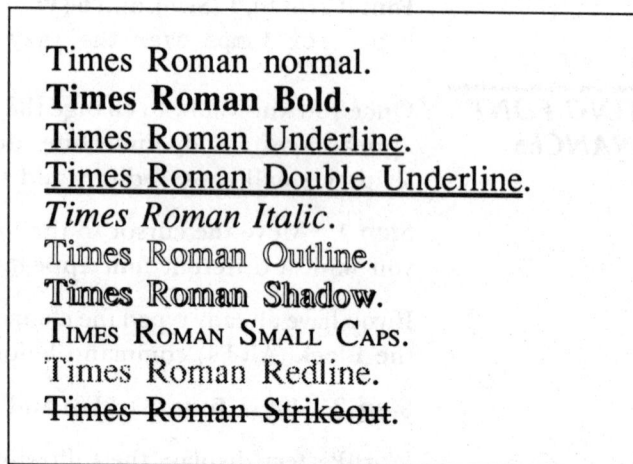

Times Roman normal.
Times Roman Bold.
<u>Times Roman Underline</u>.
<u>Times Roman Double Underline</u>.
Times Roman Italic.
Times Roman Outline.
Times Roman Shadow.
TIMES ROMAN SMALL CAPS.
Times Roman Redline.
~~Times Roman Strikeout~~.

Figure 11.6 The nine font appearances for the base font of 18-point Times Roman.

Times Roman normal.
Times Bold and Underline.
Times Small Caps, Outline, Italics.
Times Bold and Shadow.

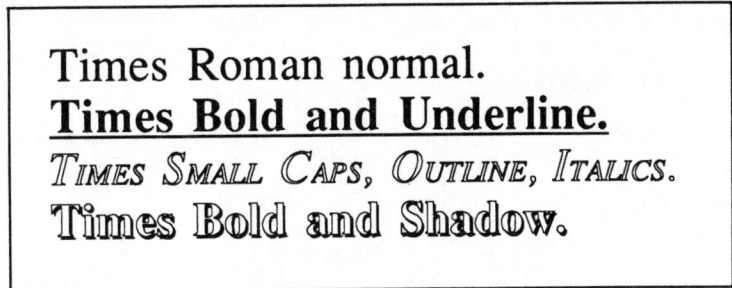

Figure 11.7   Mixing font appearances.

CHOOSING FONT COLORS AND GRAY SHADING

With WordPerfect, you can select font colors and gray shading by following these steps:

Step 1.   Move the cursor to the location in your document where you want a different font color or gray shading.

If you have already typed the characters, highlight (block) them using the **Block** (Alt-F4) command before proceeding to the next step.

Step 2.   Press **Font** (Ctrl-F8) and **5** (Print **C**olor).

WordPerfect displays the Print Color menu shown in Figure 11.8.

Step 3.   Select a color by pressing **1** through **9**, **A**, or **N**; or press **O** (**O**ther) to create your own mix of the primary colors (red, green, and blue).

If you have a normal (noncolor) laser printer, you can create gray shading by selecting **O** (**O**ther) and typing, for example, 50% Red, 50% Green, and 50% Blue to create 50% gray shading. Examples are shown in Figure 11.9.

Step 4.   Type the text you want in the modified print color.

Step 5.   To return to the default color (black), press **Right Arrow** or press **Font** (Ctrl-F8), **5** (Print **C**olor), **1** (**B**lack).

PRINTING REVERSED TYPE

Reversed type (also called *dropout* or *surprinted* type) is text that appears white on a dark background. You can use the Print Color command and text boxes to create reversed type or to make other effects, such as light gray on a dark gray background. See Figure 11.10.

```
Print Color

                            Primary Color Mixture
                        Red       Green       Blue

        1 - Black        0%         0%          0%
        2 - White      100%       100%        100%
        3 - Red         67%         0%          0%
        4 - Green        0%        67%          0%
        5 - Blue         0%         0%         67%
        6 - Yellow      67%        67%          0%
        7 - Magenta     67%         0%         67%
        8 - Cyan         0%        67%         67%
        9 - Orange      67%        25%          0%
        A - Gray        50%        50%         50%
        N - Brown       67%        33%          0%
        O - Other

        Current Color    0%         0%          0%


Selection: 0
```

Figure 11.8   The Print Color menu.

To create reversed text, follow these steps:

Step 1.   Press **Graphics** (Alt-F9), **3** (Text **B**ox), **4** (**O**ptions).

The Options: Text Box menu appears on the screen; see Figure 7.9 in Chapter 7, "Drawing Lines and Boxes."

Step 2.   Press **1** (**B**order Style) and **1** (**N**one) four times to set the border to None.

Step 3.   Press **9** (**G**ray Shading), type 100, press **Enter** to make a black-filled box, and press **Exit** (F7) to return to the document screen.

If you want the background gray instead of black, type a number less than 100.

Step 4.   Press **Graphics** (Alt-F9), **3** (Text **B**ox), and **1** (**C**reate).

The Definition: Text Box menu appears on the screen.

100% Gray Shading (no color)
95% Gray Shading (5% color)
90% Gray Shading (10% color)
80% Gray Shading (20% color)
70% Gray Shading (30% color)
60% Gray Shading (40% color)
50% Gray Shading (gray color)
40% Gray Shading (60% color)
30% Gray Shading (70% color)
20% Gray Shading (80% color)
10% Gray Shading (90% color)
5% Gray Shading (95% color)
1% Gray Shading (99% color)

Figure 11.9   Examples of gray shading of text.

Step 5.   Press **3** (Type), **2** (Page), **4** (Vertical Position), **2** (Top), **5** (Horizontal Position), **5** (Margins), **3** (Center), **6** (Size), **1** (Width (auto height)), type a desired width for the text, press **Enter**, and **8** (Edit).

These commands define the attributes of the text box and display the text box edit menu.

Step 6.   Press **Font** (Ctrl-F8), **5** (Print Color), **2** (White), and **Enter**.

This makes the text white, to produce white-on-black characters. If you want the text gray, instead of pressing **2** (White), press **O** (Other) and set Red, Green, and Blue all to the same value greater than zero. The higher the values, the lower the gray scale. Thus, setting Red,

100% Gray Shading (black color)
95% Gray Shading (5% color)
90% Gray Shading (10% color)
80% Gray Shading (20% color)
70% Gray Shading (30% color)
60% Gray Shading (40% color)

40% Gray Shading (60% color)
30% Gray Shading (70% color)
20% Gray Shading (80% color)
10% Gray Shading (90% color)
5% Gray Shading (95% color)
1% Gray Shading (99% color)
0% Gray Shading (white color)

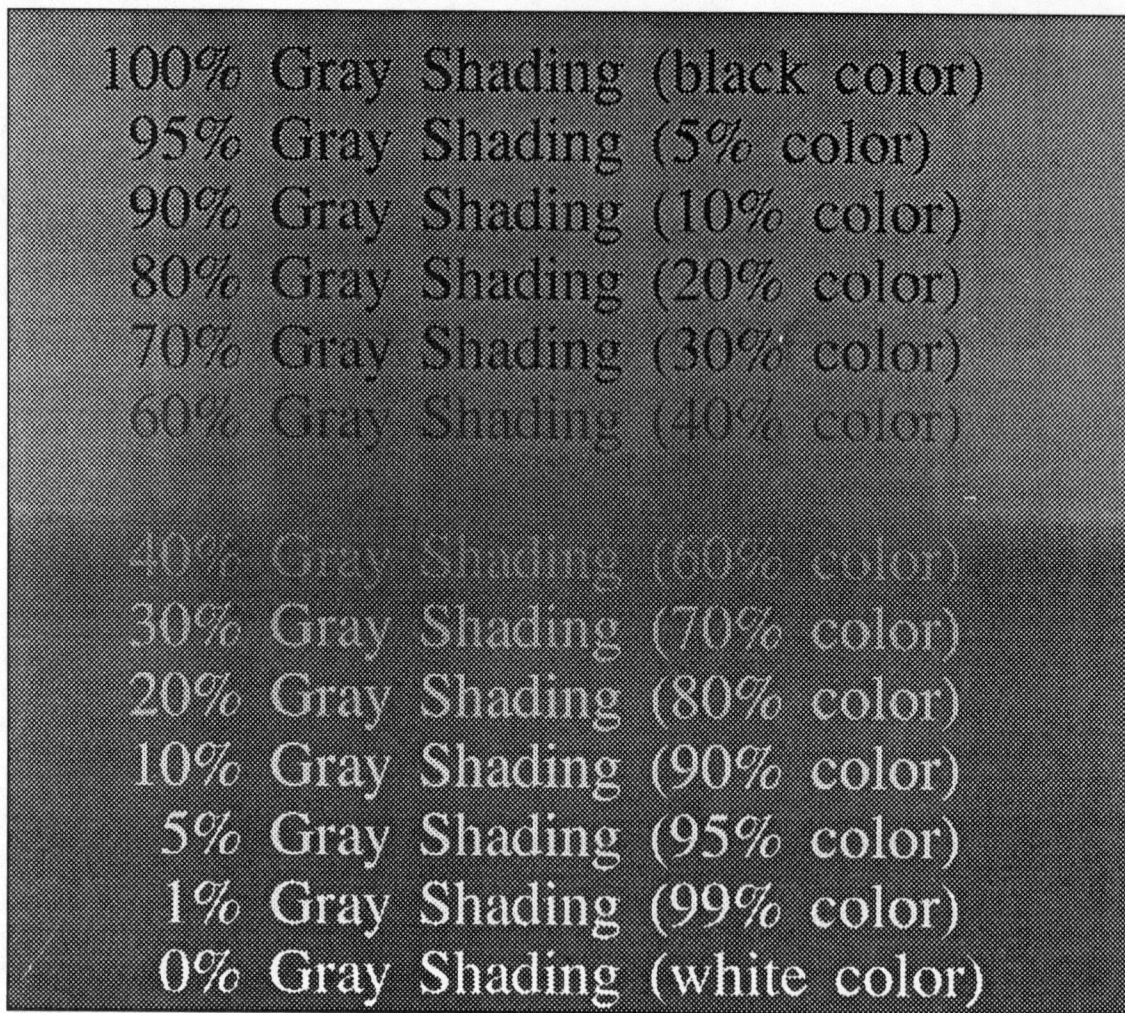

Figure 11.10   Reversed text. Same as Figure 11.9 except on a 50% gray background.

Green, and Blue to 20%, 20%, and 20% will create an 80% gray shading. See Figures 11.9 and 11.10.

Step 7.   Press **Font** (Ctrl-F8), **4** (Base **F**ont), and select the desired typeface and size; then press **Font** (Ctrl-F8), **1** (**S**ize), and **7** (**E**xt Large).

Step 8.   Type the phrase into the text box and press **Exit** (F7).

Step 9.   Press **Exit** (F7) twice to return to your document.

KERNING AND LETTER SPACING

For information on kerning and on spacing between words and letters, see "Kerning" and "Spacing Between Words and Letters" in Chapter 4, "Formatting Documents."

AVOIDING FONT PITFALLS

Just because you *can* vary the font size and appearance doesn't mean you *should*. The purpose of type design is to make your documents attractive and easy to read. See Chapter 3, "Designing Documents."

Keep your text clean and simple. Avoid excessive changes in font sizes and appearances that distract your reader from the real intent of the text. For example, compare the two documents in Figure 11.11. The document in Figure 11.11B violates its own rules, while the one in Figure 11.11A follows the basic principles of design.

Font Guidelines

The following are some general guidelines on typefaces to help you create attractive, easy-to-read documents:

- *Select an appropriate base font and (except for titles, headings, and special effects) stick to it.* For example, Figure 11.11A uses the base font of New Century Schoolbook and varies from that font only in the title and heading (which are in Helvetica).

- *Be consistent.* Don't change the font typeface, size, appearance, or color unless you have a good reason to do so. And when you do make a change—for example, in a heading—make sure the change is applied consistently in all headings. In Figure 11.11A, the main point of each bulleted item of style guidelines is in italics for emphasis. Note that this style is applied consistently for every item in the list.

- *Limit each page to two or three typefaces.* Documents with *excessive* type changes look gaudy and amateurish. For variation and contrast, use different font sizes in the same typeface.

- *Use a serif font* (e.g., Times Roman or New Century Schoolbook) *as your base font in long documents.* Serif fonts have horizontal base lines that help the eye flow from one word to the next. Sans serif fonts (e.g., Helvetica and Avant Garde Gothic Book) have predominantly vertical lines that accentuate individual words. Use sans serif fonts, therefore, in titles and headings.

- *Use medium-weight typefaces.* Very light and very heavy typefaces are harder to read than a medium-weight typeface.

Typeface Guidelines

Just because you *can* vary the font size and appearance doesn't mean you *should*.

The purpose of type design is to make your documents attractive and easy to read. So keep your text clean and simple. Avoid excessive changes in font sizes and appearances that distract your reader from the real intent of the text.

Style Guidelines

The following are some general guidelines on typefaces to help you create attractive, easy-to-read documents:

- *Select an appropriate base font and stick to it*. Change the font only for titles, headings, or occasional emphasis.

- *Be consistent*. Don't change the font typeface, size, appearance, or color unless you have a good reason to do so. And when you do make a change—for example, in a heading—make sure the change is applied consistently in all headings.

- *Limit each page to 2 or 3 typefaces*. Documents with *excessive* type changes look gaudy and amateurish. For variation and contrast, use different font sizes in the same typeface.

- *Use a serif font (e.g., Times or Schoolbook) as your base font in long documents*. Serif fonts have horizontal base lines that help the eye flow from one word to the next. Sans serif fonts have predominantly vertical lines that accentuate individual words. Use sans serif fonts, therefore, in titles and headings.

- *Use medium-weight typefaces*. Very light and very heavy typefaces are harder to read than a medium-weight typeface.

- *Avoid all caps*. Phrases in all capital (uppercase) letters are less legible than those in lowercase letters (or mixed uppercase and lowercase). Especially avoid using all caps in sans serif fonts.

Figure 11.11A A document that follows the rules of design.

- *Avoid all caps*. Phrases in all capital (uppercase) letters are less legible than those in lowercase letters (or mixed uppercase and lowercase). Especially avoid using all caps in sans serif fonts. See Figure 11.12.

Typeface Guidelines

Just because you *can* vary the font **size** and appearance doesn't mean you *should*.

*The purpose of type design is to make your documents attractive and easy to read. So keep your text **clean** and simple. Avoid EXCESSIVE changes in font sizes and appearances that distract your reader from the real intent of the text.*

STYLE GUIDELINES

The following are some general guidelines on typefaces to help you create *attractive*, **easy-to-read** documents:

♥ *Select an appropriate base font and stick to it*. Change the font only for titles, headings, or occasional emphasis.

♦ *Be consistent*. Don't change the font *typeface*, size, appearance, or color unless you have a good reason to do so. And when you do make a change—for example, in a heading—make sure the change is applied consistently in all headings.

♣ *Limit each page to 2 or 3 typefaces*. Documents with *excessive* type changes look gaudy and amateurish. For variation and contrast, *use different font sizes in the same typeface*.

♠ Use a serif font (e.g., Times or Schoolbook) as your base font in long documents. Serif fonts have horizontal base lines that **help the eye** flow from one word to the next. Sans serif fonts have predominantly vertical lines that accentuate individual words. Use sans serif fonts, therefore, in titles and headings.

• *Use medium-weight typefaces*. **Very light and very heavy typefaces are harder to read than a medium-weight typeface.**

Avoid all caps. Phrases in ALL CAPITAL (UPPERCASE) LETTERS ARE LESS LEGIBLE THAN THOSE IN lowercase letters (or mixed uppercase and lowercase). Especially avoid using all caps in sans serif fonts.

Figure 11.11B A document that violates the rules of design.

• *If readability is your primary goal, use ragged right instead of justified text*. Some documents require justification, but ragged right margins are perfectly acceptable, even in some formal publications. Lines of text with a ragged right margin are easier for the eye to follow than justified text.

• *In justified text, avoid large gaps ("rivers") between letters and words.* Figure 11.14 show the same two paragraphs, one with rivers and one without. The cure for rivers is to adjust the word and letter spacing as described in "Spacing Between Words and Letters" in Chapter 4, "Formatting Documents," and to turn *on* hyphenation.

With experimentation and care, you will be able to produce attractive, legible, published documents, using appropriate font typefaces, sizes, and appearances.

NOWHERE IS OUR NATION'S HERALDED EMERGENCE INTO THE INFORMATION AGE MORE APPARENT THAN IN THE USE OF THE COMPUTER IN WRITTEN COMMUNICATION. FIVE YEARS AGO, THE TERM "WORD PROCESSOR" WAS RARELY USED AND EVEN MORE RARELY UNDERSTOOD. NOW, AS A RESULT OF THE WIDESPREAD ACCEPTANCE OF THE PERSONAL COMPUTER, THE TERM IS PART OF OUR EVERYDAY VOCABULARY.

Nowhere is our nation's heralded emergence into the Information Age more apparent than in the use of the computer in written communication. Five years ago, the term "word processor" was rarely used and even more rarely understood. Now, as a result of the widespread acceptance of the personal computer, the term is part of our everyday vocabulary.

Figure 11.12   Demonstration of the effect of all caps on readability.

Excessive Raggedness:

Nowhere is our nation's heralded emergence into the Information Age more apparent than in the use of the computer in written communication. Five years ago, the term "word processor" was rarely used and even more rarely understood. Now, as a result of the widespread acceptance of the personal computer, the term is part of our everyday vocabulary.

Better:

Nowhere is our nation's heralded emergence into the Information Age more apparent than in the use of the computer in written communication. Five years ago, the term "word processor" was rarely used and even more rarely understood. Now, as a result of the widespread acceptance of the personal computer, the term is part of our everyday vocabulary.

Figure 11.13   Demonstration of the effect of excessive raggedness in unjustified text.

Excessive Gaps and "Rivers":

Nowhere is our nation's heralded emergence into the Information Age more apparent than in the use of the computer in written communication. Five years ago, the term "word processor" was rarely used and even more rarely understood. Now, as a result of the widespread acceptance of the personal computer, the term is part of our everyday vocabulary.

Better:

Nowhere is our nation's heralded emergence into the Information Age more apparent than in the use of the computer in written communication. Five years ago, the term "word processor" was rarely used and even more rarely understood. Now, as a result of the widespread acceptance of the personal computer, the term is part of our everyday vocabulary.

Figure 11.14   Demonstration of the effect of "rivers" in justified text.

SUMMARY

In this chapter you have learned how to select different fonts (typefaces) within your document by pressing **Font** (Ctrl-F8) and **4** (Base Font), highlighting the desired font, and pressing **1** (Select).

You can change the size of the font either by changing the base font or, more simply and temporarily, by pressing **Font** (Ctrl-F8), **1** (Size), and selecting the desired size—superscript, subscript, fine, small, large, very large, or extra large.

To select a new font appearance, press **Font** (Ctrl-F8), **2** (Appearance), and select the desired appearance—bold, underline, double underline, italics, outline, shadow, small caps, redline, or strikeout.

You can set the color or gray shading of a font by pressing **Font** (Ctrl-F8), **5** (Print **C**olor), and selecting the desired color. For gray shading, use the color **O**ther and set the percent of red, green, and blue.

You can create attractive documents if you understand and follow the principles of design in selecting typefaces.

Chapter 12

Inserting Special Characters

A major requirement of desktop publishing is the ability to insert special characters into a document. In this requirement, WordPerfect excels.

In this chapter you will learn the following:

- What special characters are required in desktop publishing that aren't necessary (or available) in normal word processing.

- What special characters are available using WordPerfect with your printer.

- How to insert these special characters into your document.

USING SPECIAL CHARACTERS

Special characters are required for the following types of text:

- Mathematical and scientific formulas and equations.

$$^{238}_{92}\text{U} \rightarrow {}^{4}_{2}\alpha + {}^{234}_{90}\text{Th}$$

- Foreign phrases.

  ¿Estarás aquí mañana?

- Currency symbols.

  Dollar (\$), cent (¢), pound (£), yen (¥).

- Typographical characters.

  Em dash (—), en dash (–), left and right quote marks (" . . . "), other symbols (™, ®, ©, ¶, §).

WordPerfect's Support of Special Characters

WordPerfect supports digraphs (Æ, œ), diacriticals (ñ, é), and other special characters (α, ©, →, £, ¿, ±) through the **Compose** command, initiated by pressing **Ctrl-2** or **Ctrl-V**. A complete list of the characters accessible through WordPerfect is given in Appendix P of the WordPerfect user's manual.

Your Printer's Support of Special Characters

Your printer doesn't ordinarily support all the WordPerfect special characters. If your printer supports graphics, however, WordPerfect will create a bit-mapped shape for any character that isn't built into your printer. These bit-mapped characters usually don't have the same quality as, and take longer to print than, the built-in characters.

Figure 12.1 shows the file CHARMAP.TST printed on the Hewlett-Packard LaserJet Series II with font cartridge J (Math Elite) and the font Prestige Elite 10 pt., with graphics turned *off*.

This prints all characters in Character Map 0

```
        0                   1
        0 1 2 3 4 5 6 7 8 9 0 1 2 3 4 5 6 7 8 9 |

030         ! " # $ % & ' ( ) * + , - . / 0 1 |

050     2 3 4 5 6 7 8 9 : ; < = > ? @ A B C D E |

070     F G H I J K L M N O P Q R S T U V W X Y |

090     Z [ \ ] ^ _ ` a b c d e f g h i j k l m |

110     n o p q r s t u v w x y z { | } ~       |

        0 1 2 3 4 5 6 7 8 9 0 1 2 3 4 5 6 7 8 9 |
        0                   1
```

This prints all characters in Character Map 1

```
        0                   1
        0 1 2 3 4 5 6 7 8 9 0 1 2 3 4 5 6 7 8 9 |

000     ` · ˜ ^ - / ´ ¨ ¯ '       ,   ° · "  .    ˇ |

020       ¯ ˘           Á á Â â Ä ä À à Å å Æ æ Ç ç |

040     É é Ê ê Ë ë È è Í í Î î Ï ï Ì ì Ñ ñ Ó ó |

060     Ô ô Ö ö Ò ò Ú ú Û û Ü ü Ù ù Ÿ ÿ Ã ã Đ đ |

080     Ø ø Õ õ Ý ý Đ đ Þ þ     Ā ā     Ć ć     |

100     Ĉ ĉ c         E e Ē ē     Ġ ġ           |

120     Ģ ģ Ĝ ĝ Ģ ģ Ĥ ĥ Ħ ħ ı   Ī         Į     |

140     Ĵ     Ķ ķ Ĺ ĺ     Ļ ļ Ļ ļ     Ń ń   ħ   |

160     Ŋ ŋ ö̈ ö̈ ō ō     Ŕ ŕ     Ŗ ŗ Ś ś Š š Ş ş |

180     Ŝ ŝ     Ţ ţ Ŧ ŧ     Ü ü Ū ū     Ů ů Ũ ũ |

200     Ŵ ŵ Ŷ ŷ Ź ź     z z     Ḍ ḍ Ī ī Ñ ñ Ř ř |

220     s̄ s̄ Ŧ ŧ     Ỳ ỳ                         |

        0 1 2 3 4 5 6 7 8 9 0 1 2 3 4 5 6 7 8 9 |
        0                   1
```

Figure 12.1   Printout of the WordPerfect file CHARMAP.TST using the Hewlett-Packard LaserJet Series II, font cartridge J (Math Elite) and the font Prestige Elite 10 pt. Character maps 10 through 12 contain no printable characters.

```
This prints all characters in Character Map 2

        0                     1
        0 1 2 3 4 5 6 7 8 9 0 1 2 3 4 5 6 7 8 9 |
000     .   °         <  _                     '   |

020                                                |

        0 1 2 3 4 5 6 7 8 9 0 1 2 3 4 5 6 7 8 9 |
        0                     1


This prints all characters in Character Map 3

        0                     1
        0 1 2 3 4 5 6 7 8 9 0 1 2 3 4 5 6 7 8 9 |
000     ▒ ▓ █ █ ▌ █ ▀ ▄ █ – | ┌ ┐ ┘ └ ├ ┬ ┤ ┴ ┼ = |
020     ║ ╓ ╖ ╜ ╙ ╟ ╥ ╢ ╨ ╧ ╔ ╗ ╝ ╚ ╠ ╦ ╣ ╩ ┠ ┰ |
040     ┨ ┸ ┝ ┯ ┥ ┷ ┿ ╂ – | – ╷ = ║ ═ ╟ ┈ ┄ ╎ ╏ |
060     ┞ ┟ ┡ ┢ ┰ ┰ ┰ ┰ ┦ ┧ ┩ ┪ ┴ ┸ ┴ ┸ ┼ ┼ ┿ ┿ |
080     ╁ ╁ ╀ ╀ ╂ ╂ ╂                              |

        0 1 2 3 4 5 6 7 8 9 0 1 2 3 4 5 6 7 8 9 |
        0                     1


This prints all characters in Character Map 4

        0                     1
        0 1 2 3 4 5 6 7 8 9 0 1 2 3 4 5 6 7 8 9 |
000     • ○ ■ ·     ¶ § ¡ ¿ « » £ ¥ ₨ ƒ ª º ½ ¼ ¢ |
020     ² η ® © ¤   ³   ' '   " "  - – < > ○ □ † |
040     ‡ ™ ℠ ℞   ○ ■ ·     –                     |
060       £               ⊛                       |

        0 1 2 3 4 5 6 7 8 9 0 1 2 3 4 5 6 7 8 9 |
        0                     1
```

Figure 12.1 *Continued*

This prints all characters in Character Map 5

This prints all characters in Character Map 6

Figure 12.1 *Continued*

```
This prints all characters in Character Map 7

     0                   1
     0 1 2 3 4 5 6 7 8 9 0 1 2 3 4 5 6 7 8 9 |

000  ⌈ ⌋ |   √ ¯ Σ Π ⊔     |       | ‖         |
020  ‖           ⌈ { ⌊ |         ⌉ } ⌋ | ⌊      |
040    ⌊ | ⌋       ⌋ | ⌈       ⌈ | ⌉       ⌉ |
060  | ∪ ∩ φ ¯ ¯ ⌝ \ 〉 / ∠ _ ⌟               |
080      ⌋ | ⌈ → ← ─       ⇒ ⇐ ─ ↑ ↓ | ⇑ ⇓ ‖ |
100        ⌈ ⌊ |         ⌉ ⌋ |         ⌈ ⌊ |
120  |         ⌉ ⌋ | 〈       〉       /       |
140  \                                        |
160  ⌠ ⌡   ─ ⌊ ⌋ ─                            |
180          ⟦         ⟦ ⟦ ‖ ⟧       ‖ ⟧ ‖    |
200                                           |
220                                           |

     0 1 2 3 4 5 6 7 8 9
```

Figure 12.1 *Continued*

Figure 12.2 shows the file CHARMAP.TST printed on the Apple LaserWriter using 12-point Times Roman, with graphics turned *off*.

With graphics turned *on*, WordPerfect would print all the characters shown in Appendix P of the WordPerfect user's manual.

To read the maps in Figures 12.1 and 12.2 or the maps in the appendix of the WordPerfect user's manual, follow these steps:

Step 1. Find the character that you want inserted into your document.

Step 2. Press **Compose** (Ctrl-2 or Ctrl-V).

Step 3. Type the number of the character set (character map) that contains the desired character.

Step 4. Type a comma (,) and then type the number of the character within the set (or map).

This prints all characters in Character Map 8

```
     0                   1
     0 1 2 3 4 5 6 7 8 9 0 1 2 3 4 5 6 7 8 9 |

000  A α B β в    Γ γ Δ δ E ε Z ζ H η Θ θ I ι |

020  K κ Λ λ M μ N ν Ξ ξ O o Π π P ρ Σ σ Σ ς |

040  T τ T υ Φ φ X χ Ψ ψ Ω ω                   |

060      ε ϑ           φ ω                      |

080                                            |

100                                            |

120                                            |

140                                            |

160                                            |

180                                            |

200                                            |

     0 1 2 3 4 5 6 7 8 9 0 1 2 3 4 5 6 7 8 9 |
     0                   1
```

This prints all characters in Character Map 9

```
     0                   1
     0 1 2 3 4 5 6 7 8 9 0 1 2 3 4 5 6 7 8 9 |

000  א ב ג                                      |

020                                            |

040                                            |

     0 1 2 3 4 5 6 7 8 9 0 1 2 3 4 5 6 7 8 9 |
     0                   1
```

Figure 12.1 *Continued*

This prints all characters in Character Map 0

```
        0                   1
        0 1 2 3 4 5 6 7 8 9 0 1 2 3 4 5 6 7 8 9 |

030           ! " # $ % & ' ( ) * + , - . / 0 1 |

050     2 3 4 5 6 7 8 9 : ; < = > ? @ A B C D E |

070     F G H I J K L M N O P Q R S T U V W X Y |

090     Z [ \ ] ^ _ ' a b c d e f g h i j k l m |

110     n o p q r s t u v w x y z { | } ~       |

        0 1 2 3 4 5 6 7 8 9 0 1 2 3 4 5 6 7 8 9 |
        0                   1
```

This prints all characters in Character Map 1

```
        0                   1
        0 1 2 3 4 5 6 7 8 9 0 1 2 3 4 5 6 7 8 9 |

000     ` . ˜ ^ —/ ´ ¨ ¯           • ˙ ˘ ˛ . ˇ |

020         ˘ ₁ Á á Â â Ä ä À à Å å Æ æ Ç ç |

040     É é Ê ê Ë ë È è Í í Î î Ï ï Ì ì Ñ ñ Ó ó |

060     Ô ô Ö ö Ò ò Ú ú Û û Ü ü Ù ù Ÿ ÿ Ã ã Ð đ |

080     Ø ø Õ õ Ý ý             Ă ă Ā ā Ą ą Ć ć Č č |

100     Ĉ ĉ Ċ ċ Ď ď Ě ě Ė ė Ē ē Ę ę Ǵ ǵ Ğ ğ Ğ ğ |

120     Ģ ģ Ĝ ĝ Ġ ġ Ĥ ĥ Ħ ħ Ì ì i ì Ī ī Į į Ĩ ĩ   |

140     Ĵ ĵ   Ķ ķ Ĺ ĺ Ľ ľ Ļ ļ Ł ł Ł ł Ń ń       Ň ň |

160     Ņ ņ Ő ő Ō ō Œ œ Ŕ ŕ Ř ř Ŗ ŗ Ś ś Š š Ş ş |

180     Ŝ ŝ Ť ť Ţ ţ Ŧ ŧ Ŭ ŭ Ű ű Ū ū Ų ų Ů ů Ũ ũ |

200     Ŵ ŵ Ŷ ŷ Ź ź Ž ž Ż ż       Ḍ ḍ Ḹ ḹ Ñ ñ Ŗ ŗ |

220     Ŝ ŝ Ṫ ṫ Ẏ ẏ Ỳ ỳ                         |

        0 1 2 3 4 5 6 7 8 9 0 1 2 3 4 5 6 7 8 9 |
        0                   1
```

Figure 12.2   Printout of the WordPerfect file CHARMAP.TST using the Apple LaserWriter and 12-point Times Roman font. Character maps 2, 3, and 9 through 12 contain no characters.

This prints all characters in Character Map 4

```
          0                   1
          0 1 2 3 4 5 6 7 8 9 0 1 2 3 4 5 6 7 8 9 |

000       •       ·     ¶ § ¡ ¿ « » £ ¥   ƒ ª º         ¢ |

020           ® © ¤             '       " " – —‹ ›       † |

040       ‡ ™                           fi fl ...         |

060         , „                         ‰               |

          0 1 2 3 4 5 6 7 8 9 0 1 2 3 4 5 6 7 8 9 |
          0                   1
```

This prints all characters in Character Map 5

```
          0                   1
          0 1 2 3 4 5 6 7 8 9 0 1 2 3 4 5 6 7 8 9 |

000       ♥ ♦ ♣ ♠                                     |

020       ↵                                           |

          0 1 2 3 4 5 6 7 8 9 0 1 2 3 4 5 6 7 8 9 |
          0                   1
```

Figure 12.2 *Continued*

To determine the character number within a set (or map), add the row number (the numeric value at the left of each row) and the column number (the numeric value along the top of each column). For example, to select the character number of a Greek omega (ω), find the row value (40 in Figure 12.1) and the column value (11 in Figure 12.1), and add the two: 51. Thus, to insert an omega, type 8,51.

Step 5. Press **Enter**.

The special character appears in the document.

USING SPECIAL CHARACTERS IN DESKTOP PUBLISHING

Desktop publishing requires that you break some old habits and form some new ones. The following are rules for desktop publishing that deal with special characters (see Figure 12.3):

• Use an em dash (—) rather than double hyphens (--) for elements added for emphasis or explanation.

This prints all characters in Character Map 6

```
             0                 1
             0 1 2 3 4 5 6 7 8 9 0 1 2 3 4 5 6 7 8 9 |

000          – ± ≤ ≥ ∝ / /     +   ⟨ ⟩ ~ ≈ ≡ ∈ ∩     Σ ∞ |

020          ¬ → ← ↑ ↓ ↔                       °         × |

040          ∫ ∏   ∇ ∂ ′ ″       ℑ ℜ ℘       ⇒ ⇐ ⇑ ⇓ |

060          ⇔             ∪ ⊂ ⊃ ⊆ ⊇ ∌ Ø           ∠ |

080          ⊗ ⊕       ∧ ∨     ⊥           ◊       ≠ |

100              ∴                         ≅     |

120          ∃ ∀                               |

140                                          |

160                                          |

180                                          |

200                            ∉             |

             0 1 2 3 4 5 6 7 8 9 0 1 2 3 4 5 6 7 8 9 |
             0                 1
```

Figure 12.2 *Continued*

Example: The Ocean Breeze Bookstore philosophy is summarized in two words—quality service. **Not**: The Ocean Breeze Bookstore philosophy is summarized in two words--quality service. (It is called an *em dash* because it is the width of a capital M.)

- Use an en dash (–) rather than a normal hyphen to mean "to" in a range of values.

  Example: Pages 16–21. **Not**: Pages 16-21. (It is called an *en dash* because it is the width of a capital N. An en dash is slightly wider than a normal keyboard hyphen.)

- Use left and right quote marks (" . . . "), not common keyboard quote marks (" . . . ").

  Example: If your computer "bombs" or your hard disk "crashes," don't give up. **Not**: If your computer "bombs" or your hard disk "crashes," don't give up.

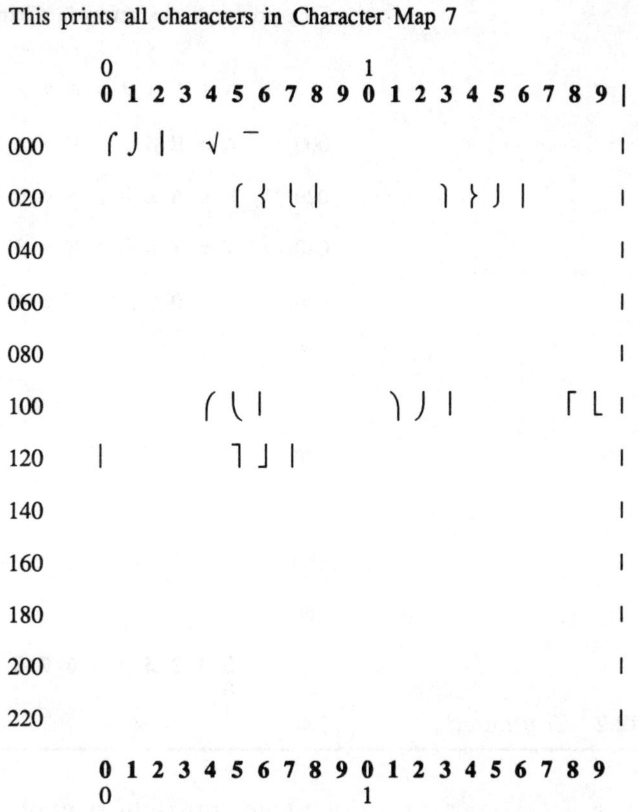
This prints all characters in Character Map 7
000
020
040
060
080
100
120
140
160
180
200
220

Figure 12.2 *Continued*

- Use left and right single quotes (' . . . '), not just apostrophes.

  Example: I asked my friend, "Did you see my article, 'Macro Magic'?" **Not**: I asked my friend, "Did you see my article, 'Macro Magic'?"

- In bulleted lists, use a true bullet symbol (•), not just a lower-case o or a dash (-).

- Use a times symbol (×), not just an x, for multiplication or in dimensions.

  Example: 12 × 12 = 144. **Not**: 12 x 12 = 144.

- Use a true inch symbol (″), not a quote mark ("), to mean inches.

  Example: 2″ × 4″. **Not**: 2" x 4".

- Use a true arrow (→), not a dash and the greater-than sign (->).

This prints all characters in Character Map 8

	0									1									
	0	1	2	3	4	5	6	7	8	9	0	1	2	3	4	5	6	7	8	9
000	A	α	B	β			Γ	γ	Δ	δ	E	ε	Z	ζ	H	η	Θ	θ	I	ι
020	K	κ	Λ	λ	M	μ	N	ν	Ξ	ξ	O	o	Π	π	P	ρ	Σ	σ		ς
040	T	τ	Y	υ	Φ	φ	X	χ	Ψ	ψ	Ω	ω								
060			ϑ				Υ	φ	ϖ											
080																				
100																				
120																				
140																				
160																				
180																				

0 1 2 3 4 5 6 7 8 9 0 1 2 3 4 5 6 7 8 9 |
0   1

Figure 12.2 *Continued*

- Use a true copyright symbol (©), not (c).

This list is more representative than exhaustive. Your experience and attention to detail will lead you to other typographic rules dealing with special characters.

INSERTING SPECIAL CHARACTERS INTO YOUR DOCUMENT

To insert a special character into your document, follow these steps:

Step 1. Locate the character map (or set) in which the desired character is found.

For example, if you want to insert the Greek letter α, you would find it in character map 8. See Figure 12.1 or 12.2.

Step 2. Identify the character number in the character map.

For example, α is character number 1 in character map 8. The Spanish letter ñ is character number 57 in character map 1. You may have to spend a little time figuring out the grid system used for numbering each of the characters in a character set.

Typographic Symbols

Incorrect	Correct	Symbol Name	Character Numbers
--	—	em dash	4,34
-	–	en dash	4,33
"	"	left quote	4,32
"	"	right quote	4,33
'	'	left single quote	0,96
'	'	left single quote	0,9
-	•	bullet	4,0
x	×	times symbol	6,39
"	"	inch symbol	6,46
->	→	arrow	6,21
(c)	©	copyright symbol	4,23

Figure 12.3 Typographic symbols used in desktop publishing. The character numbers are used with the **Compose** command to insert the character into a document.

Step 3. Move the cursor to the location in your document where you want to insert the special character.

Step 4. Press **Compose** (Ctrl-V) by holding down the **Ctrl** key and tapping **v**.

When you press **Compose** (Ctrl-V), WordPerfect gives the prompt **Key =** on the status line. You may also press **Ctrl-2** to evoke the **Compose** feature (by holding down the control key and tapping **2**, in which case WordPerfect gives no prompt).

Step 5. Type the character map number, a comma, the character number (in the character map), and press **Enter**.

For example, to insert α, press **Compose** (Ctrl-V), type 8,1, and press **Enter**. WordPerfect inserts the character into your document.

INSERTING DIGRAPHS AND DIACRITICALS

Digraphs are special characters composed of two normal characters. For example, Æ (a digraph) is composed of **A** and **E**; £ is composed of **-** and **L**; and œ is composed of **o** and **e**. *Diacritics* are special characters composed of a diacritical mark (´, ~, `, ¨, etc.) and a normal letter. For example, ñ is composed of ~ and **n**; û is composed of ˆ and **u**; and é is composed of ´ and **e**.

You can insert digraphs and diacriticals into your document in the same way as you inserted special characters, as described in the previous section (i.e., by pressing **Compose** (Ctrl-V) and typing the character number, a comma, and the character set). The digraphs and diacriticals are found mostly in character map 1.

But WordPerfect offers a simple, easier-to-remember method:

Step 1.   With your cursor at the location where you want the digraph or diacritical, press **Compose** (Ctrl-V or Ctrl-2).

Step 2.   Type the first of the two characters in the digraph or the diacritical mark in the diacritical character.

For example, press ~ to start the character ñ, or press **A** to start the character Æ. If you use the Ctrl-V method, WordPerfect displays this first character (~ or A) on the status line; if you use the Ctrl-2 method, WordPerfect displays nothing.

Step 3.   Type the second character in the digraph or the diacritical.

For example press **n** to complete the character ñ, or press **E** to complete the character Æ.

That's it, fast and simple. You do *not* type a comma between the characters or press **Enter** after the second character.

SUMMARY

In this chapter you have learned that several special characters are required in desktop publishing that aren't necessary (or available) in normal word processing. You have also learned how to print the WordPerfect document CHARACTR.DOC or CHARMAP.TST to determine which special symbols your printer supports and which it doesn't.

Most importantly, you have learned how to use the **Compose** command (**Ctrl-V** or **Ctrl-2**) to insert special characters into your document.

Chapter 13

Typing Tables and Equations

In the days before WordPerfect 5.1, typing tables and equations was one of the most difficult tasks in word processing and desktop publishing. Now, with WordPerfect 5.1's new Tables and Equation commands, tables and equations are a snap.

In this chapter you'll learn the following:

- How to create and edit tables.

- How to exchange columns within a table.

- How to create equations using WordPerfect's equation editor.

MAKING TABLES

The general steps for creating a table are as follows:

Step 1.   Press **Columns/Table** (Alt-F7).

This evokes the one-line menu **1** **C**olumns; **2** **T**ables; **3** **M**ath: **0**.

Step 2.   Press **2** (Tables).

The menu **Table: 1** **C**reate; **2** **E**dit: **0**.

Step 3.   Press **1** (**C**reate).

WordPerfect then asks you for the number of columns in the table.

Step 4.   Type the number of columns and press **Enter**.

If you're unsure of the number of columns, just estimate a number. You can always insert, delete, or join columns later. WordPerfect then asks you for the number of rows in the table.

Step 5.   Type the number of rows and press **Enter**.

Again, if you're unsure of how many rows you'll need in the table, just estimate a number. You can insert or delete rows later. WordPerfect then displays the Table Edit screen, shown in Figure 13.1 and explained below.

Step 6.   Edit the table as desired, using any of the commands at the bottom of the Table Edit screen.

Step 7.   Press **Exit** (F7) to exit the Table Edit screen and return to the document screen.

The outline of the table stays on the screen.

Step 8.   Fill in the table cells with the table data.

The Table Edit Commands

The Table Edit screen (Figure 13.1) supports a powerful set of commands. You can use these commands on a single cell within the table or on a block of cells. To select a block of cells from Table Edit mode, press **Block** (Alt-F4) and move the cursor with the arrow keys in the usual manner. WordPerfect highlights all the selected cells.

The following is an explanation of most of the Table Edit commands:

• Standard cursor movement keys allow you to move the cursor through the table. For example, **Right Arrow** moves the cursor to the next cell in the row. **Home, Home, Up Arrow** moves the cursor to the first cell (upper left corner) of the table.

• **Ctrl-Right Arrow** increases the column width and **Ctrl-Left Arrow** decreases the column width of the column in which the cursor (highlight bar) is currently located. This allows you to easily increase or decrease the column width to the size of the largest entry within the column.

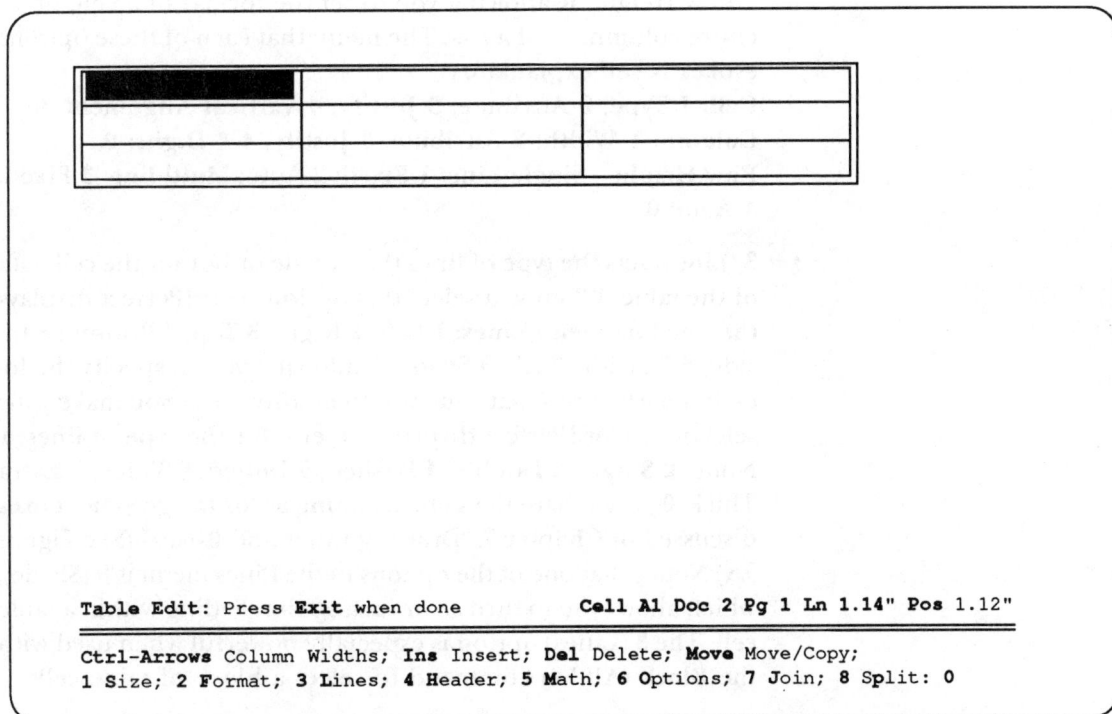

Figure 13.1 Table Edit screen

- **Ins** inserts one or more columns or rows into the table. When you press **Ins**, WordPerfect prompts you with the message **Insert: 1 R**ows; **2 C**olumns: **0**, after which you can specify the number of rows or columns that you would like to insert into the table.

- **Del** deletes one or more columns or rows from the table.

- **Move** (Ctrl-F4) allows you to move, copy, delete, or retrieve a column, row, or block of table data. The command works similar to the **Move** (Ctrl-F4) command for the normal document screen, except that in Table Edit mode, you can specify rows and columns rather than sentences, paragraphs, or pages to move, copy, delete, or retrieve.

- **1** (**S**ize) re-designates the number of rows and columns in the table. *Caution!* If you use **1** (**S**ize) to decrease the number of rows or columns, you may lose information that you have typed into the table.

- **2** (**F**ormat) evokes the one-line menu **Format: 1 C**ell; **2 C**olumn; **3 R**ow Height: **0**, allowing you to set the format of a cell, of an entire column, or of a row. The menu that each of these options evokes is self-explanatory:
  Cell: 1 Type; **2 A**ttribute; **3 J**ustify; **4 V**ertical Alignment: **0**.
  Column: 1 Width; **2 A**ttribute; **3 J**ustify; **4 #** Digits: **0**.
  Row Height—Single Line: 1 Fixed; **2 A**uto; **Multi-line: 3 F**ixed; **4 A**uto: **0**.

- **3** (**L**ines) sets the type of lines that divide or border the cell data of the table. When you select this option, WordPerfect displays the one-line menu **Lines: 1 L**eft; **2 R**ight; **3 T**op; **4 B**ottom; **5 I**nside; **6 O**utside; **7 A**ll; **8 S**hade: **0**, allowing you to specify the location of the lines that you want to modify. After you make your selection, WordPerfect displays a menu for the type of lines: **1 N**one; **2 S**ingle; **3 D**ouble; **4 D**ashed; **5 D**otted; **6 T**hick; **7 E**xtra Thick: **0**, which have the same meaning as for the graphics boxes discussed in Chapter 7, "Drawing Lines and Boxes." (See Figure 7.8.) Notice that one of the options in the Lines menu is **8** (**S**hade), which allows you to turn *on* or turn *off* the shading within a table cell. The **3** (**L**ines) option is especially powerful when used with the **Block** (Alt-F4) command to select a block of table cells.

- **4** (**H**eader) specifies a row that is repeated at the top of every page for tables that span more than one page.

- **5** (**M**ath) allows you to use the table as a mini-spreadsheet. When you select **5** (**M**ath), WordPerfect displays the one-line menu **Math: 1 C**alculate; **2 F**ormula; **3 C**opy Formula; **4** +; **5** =; **6** *: **0**, where **1** (**C**alculate) carries out the math calculations, **2** (**F**ormula) lets you specify a math formula within a cell, and **3** (**C**opy Formula) lets you copy a formula from one cell to another or from one block of cells to another block. Options **4** (+), **5** (=), and **6** (*) are special math functions for Subtotal (+), Total (=), and Grand Total (*); consult your WordPerfect user's manual for more information.

- **6** (**O**ptions) evokes the menu shown in Figure 13.2, which allows you to specify various options for the table. If you have questions about these options, consult the WordPerfect user's manual.

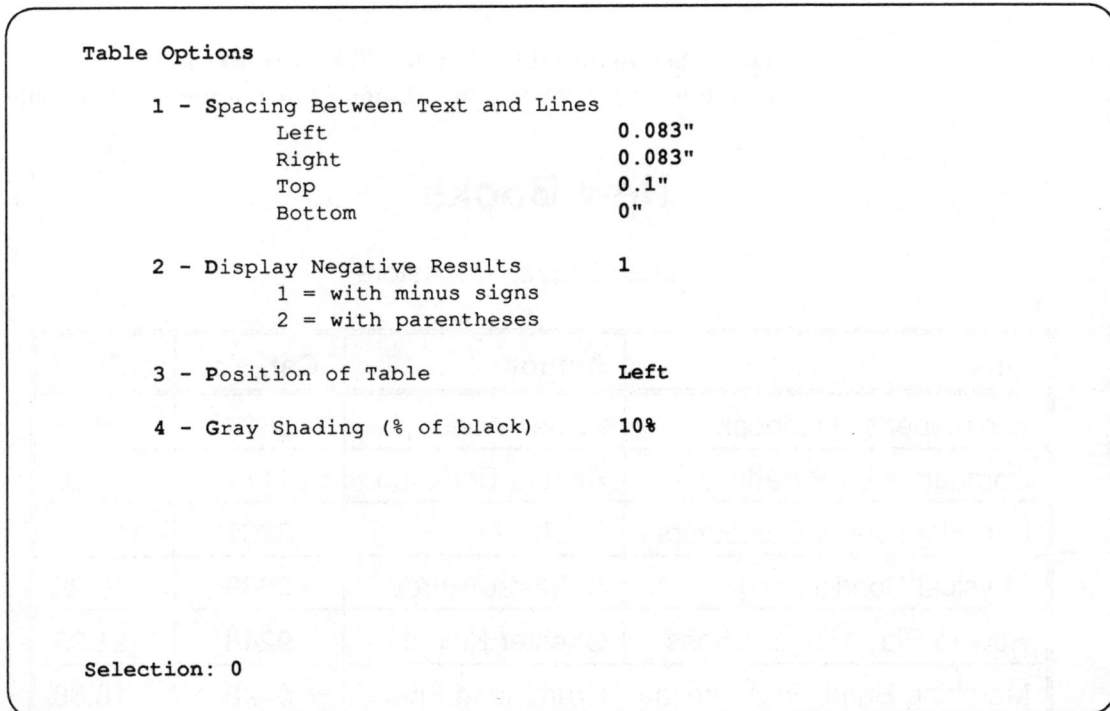

```
Table Options

    1 - Spacing Between Text and Lines
            Left                    0.083"
            Right                   0.083"
            Top                     0.1"
            Bottom                  0"

    2 - Display Negative Results    1
            1 = with minus signs
            2 = with parentheses

    3 - Position of Table           Left

    4 - Gray Shading (% of black)   10%




    Selection: 0
```

Figure 13.2 The Table Options menu.

- **7** (**J**oin) allows you to join a block of table cells into one cell.

- **8** (**Sp**lit) allows you to split a cell into multiple columns or rows.

The best way to learn the details of these various options is to experiment with them and to read about them in the WordPerfect user's manual.

Creating a Table

Figure 13.3 shows the typical kind of table that you would want to create for a publication. If you haven't used WordPerfect's Table feature, you'll be pleasantly surprised at how easily you can create the New Books list. Just follow these steps:

Step 1. Clear the WordPerfect document screen (if necessary), type the heading before the table (New Books at Ocean Breeze Bookstore), and move the cursor to the location where you want the table to start.

Step 2. Set up the table: **Columns/Table** (Alt-F7), **2** (**T**ables), **1** (**C**reate), 4 (the number of columns), **Enter**, 8 (the number of rows), **Enter**.

New Books

at Ocean Breeze Bookstore

Title	Author	Cat. No.	Price
Zookeeper's Handbook	Foster Wilde	3812	48.25
Computers on Parade	Roland Compton	4111	8.95
Encyclopedia of Computers	Noah Ahl	8267	117.50
Physical Conditioning	B. Moore Hardy	0689	8.95
How to Play Master Chess	Chester Knight	9248	21.95
Marching Bands in America	Drummond Fife	5428	18.88
How to Pray	Neil Downey	1432	12.95

Figure 13.3   A sample table.

WordPerfect displays the Tables Edit screen, like the one shown in Figure 13.1, except the table has four columns and eight rows.

Step 3. With the cursor in the upper left cell (A1) of the table, press **Block** (Alt-F4) and press **Right Arrow** three times to highlight the top row of the table.

Notice that the relative widths of the columns are not the same as shown in Figure 13.3. You'll adjust the column widths later.

Step 4. Create double lines between the top row and the second row: Press **3** (Lines), **4** (Bottom), and **3** (Double).

Step 5. Specify that data entered in column C will be centered within the cells: move the cursor to cell C1, press **2** (Format), **2** (Column), **3** (Justify), **2** (Center).

Step 6. Specify that data entered in column D will be right justified: move the cursor to cell D1, press **2** (Format), **2** (Column), **3** (Justify), **3** (Right).

Step 7. Press **Exit** (F7) to exit the Table Edit screen and return to the document screen.

Step 8. Type the headings in the top row of the table: move the cursor to cell A1, press **Bold** (F6), Title, **Bold** (F6), move to B1, **Bold** (F6), Author, **Bold** (F6), move to C1, **Bold** (F6), Cat. No., **Bold** (F6), move to D1, **Bold** (F6), Price, **Bold** (F6).

Step 9. Type the data into the table.

To move from one cell to the next in the same row, use **Right Arrow, Left Arrow, Tab,** or **Shift-Tab**. To move from one cell to the next in the same column, press **Up Arrow, Down Arrow**, or other cursor movement keys. As you type some of the titles, WordPerfect will expand the cell height to accommodate all the words.

Step 10. Adjust the column widths: Make sure the cursor is within the borders of the table and press **Columns/Table** (Alt-F7) to get back to the Table Edit screen; then move the cursor to cell A4 and press **Ctrl-Right Arrow** several times until all the book titles fit on one line within each cell. Move the cursor to the other columns and press **Word Right** (Ctrl-Right Arrow) to expand the column widths or **Word Left** (Ctrl-Left Arrow) to decrease the column widths so that your table looks like the one in Figure 13.3.

Step 11. Save the file to the disk using the filename NEW-BOOKS.TAB.

That completes the creation of the New Books table. Now you'll see how easily you can move columns within this or any WordPerfect table.

Moving Columns

Sometimes, after you have created a table, you decide that the columns are out of order. Suppose, for example, that you want to interchange the Cat. No. column and the Price column in the table in Figure 13.3. Just follow these steps:

Step 1. Move the cursor to cell D1 and press **Columns/Table** (Alt-F7).

WordPerfect puts you into the Table Edit screen.

Step 2. Press **Move** (Ctrl-F4).

The one-line menu **Move: 1 B**lock; **2 R**ow; **3 C**olumn; **4 R**etrieve: **0** appears on the screen.

Step 3. Press **3** (**C**olumn).

1 Move; **2 C**opy; **3 D**elete: **0** appears on the status line.

Step 4. Press **1** (**M**ove).

The column disappears and the message **Move cursor; press Enter to retrieve** appears on the screen.

Step 5. Move the cursor to cell C1, the location at which you want to insert the Price column.

Actually, if you've followed all the steps exactly as given, the cursor should already be residing at cell C1.

Step 6. Press **Enter** to retrieve the column.

That completes the column move. The only problem now is that the table has a double line instead of a single line between columns C and D.

Step 7. Convert the double line to a single line between columns C and D: Move the cursor to C1, press **Block** (Alt-F4), move the cursor to C8, press **3** (**Lines**), **2** (**Right**), and **2** (**Single**).

As you can see, the power of WordPerfect 5.1 makes creating tables fast and simple.

TYPING SIMPLE EQUATIONS

Many technical reports contain mathematical, statistical, chemical, and nuclear formulas or equations that are difficult to type. They often contain Greek letters, special symbols, subscripts, and superscripts. WordPerfect 5.1 can easily handle all of these difficulties.

You can use two different approaches for typing equations:

- Use normal WordPerfect edit features, such as special symbols, superscripts, subscripts, and overstrikes. This is the best method for creating simple equations.

- Use the new WordPerfect 5.1 equation editor. This is the best method for creating complex, multilevel equations.

You'll first see how to employ special symbols, superscripts, subscripts, and overstrikes to create simple equations.

Special Symbols

To type a Greek letter or other special symbol, use the **Compose** (Ctrl-V or Ctrl-2) feature. For example, to create a Greek alpha (α) press **Compose** (Ctrl-V or Ctrl-2), type 8,1, and press **Enter**. The pair of numbers 8,1 gives the character set (8) and the character number (1), as listed in Appendix P, "WordPerfect Characters," of the WordPerfect user's manual. For more details, see Chapter 12, "Inserting Special Characters."

Subscripts

Subscripts and superscripts occur in many chemical and mathematical equations. For example, the chemical equation for "rusting" (the oxidation of iron to iron oxide), shown in Figure 13.4, Item A, contains subscripts (characters that appear *below* the level of other characters and are usually smaller in size). Follow these steps to type this equation using WordPerfect's subscript feature:

Step 1. Clear the screen, and start the equation by typing 4Fe + 30 (leaving two spaces before and after the +).

The cursor is now at the position of the first subscript.

Item A: $4Fe + 3O_2 \rightarrow 2Fe_2O_3$

Item B: $^{238}_{92}U \rightarrow ^{4}_{2}He + ^{234}_{90}Th$

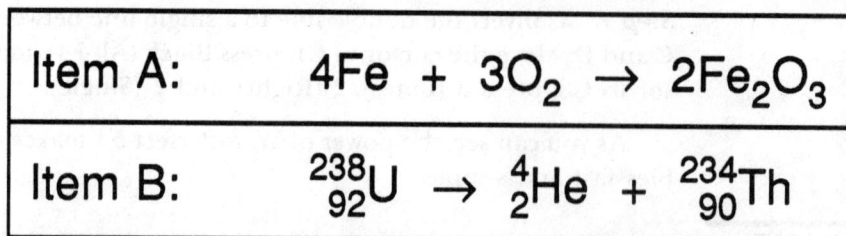

Figure 13.4 Sample formulas. Item A uses the Subscript feature; Item B uses the Overstrike feature.

Step 2. Press **Font** (Ctrl-F8), **1** (**S**ize), **2** (Subscpt).

The Pos number on the status line changes color (or pattern) to indicate subscript.

Step 3. Type 2 (the subscript 2), and press **Right Arrow** to move the cursor past the subscript code.

You can see the codes [SUBSCPT] and [subscpt] with **Reveal Codes** (Alt-F3). After pressing **Right Arrow** to move past [subscpt], the Pos number on the status line returns to normal. You can also exit subscript mode by selecting Subscript again or by pressing **Font** (Ctrl-F8), **3** (**N**ormal). The subscript characters do *not* appear below the normal text line on the document screen, but do appear as a subscript when printed or when viewed on the View Document screen.

Step 4. Press the **Space Bar** twice, then press **Compose** (Ctrl-V), and type 6,21 to produce a right arrow symbol (the chemical reaction "yield" sign).

Step 5. Finish typing the chemical formula, using the subscript feature where required.

After you have finished typing the chemical equation, print the result by pressing **Print** (Shift-F7), **1** (**F**ull Document).

Superscripts

To make a superscript (characters that must appear *above* the level of other characters), follow the similar steps as those for making a subscript: Press **Font** (Ctrl-F8), **1** (**S**ize), and **1** (Suprscpt). To exit superscript mode, press **Right Arrow** past the [suprscpt] code or press **Font** (Ctrl-F8), **3** (**N**ormal).

Changing the Size of Subscripts and Superscripts

WordPerfect 5.1 allows you to modify the relative size of subscripts and superscripts. Just press **Setup** (Shift-F1), **4** (Initial Settings), **8** (**P**rint Options), and **6** (**S**ize Attribute Ratios). Press **Enter** for each of the attributes that you want kept the same and enter a new attribute for each of the ones you want to change. For example, you may wish to change the subscript/superscript size ratio to 75%.

Overstrikes

Nuclear equations are another type of simple formula, as shown in Figure 13.4, Item B (the nuclear equation for the spontaneous radioactive decay of uranium-238). To create this simple equation, follow these steps:

Step 1. Press **Font** (Ctrl-F8), **1** (**S**ize), **1** (**S**uprscpt), **2** (to create the superscript 2), **Right Arrow** (to move past the [suprscpt] code and return to normal type).

Now comes the problem of creating a superscript 3 and a subscript 9 at the same location.

Step 2. Press **Format** (Shift-F8), **4** (**O**ther), **5** (**O**verstrike).

The one-line menu **1 C**reate; **2 E**dit: **0** appears on the status line. To make a new overstrike combination, you would select option 1; to edit an existing overstrike, you would select option 2.

Step 3. Press **1** (**C**reate).

WordPerfect displays the prompt [Ovrstk] on the status line and waits for you to type the characters that you want at the same position.

Step 4. Press **Font** (Ctrl-F8), **1** (**S**ize), **1** (**S**uprscpt) (to insert the begin superscript code [SUPRSCPT]), **3** (the desired superscript character), **Font** (Ctrl-F8), **1** (**S**ize), **1** (**S**uprscpt) (to insert the end superscript code [suprscpt]), **Font** (Ctrl-F8), **1** (**S**ize), **2** (**S**ubscpt) (to insert the begin subscript code [SUBSCPT]), **9** (the desired subscript), **Font** (Ctrl-F8), **1** (**S**ize), **2** (**S**ubscpt) (to insert the end subscript code [subscpt]), **Enter** (to accept the overstrike characters and code), and **Exit** (F7) to return to the document.

WordPerfect displays only the last overstrike character on the document screen. To see the actual overstrike symbols, press **Print** (Shift-F7), **6** (**V**iew Document).

Step 5.   Repeat step 4, only this time overstrike a superscript 8 with a subscript 2, then press **U** (to finish the formula for uranium-238), **Space Bar** twice, **Compose** (Ctrl-V), 6,21 (to insert an arrow), and **Space Bar** twice.

You are now ready to type the symbol for helium (He).

Step 6.   Complete the nuclear equation using the techniques explained in the previous steps.

If you desire, print the formula. Not all printers support overstrike (or even superscripts and subscripts). If you are a scientist or engineer who frequently types nuclear equations, you can use a macro to create superscripts and subscripts, as explained in Chapter 15, "Using Macros."

TYPING COMPLEX EQUATIONS

To create complex equations, use WordPerfect's new equation editor. However, a complete explanation of the equation editor is beyond the scope of this book. (Please refer to the "Equations" sections of the WordPerfect user's manual for more information.) Here is an example of how to use the equation editor.

The equation in Figure 13.5 would be almost impossible to type using the normal WordPerfect document screen, but with the equation editor, it's simple. Follow these steps:

Step 1.   Press **Graphics** (Alt-F9) and **6** (Equation) to evoke the one-line menu **Equations: 1** Create; **2** Edit; **3** New Numbers; **4** Options: **0.**

$$\int \frac{dx}{\alpha^2 + x^2} = \frac{1}{\alpha}\tan^{-1}\left(\frac{x}{\alpha}\right)$$

Figure 13.5   A sample equation created by WordPerfect's Equation Editor.

Step 2. Press **1** (Create).

WordPerfect displays the Definition: Equation menu, which is similar to the Definition: Figure menu in Figure 9.2. See Chapter 9, "Displaying Graphics," for an explanation of the meaning of the menu items.

Step 3. Press **9** (Edit).

WordPerfect now displays the Equation Edit screen, similar to Figure 13.6, except that the equation edit window and the equation display window are blank. The cursor is located within the edit window.

Step 4. Type the following: INT {dx OVER {ITAL alpha^2~+~x^2}}~=~1 OVER ITAL alpha tan^{-1} LEFT (x OVER ITAL alpha RIGHT)

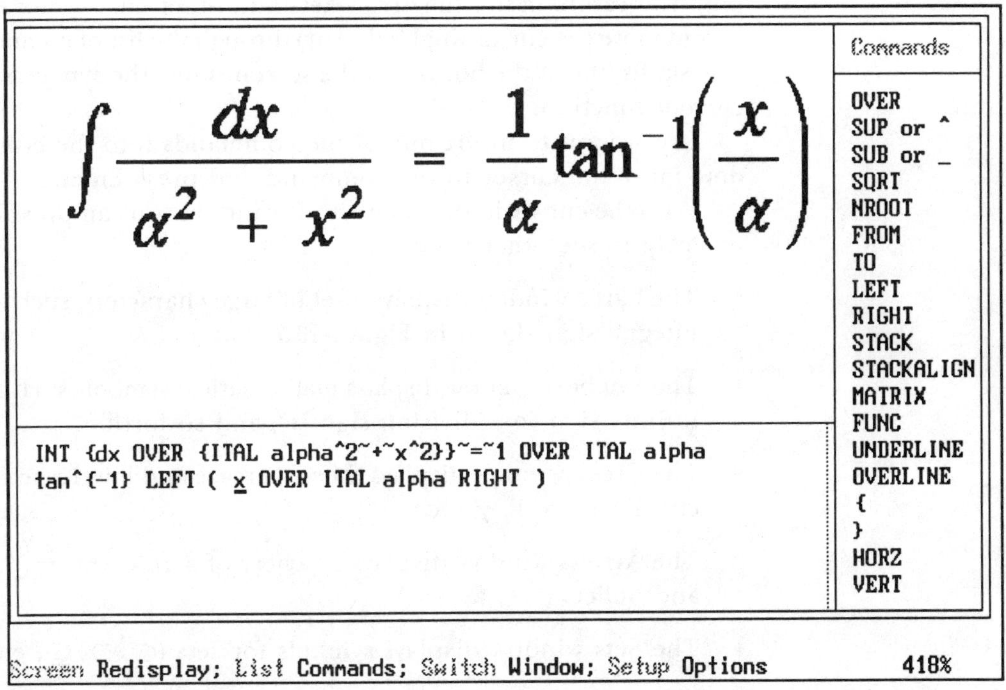

Figure 13.6 The Equation Editor screen.

This set of commands and symbols is shown in the edit window of Figure 13.6. To understand the meaning of the commands, consult your WordPerfect user's manual "Equations, Commands and Symbols."

Step 5. Press **Screen** (Ctrl-F3) to display the equation in the display window.

Now your screen should like exactly like Figure 13.6. If any discrepancies exist, carefully check and edit the commands and symbols in the edit window.

If you know all the desired equation commands and codes, you can simply type them into the edit window of the equation editor. However, WordPerfect provides a Commands window at the right to help you remember the desired commands and to insert them into the edit window. To access the Commands window, press **List** (F5). You can then use the arrow keys and other cursor-movement keys to move the cursor (highlight bar) through the list of commands. The status line at the bottom of the screen shows the syntax for the current function.

If you want to insert one of the commands into the edit window, move the cursor to the command and press **Enter**.

With the cursor in the Commands window, you can press **PgDn** or **PgUp** to see other windows:

- The Large window displays a set of large characters, such as the integral sign shown in Figure 13.5.

- The Symbols window displays mathematical symbols such as the infinity sign (∞), division sign ($\div$), and so forth.

- The Greek window displays the uppercase and lowercase Greek characters (α, ß, γ, etc.).

- The Arrows window displays a variety of arrows ($\rightarrow$, $\leftarrow$, $\uparrow$, etc.) and bullets ($\circ$, $\bullet$, ■, etc.).

- The Sets window displays symbols for sets ($\subset$, $\supset$, $\subseteq$, etc.).

- The Other window displays several other symbols.

To use any of these symbols, just move the cursor to the desired symbol and press **Enter**. You can also just type the name of the symbol. For example, typing `alpha` inserts a Greek alpha into the equation.

To change the options of the equation, press **Setup** (Shift-F1) from within the Equation Editor. You can then select how the equation is printed (as text or as graphics), the size of the equation (by setting the point size of the base font), and the location of the equation within the equation box.

SUMMARY

Typing tables is simple with WordPerfect's powerful tables feature. Just press **Columns/Table** (Alt-F7), **2** (**T**ables), **1** (**C**reate) and answer the questions about the size of your table to get into the table editor.

WordPerfect provides two methods for typing equations: 1) the normal document screen for creating simple equations and 2) the equation editor for creating complex, multilevel equations. For simple equations, you can use special characters, subscripts, superscripts, and overstrikes. For complex equations, you can access the equation editor by pressing **Graphics** (Alt-F9), **6** (**E**quation), **1** (**C**reate), and **9** (**E**dit).

Chapter 14

Using Styles

When we say *styles*, we're not talking about designer jeans, French evening gowns, or coiffures. We're talking about WordPerfect *styles*, that is, user-defined commands for generating a set of WordPerfect functions, such as formats, fonts, characters, marks, and graphics. A style is one of those WordPerfect features that seems like an unnecessary luxury—until you start to use it. Then you wonder how you ever got along without it.

In this chapter you will learn the following:

- What a WordPerfect style is.

- How you can benefit from using styles.

- How to define a style.

- How to use a style.

- How to use style examples to create a document with a consistent format.

After reading this chapter you will be able to apply styles to your letters, memos, forms, reports, chapters, and books.

DOING IT WITH STYLE

Let's suppose that you are the Ocean Breeze Bookstore personnel manager with the task of writing job descriptions for all bookstore employees. You want to use a standard format so that any supervisor, worker, or job applicant can easily understand exactly what the job entails and how it relates to other jobs in the company.

Why Styles?

Using WordPerfect styles to design the job description format and write the job descriptions has several benefits:

- WordPerfect styles generate a standard format for documents, regardless of who types them. Once you define the styles, anyone in the secretarial pool can create documents with the same uniform look.

- Typing the document titles and headings is faster and more accurate when you (or your secretaries) use styles.

- Styles provide greater flexibility in the appearance of your documents. For example, if you decide to change how a document looks, you do not have to retype or do extensive editing but simply change the WordPerfect styles; and the styles are automatically changed throughout that document as well as other documents that later use the same set of styles.

The job description sheet in Figure 14.1 is a good illustration of the use of styles. To create this job description sheet, you will need to define and use five WordPerfect styles:

- The *Job Start* style, used once at the beginning of each job description sheet to format the document.

  This style sets the margins, base font, and tabs for the document.

- The *Job Title* style, used to create the job title, the Ocean Breeze Bookstore logo, and the current date.

  This style automatically generates the text, font changes, and graphics line from the top of the document to the date in Figure 14.1. The user only types Sales Clerk; the style does everything else.

- The *Duty Start* style, used to insert the **Duties** header (including graphics line) and to define the start of the bulleted list.

- The *Duty Next* style, used to create the hanging indented, bulleted list items in the duties list.

  The Duty Start style is used for the first item in the duties list, and the Duty Next style is used for subsequent duties.

- The *Head* style, used to generate all headers (except **Duties**).

  This style inserts the horizontal line and the proper format and font codes for the header name. The user only has to type the header name, such as Hours, Salary, or Supervisory.

DEFINING STYLES

The general steps in creating a style are as follows:

Step 1. From within WordPerfect, press **Style** (Alt-F8).

This accesses the Styles menu, a listing of all the styles that you have defined (which at this point is none, unless you have specified a style library in WordPerfect **Setup** (Shift-F1) under Location of Auxiliary Files), and the Styles command line at the bottom of the screen: **1 O**n; **2 O**ff; **3 C**reate; **4 E**dit; **5 D**elete; **6 S**ave; **7 R**etrieve; **8 Update: 1**

These menu items have the following functions:

> **1 O**n turns *on* the highlight style from the style list. Obviously you can't use this command until you have defined at least one style.

Job Title: Sales Clerk

Ocean Breeze Bookstore
February 8, 1989

Duties:

- Handle cash register purchases.
- Know procedures for cashing checks, accepting credit cards, accepting in-store credit for approved customers.
- Take orders on new books.
- Shelve new books.
- Call or mail book order notices to patrons.
- Perform book inventory on showroom floor.
- Answer patron's questions regarding book locations and book recommendations.

Hours:

9:00 a.m. to 6:00 p.m., five days/week. Off every Sunday, off every other Saturday.

Salary:

Starting: $5.12/hour.
Maximum: $6.55/hour.

Supervisory:

Supervisor: Sales Manager
Supervises: none

Figure 14.1 An Ocean Breeze Bookstore Job Description Sheet, an example of using WordPerfect styles in documents.

2 Off turns *off* the current paired style. A *paired* style is one that has a paired set of commands, one set that becomes active when you turn *on* the style and stays active while you type input, and another set that becomes active after you type input. A paired style is analogous to the WordPerfect commands **Bold** (F6) or **Underline** (F8), in which one command code turns *on* the feature and another code turns *off* the feature. Once you turn *on* a paired style and have typed the desired input, you can turn it *off* by pressing **2** (Off) or by moving the cursor past the [Style Off] code.

3 Create allows you to define a new style.

4 Edit allows you to modify an existing style.

5 Delete erases an existing style from the list of styles.

6 Save copies the list of styles from the current document to a disk file. After you define a set of styles, you should save the styles to the disk to be used in later documents.

7 Retrieve loads a styles file (saved using the **6** (Save) command from the disk into the current document.

8 Update loads the default library (specified in the **Setup** Location of Auxiliary Files command) into the current document, adding the default library styles to the current list of styles and overwriting any styles in the current style sheet that have the same name. The purpose of this command is to update the styles in the current document with a more recent version of the default style library.

Step 2. Press **3** (Create) to create a new style.

WordPerfect displays the Styles: Edit menu shown in Figure 14.2. These menu items have the following functions:

1 - Name allows you to give the style a name. You can use up to 11 characters in the name.

2 - Type allows you to set the style type, either paired or open. Paired styles have paired sets of commands, one set that becomes active when you turn *on* the style and stays active while you type input, and another set that becomes active after you type input. A paired style is analogous to Bold (F6) or

```
Styles: Edit

    1 - Name

    2 - Type            Paired

    3 - Description

    4 - Codes

    5 - Enter           HRt







Selection: 0
```

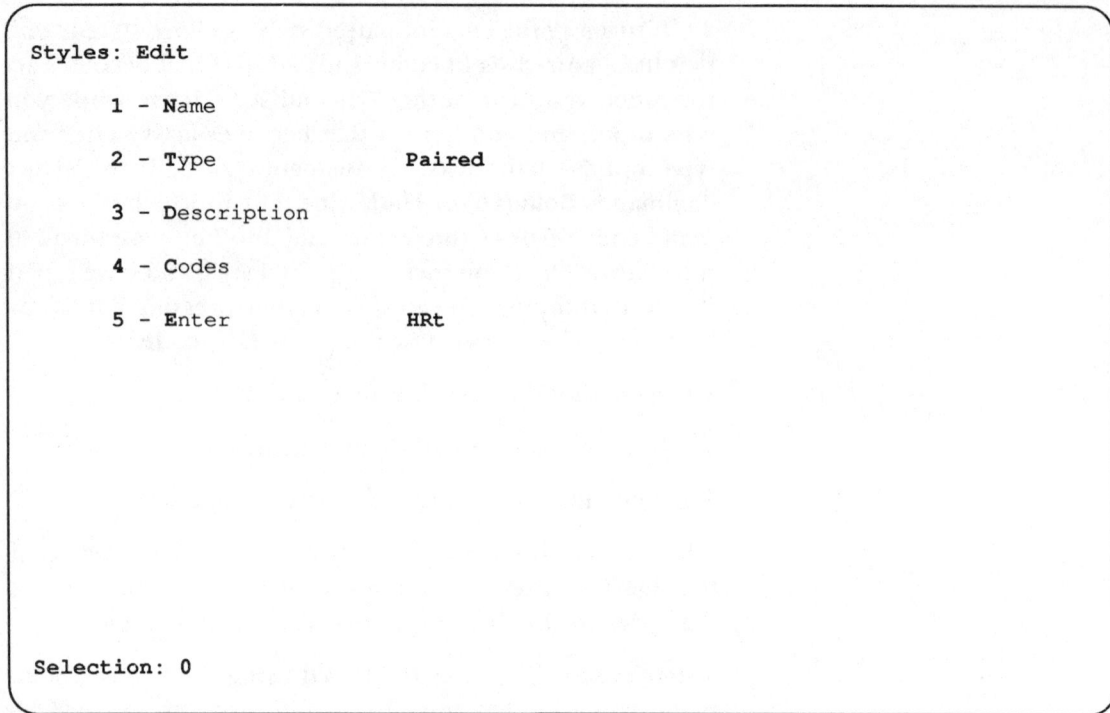

Figure 14.2 The Styles: Edit Menu used to create or edit a style.

Underline (F8), in which one command code turns *on* the feature and another code turns *off* the feature. Open styles set WordPerfect features that become active from that point on in the text. An open style is analogous to setting the margins (or the justification), which stay active until they are explicitly changed. You do not turn *off* an open style. The differences between paired and open styles will become clearer in the examples below.

3 - Description allows you to type a description of the style to help you remember its purpose and function. The description may contain up to 55 characters.

4 - Codes allows you to define the codes (WordPerfect functions such as the Format, Font, Graphics, and Date features). The codes can contain anything from a single character to a complex set of functions, graphics, and text.

5 · Enter allows you to set how the style handles the Enter key in a paired style (this option is not necessary, nor allowed, in open styles). With a paired style *on*, WordPerfect can interpret the input of Enter in one of three ways: as a hard return (inserting the [HRt] code into the input portion of the paired style), as a means of turning the style *off* (but not inserting [HRt]), or as a means of turning the style *off* and then immediately turning it *on* again.

Step 3. Press **1** (**N**ame) and enter the name of the style.

Step 4. Press **2** (**T**ype) and select the style type, paired or open.

Step 5. Press **3** (**D**escription) and enter a line of text that describes the function of the style.

Step 6. Press **4** (**C**odes) and specify the functions within the style. You can use any WordPerfect feature that generates codes, such as margins, widow/orphan protection, justification, bold, underline, date code, table of contents mark text, automatic paragraph number, and graphics. The examples below will show how this is done.

Step 7. If the style is of type *paired*, press **5** (**E**nter) and select the meaning of **Enter**. This will be explained below.

After you have defined a set of styles that you want to use in other documents, save the styles to the disk by pressing **Style** (Alt-F8) and **6** (**S**ave), and entering the name of the style (a legal disk filename).

You can also define a style from existing codes in a document by following these steps:

Step 1. Move the cursor to the beginning of the codes, press **Block** (Alt-F4) and move the cursor to the end of the codes.

Step 2. Press **Style** (Alt-F8) and **3** (**C**reate).

Now continue with step 3 from the procedure above. In step 6 above, the desired codes will already be present in the Styles Code window, so you don't have to insert them manually. The advantage of using existing codes is that you can see the effect of the codes on your document before you insert them into the Styles Code window.

USING STYLES

When you get ready to use a style, follow these simple steps:

Step 1. Move the cursor to the location in your document where you want the style.

Step 2. Press **Style** (Alt-F8) to access the Styles menu.

Step 3. Use the **Up Arrow** or **Down Arrow** to move the highlight bar to the desired style.

You can also move the highlight bar to the desired style by pressing **Search** (F2) and typing the first few letters of the style name (or the complete name) and pressing **Enter**.

Step 4. Press **1** (**On**) or **Enter**.

Step 5. If the style is of type *paired*, type the text that you want between the pairs (such as a header) and then turn *off* the style in one of the following ways: pressing **Enter** (if you defined the Enter key for *off*), pressing **Style** (Alt-F8) and **2** (**Off**) or pressing **Right Arrow** to move the cursor past the [Style Off] code.

That's all there is to it. In fact, as you will see in Chapter 15, "Using Macros," you can define a macro to execute a style, which makes using styles even easier.

STYLE EXAMPLES

We will now create the style examples used in the Ocean Breeze Bookstore Job Description Sheet (Figure 14.1). These styles, as listed above, have the names *Job Start, Job Title, Duty Start, Duty Next*, and *Head*.

Creating the Job Start Style

We will begin with the Job Start style, the simplest of our style examples, and the first one you will use whenever you type a new job description sheet.

Step 1. From the WordPerfect document screen, press **Style** (Alt-F8).

WordPerfect displays the Styles menu, as explained above.

Step 2. Press **3** (**Create**).

WordPerfect displays the Styles: Edit menu shown in Figure 14.2.

Step 3. Press **1** (**Name**), type Job Start and press **Enter** to give the style a name.

We could have chosen any name that effectively described the function of the style.

Step 4. Press **2** (**T**ype) and **2** (**O**pen) to specify that Job Start is of type *open* (rather than *paired*).

We chose type open since the format codes in Job Start are to be effective from this point on in the document.

Step 5. Press **3** (**D**escription) and enter `Start of Job Description Sheet`.

This phrase succinctly describes the function of the style.

Step 6. Press **4** (**C**odes).

WordPerfect displays the Style Codes screen shown in Figure 14.3.

Step 7. Press **Font** (Ctrl-F8) to select a new font, **4** (**B**ase **F**ont) to select a new base font for the document), **N** (**N**ame search) to search for the font name), type `Helvetica` and press **Enter** to highlight the Helvetica font name, press **1** (**S**elect), type `12` (if prompted for the font size), and press **Enter**.

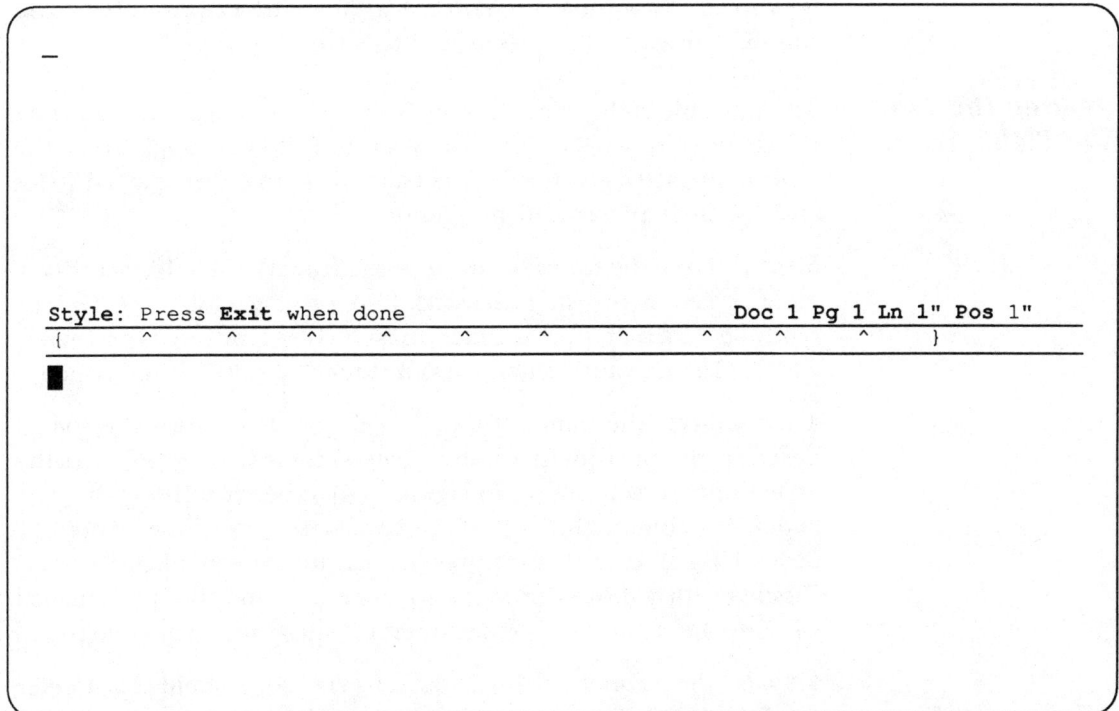

```
 —




















Style: Press Exit when done                    Doc 1 Pg 1 Ln 1" Pos 1"
{      ^       ^       ^       ^       ^       ^       ^       ^       ^       }
█
```

Figure 14.3 The Style Codes screen used to input codes for a style of type *open*.

This step sets the base font to Helvetica 12 point. If your printer doesn't support this font, set the base font to a different one.

Step 8. Press **Format** (Shift-F8), **1** (Line), **7** (Margin), type `1.5` and press **Enter**, type `1.0` and press **Enter**, and press **Enter** twice more to return to the Styles Code screen.

This step sets the left margin to 1.5″ and the right margin to 1.0″. We selected a 1.5″ margin to allow room to put the job description sheets in a three-ring binder.

Step 9. Press **Format** (Shift-F8), **1** (Line), **8** (Tab Set), **0** and **Enter** to move the cursor to the 0 position, **Ctrl-End** (to delete all the tab codes), **Tab** (to set a tab at 0), type `0.8` (don't omit the zero) and press **Enter**, type `1.2` and press **Enter** (to set a tab at 1″), and continue entering values to set the tabs at +1.6 and +2.0. After entering the last tab stop, press **Exit** and **Enter** to return to the Style Codes screen.

This completes the definition of the style Job Start. If it seemed like a lot of work, you can imagine how much time it will save in the future. Every time you want to start a job description sheet, you simply turn *on* the style (see "Using Styles" above).

Creating the Job Title Style

The Job Title style is the most complex of the styles used to create job description sheets. Take the time to follow through all of the steps below so that you will understand how to define paired styles and see their power and potential.

Step 1. From the Styles menu (accessed from the WordPerfect document screen by pressing **Style** (Alt-F8)), press **3** (Create), **1** (Name), type `Job Title` and press **Enter**, press **3** (Description), type `Insert Job Title` and press **Enter**, press **5** (Enter), **2** (Off), and **4** (Codes).

This step sets the name of the style to Job Title, gives the style a description, specifies that Enter turns *off* the style, and accesses the Style Codes screen (shown in Figure 14.4) to begin defining the style codes. The comment `Place Style On Codes above,` and `Style Off Codes below` means that features (such as font size, bold, and center) should be turned *on* prior to the comment box and should be turned *off* after the comment box (as demonstrated in the next step).

Step 2. Press **Font** (Ctrl-F8), **1** (Size), **6** (Vry Large), **Bold** (F6), **Center** (Shift-F6), type `Job Title:`, **Space Bar**, **Right Arrow** (to move the cursor past the comment box, i.e., to the right of the comment code),

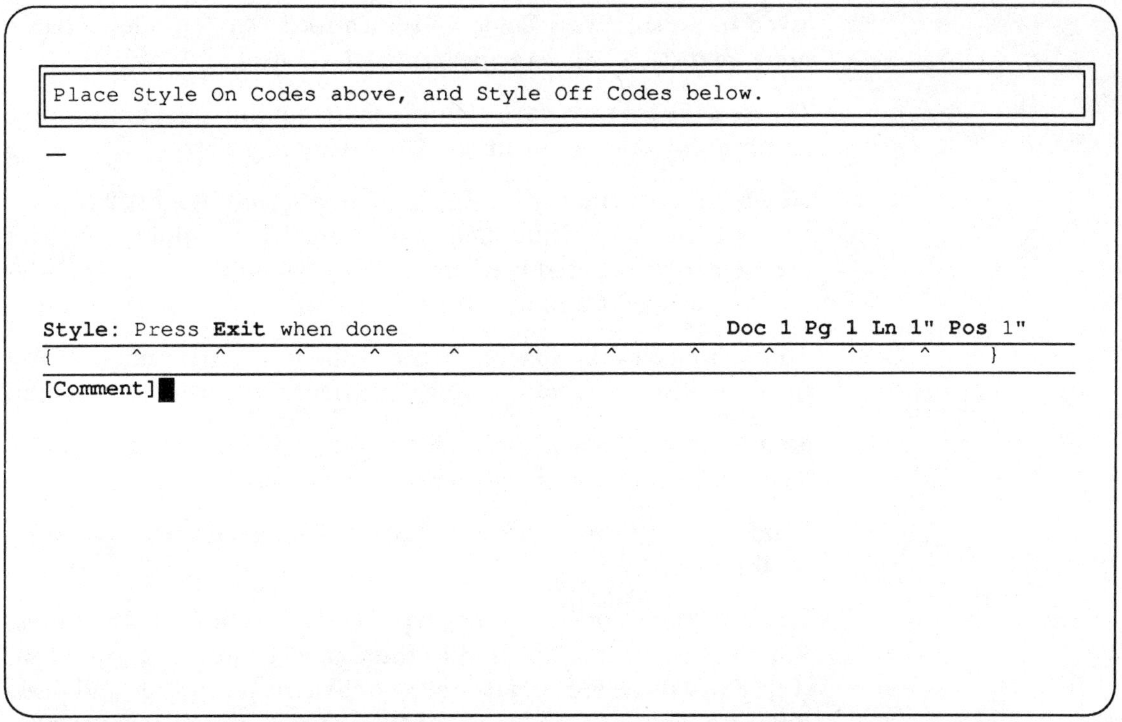

```
┌─────────────────────────────────────────────────────────────────────┐
│ ┌───────────────────────────────────────────────────────────────┐ │
│ │ Place Style On Codes above, and Style Off Codes below.        │ │
│ └───────────────────────────────────────────────────────────────┘ │
│ ─                                                                   │
│                                                                     │
│                                                                     │
│                                                                     │
│                                                                     │
│ Style: Press Exit when done                    Doc 1 Pg 1 Ln 1" Pos 1" │
│ {    ^    ^    ^    ^    ^    ^    ^    ^    ^    ^    ^    }        │
│ [Comment]█                                                          │
│                                                                     │
│                                                                     │
└─────────────────────────────────────────────────────────────────────┘
```

Figure 14.4 The Style Codes screen used to input codes for a style of type *paired*.

Bold (F6) to turn *off* bold, **Font** (Ctrl-F8), **3** (**N**ormal) to turn *off* very large font, **Enter** (to go to the next line and turn *off* text center).

The commands in this step set the style for the top line (job title) of the job description sheet. When you turn *on* this style, whatever you type will be inserted into the position of the comment box on the Style Codes screen.

Step 3. Press **Graphics** (Alt-F9), **5** (**L**ine), **1** (**H**orizontal Line), **4** (**W**idth), type 0.1 and press **Enter**, press **5** (**G**ray Shading), type 50 and press **Enter**, and press **Enter** again (to return to the Style Codes screen).

This set of commands inserts a broad, gray, horizontal line just below the job title, as shown in Figure 14.1.

Step 4. Press **Font** (Ctrl-F8), **4** (**B**ase Font), **N** (**N**ame search) to search for the font name, type Times and press **Enter** (to highlight the Times Roman font name), press **1** (**S**elect), type 18 (to set the font size if asked to do so), press **Enter** (to return to the Style Codes screen), press **Font** (Ctrl-F8), **2** (**A**ppearance), **5** (**O**utln).

This sets the font typeface (Times), size (18-point), and appearance (outline) for the Ocean Breeze Bookstore logo.

Step 5.　Press **Format** (Shift-F8), **1** (**L**ine), **4** (Line **H**eight), **2** (**F**ixed), type 0.08 (to set the line height to normal for 12-point text) and press **Enter**, press **Enter** three times more (to return to the Style Codes screen and insert a hard return).

This step makes the spacing between the gray horizontal line and the Ocean Breeze Bookstore logo less than the normal line height.

Step 6.　Press **Format** (Shift-F8), **1** (**L**ine), **4** (Line **H**eight), and **1** (**A**uto) to set the line height back to automatic.

WordPerfect returns to the default of calculating the line height based on the font size.

Step 7.　Press **Center** (Shift-F6), type Ocean Breeze Bookstore, press **Enter** (to go down a line and to the **Center** command), press **Font** (Ctrl-F8), **4** (**B**ase Font), **N** (**N**ame search), type Helvetica and press **Enter** (to highlight the Helvetica font name), press **1** (**S**elect), type 12, press **Enter**, press **Enter** again (to go to the next line).

This step inserts the Ocean Breeze Bookstore logo (in Times outline font) and returns the font to the default Helvetica 12-point.

Step 8.　Press **Center** (Shift-F6), **Date/Outline** (Shift-F5), **2** (**D**ate **C**ode), press **Enter** twice (to go down two lines), **Exit** (to return to the Style: Edit screen), and **Enter** (to return to the Style Codes screen).

This inserts and centers the date into the document and completes the creation of the Job Title style.

You have now created two styles, one of open type (Job Start) and one of paired type (Job Title). As you can see, a *paired* style is required when user input is part of the style. In the case of Job Start (open style), the user simply turns *on* the style to set certain formats (or even insert a constant) but doesn't turn *off* the style. In the case of Job Title (paired style), the user turns *on* the style, types the name of the job (which varies from one job description sheet to another), and then turns *off* the style.

Creating the Duty Start Style

The Duty Start style will be used to start the list of duties on the Job Description Sheet. To create the style, follow these steps:

Step 1. From the Styles menu, press **3** (**C**reate to access the Styles: Edit menu), press **1** (**N**ame), type Duty Start, press **Enter**, **2** (**T**ype), **2** (**O**pen), **3** (**D**escription), type Start of List of Duties and press **Enter**, press **4** (**C**odes).

This step gives the style a name and a description, specifies its type, and accesses the Style Codes screen.

Step 2. Press **Graphics** (Alt-F9), **5** (**L**ine), **1** (**H**orizontal Line), **Enter** (to return to the Style Codes screen), and **Enter** again (to go down a line).

This creates a horizontal line above the word "Duties," as shown in Figure 14.1.

Step 3. Press **Format** (Shift-F8), **4** (**O**ther), **1** (**A**dvance), **2** (**D**own), type 0.1 (to go down 0.1″), and press **Enter**; then press **Exit** (F7).

This inserts a small space between the horizontal line and the word "Duties."

Step 4. Press **Font** (Ctrl-F8), **1** (**S**ize), **5** (**L**arge), **Bold** (F6), type Duties:, press **Space Bar**, press **Bold** (F6) to turn *off* bold, **Font** (Ctrl-F8), **3** (**N**ormal) to turn *off* large font.

Step 5. Press **Date/Outline** (Shift-F5), **6** (**D**efine), **5** (**B**ullets), and **Enter** twice (to return to codes).

This defines an automatic paragraph number for bulleted lists, as shown below "Duties" in Figure 14.1.

Step 6. Press **Format** (Shift-F8), **4** (**O**ther), **1** (**A**dvance), **2** (**D**own), type 0.1 (to go down 0.1″), and press **Enter**; then press **Exit** (F7).

This inserts a space between the word "Duties" and the first bulleted item.

Step 7. Press **Date/Outline** (Shift-F5), **5** (**P**ara Num), **1**, **Enter** (to insert the automatic paragraph number, which in this case is a bullet), and press **Indent** (F4).

Step 8. Press **Exit** (F7) to exit the Style Code screen and return to the Styles menu.

This completes the creation of the Duty Start style for the Job Description Sheet.

Creating the Duty Next Style

The Duty Start style is used to start a list of duties, but the Duty Next style, which we now define, is used to list all subsequent duties. To create this style, follow these steps:

Step 1. From the Styles menu, press **3** (**C**reate) (to access the Styles: Edit menu), press **1** (**N**ame), type Duty Next, press **Enter**, **2** (**T**ype), **2** (**O**pen), **3** (**D**escription), type Insert Next Duty in List of Duties and press **Enter**, press **4** (**C**odes).

This step gives the style a name and a description, specifies its type, and accesses the Style Codes screen.

Step 2. Press **Format** (Shift-F8), **1** (**L**ine), **4** (**L**ine Height), **2** (**F**ixed), type 0.08 (to make the line height normal for 12-point text), and press **Enter** twice.

This inserts a half-line between the previous and the next bulleted items.

Step 3. Press **Format** (Shift-F8), **1** (**L**ine), **4** (**L**ine Height), and **1** (**A**uto) (to set the line height back to automatic), **Date/Outline** (Shift-F5), **5** (**P**ara Num), **1**, **Enter** (to insert the automatic paragraph number, which in this case is a bullet), press **Indent** (F4), and finally press **Exit** (F7) to exit the Style Codes screen and return to the Styles menu.

As you can see, the Duty Next style is similar to the parts of the Duty Start style.

Having worked through these four examples, you should be able to create the Head style on your own. It is similar to, but simpler than, the Duty Start style.

Once you have created all the styles, press **6** (**S**ave), type job-desc (to give the style the library name JOBDESC), and press **Enter**. This saves a copy of the styles in a separate file on the disk.

USING THE STYLE EXAMPLES

Follow these steps to use the style examples:

Step 1. If you are still in the Style menu, press **Exit** (F7) to return to the WordPerfect document screen.

Step 2. If the screen is not clear, press **Exit** (F7), **N** (no), and **N** (no) to clear the screen.

Step 3.   With the cursor at the top of a clear screen, press **Style** (Alt-F8).

This accesses the list of styles that you created.

Step 4.   Press **Down Arrow** until the Job Start style is highlighted.

Step 5.   Press **1** (**On**) or **Enter** to turn *on* the Job Start style.

Step 6.   Press **Style** (Alt-F8), press **Down Arrow** until the Job Title style is highlighted, press **1** (**On**) (to turn *on* the Job Title style and return to your document), type Sales Clerk (the job title), and press **Enter**.

The entire heading for the Job Description sheet appears on the screen.

Step 7.   Press **Style** (Alt-F8), press **Down Arrow** until the Duty Start style is highlighted, press **1** (**On**) to turn *on* the Duty Start style and return to your document.

Note that you don't turn *off* the Duty Start style, since it is of type *open*.

Step 8.   Type the first duty: Handle cash register purchases and press **Enter**.

Step 9.   Press **Style** (Alt-F8), press **Down Arrow** until the Duty Next style is highlighted, press **1** (**On**) to turn *on* the Duty Next style and return to your document.

Step 10.   Type the second duty: Know procedures for cashing checks, accepting credit cards, accepting in-store credit from approved customers and press **Enter**.

Step 11.   Repeat steps 9 and 10 for the remainder of the duties.

Step 12.   Apply the Head style (that you created above) in a similar manner to finish typing the Job Description document.

You can now save the document to the disk and print it. When you get ready to type another Job Description sheet, clear the screen, press **Style** (Alt-F8), **7** (**Retrieve**), type jobdesc (the name of the styles you previously saved), and press **Enter**. You can now use the styles again as explained above.

SUMMARY

WordPerfect styles are user-defined commands for generating Word-Perfect functions — including fonts, formats, characters, marks, and graphics. A style increases the speed and accuracy of creating standard forms and of generating a consistent document style.

You can apply styles to any document (or set of documents) that requires a consistent set of codes. Examples include not only single-page documents (like the Job Description sheets shown above) but also lengthy documents such as reports, newsletters, chapters of books, and manuals.

Chapter 15

Using Macros

For secretaries and writers, macros are wonderful. For desktop publishers, macros are a necessity. Macros save time, increase accuracy, and help keep formats consistent. Spending a little time now learning to use macros will pay big dividends in the future.

In this chapter you will learn the following:

- How macros can help you work more efficiently.

- How to define a macro. (It's easier than you think.)

- How to use macros. You will see many examples of simple macros and several examples of complex macros.

WORKING WITH MACROS

Programmers have used macros for years, but hardly anyone other than computer scientists had heard of them until recently. Then along came Lotus 1-2-3, a wildly popular integrated spreadsheet, database, and graphics software package, which had macros. Even though few Lotus owners use macros, and even fewer understand them, the term "macros" has been thrust into the vocabulary of the business world.

What Is a Macro?

A macro is a customized series of commands executed with just a few keystrokes. For example, desktop published material often requires additional leading between lines before and after a head or before a horizontal rule. This requires the following sequence of commands: press **Format** (F8), **4** (**O**ther), **1** (**A**dvance), **2** (**D**own), type the amount of leading (for example, 0.08), and press **Enter** and **Exit** (F7) to return to your document. Wouldn't it be nice to perform only *one* command which would automatically execute these nine or ten keystrokes? WordPerfect macros can do just that.

Or suppose you work for Ocean Breeze Bookstore and have to type the phrase *Ocean Breeze Bookstore* many times a day. Wouldn't it be nice be able to execute only *one* simple command to insert the entire phrase into your document? WordPerfect macros can do that also.

These two simple examples represent only a glimpse of the power of WordPerfect macros. We will show you many examples of more sophisticated macros in this and subsequent chapters.

Who Needs Macros?

You need macros. If you do enough word processing and desktop publishing to need WordPerfect, macros can significantly increase your writing or typing productivity. Wouldn't you like to type an entire letterhead (your return address, today's date, and the salutation) with just one simple command? Wouldn't you like to write commonly used words, phrases, and even whole paragraphs with just one or two keystrokes? Wouldn't you like to execute all your standard specialized document features (spacing, margins, font typeface and size, tabs, widow/orphan protection, page number position, etc.) by pressing just a few keys?

If your answer to these questions is *no*, then you don't need macros—and you probably don't need WordPerfect either!

But if your answer is *yes*, take a few minutes to learn how to create (define) and use macros. Once you do, you can certify yourself as a word processing expert, able to tap the full potential of writing with a computer.

Once you get comfortable with the straightforward macros given in this chapter, you may wish to go one step further and learn full-blown macro programming with the WordPerfect macro language. Advanced macros are not covered in this book but are discussed in detail in our book *Working with WordPerfect, Third Edition: The Complete Guide to Word Processing and Desktop Publishing* (see Appendix C, "Additional Reading").

RECORDING YOUR KEYSTROKES

Macros are easy to make. You just follow five simple steps, as if you were making a recording with a cassette recorder:

Step 1.   Turn *on* WordPerfect's macro definition mode.

This is like pressing Record on a tape recorder.

Step 2.   Give your macro a name.

By giving a name to the macro, you can call up its services at any time.

Step 3.   Type a brief description of your macro.

A one-line description helps you remember what the macro does and how to use it.

Step 4.   Perform the keyboard strokes that you want to record.

This is like talking or singing into the microphone of your recorder. The only difference is that you press keys to record a macro.

Step 5. Turn *off* the macro definition mode.

This is like pressing Stop on your recorder.

Whenever you follow these five simple steps, WordPerfect records exactly what you did in step 4 and is able to repeat it any time you choose.

For example, one of the useful commands that WordPerfect lacks but that other word processors have is a simple function to delete text from the cursor to the *left* edge of the screen. This isn't a deficiency at all, however, since you can make a macro to simulate this command.

Get into WordPerfect, type a line of text (e.g., The quick brown fox jumps over the lazy dog.), then follow these steps:

Step 1. Turn *on* WordPerfect's macro definition mode by pressing **Macro Def** (Ctrl-F10).

WordPerfect gives the prompt **Define macro:** and waits for you to type a macro name. You may select from three different methods of naming macros:

> *Method 1*: Typing a valid DOS filename (without extension) of one to eight characters. WordPerfect automatically appends the .WPM filename extension and saves the macro to the disk. This macro type has three advantages: the macro name can be mnemonic, the macro is saved to the disk, and the macro can be edited later.

> *Method 2*: Simply pressing **Enter**. The macro defined in this way is *temporary*, lasting only until you define another macro in this manner or until you quit WordPerfect. This macro type has two advantages: it does not use disk space permanently, and it requires fewer keystrokes to execute. This macro type has two disadvantages, however: it is lost when you exit WordPerfect, and it cannot be edited.

> *Method 3:* Pressing **Alt** and an alphabetic key. The macro name consists of the **Alt** key and one of the 26 letters of the alphabet. This macro type has three advantages: it is easy to execute, it is saved to the disk, and it can be edited. This is the preferred method for frequently used macros. The two disadvantages of this type of macro are: you can have only 26 different Alt macros, and the names of the Alt macros

are not particularly mnemonic. *Note:* See "Macro Directories and Libraries" below for a method of increasing the number of Alt macros by using the **Alt, Ctrl,** and other special keys to execute macros contained within keyboard definition files.

Step 2. Type delfol (which stands for delete to first of line) and press **Enter.**

WordPerfect now checks the disk to see if you have already defined a macro by that name. (*Note:* If you have already defined a macro by that name, the prompt DELFOL.WPM is Already Defined. **1 R**eplace; **2 E**dit; **3 D**escription: **0** appears on the screen. You should press **1** (**R**eplace) if you want to replace the old macro with a new one, or press **0** (or **Enter**) if you want to keep the old macro and choose another name for the new macro. You should also press **2** (**E**dit) if you want to edit an existing macro.)

WordPerfect now displays the prompt **Description:,** after which you should type a brief one-line description of your macro.

Step 3. Type Delete from cursor to the first of the line and press **Enter.**

The flashing message **Macro Def** appears in the lower left corner of the screen. This is like turning *on* a tape recorder. From now on, until you turn *off* Macro Def, WordPerfect faithfully records every key you press. If you make a mistake with macro definition *on,* just turn *off* macro definition by pressing **Macro Def** (Ctrl-F10); then go back through all the steps again to redefine the macro.

Step 4. Press **Block** (Alt-F4).

This turns *on* the Block mode and displays the flashing message **Block on** in the lower left corner of the screen alongside **Macro Def.**

Step 5. Press **Home, Home, Home, Left Arrow.**

This moves the cursor to the extreme left edge of the line in which the cursor is located, highlighting part or all of the text on the line.

Step 6. Press **Del** (or **Backspace**) and then **Y** (Yes) to delete the block.

As you can see, the text from the cursor position on the line to the left margin was deleted, while WordPerfect recorded your keystrokes.

Step 7.   Turn *off* the macro definition mode by pressing the **Macro Def** (Ctrl-F10) again.

This also saves the macro to the disk.

Congratulations! You have successfully defined your first macro, named DELFOL. As you become more familiar with the process of defining macros, you will find it fast, fun, and fantastic! (If you weren't successful in defining the macro, just start the entire procedure again—telling WordPerfect (when it asks) that you want to replace the current definition—and carefully follow the steps again.)

Using a Macro

You can execute a macro in one of two ways:

- Press **Macro** (Alt-F10), type the macro name, and press **Enter**.

  This is the normal method for executing a macro. If, on the other hand, you used Method 2 to name the macro (which means you gave it *no* name), just press **Enter** after the prompt.

- Press **Alt-***letter*, where *letter* is one of the 26 alphabetic letters you can use to define the macro.

  Use this method if you named a macro by Method 3 above. This of course is the fastest and easiest way of executing a macro, but you can have only 26 such macros on a single disk or in a single directory.

To execute the DELFOL macro that you defined earlier, do the following:

Step 1.   Type the line of text, Macros are one of WordPerfect's most powerful features.

Step 2.   Move the cursor to the p in powerful.

Now delete the line from the cursor to the left edge of the screen using the macro DELFOL.

Step 3.   Press **Macro** (Alt-F10).

This is just like turning *on* a tape recorder to listen to what you just recorded. WordPerfect displays the prompt **Macro:**, and pauses for you to type the macro name.

Step 4. Type delfol and press **Enter**.

That's it. If you defined the macro as described in the previous section, you should now see the cursor at the left edge of the screen with only **powerful features.** remaining on the line.

Defining and Using an Alt Macro

The handiest and most-often-used macros are those defined by Method 3, that is, using the **Alt** key. For example, we will now follow the steps necessary to define a simple but useful macro, **Alt-Y**, which deletes an entire line of text. Before starting, be sure that you are in WordPerfect and that the cursor is located on a line of text in the middle of a paragraph. *Note:* If you are looking at a blank screen right now, type the following paragraph:

I am about to learn how to use the Alt key for defining and using powerful WordPerfect macros. Never again will I need to wish WordPerfect had a particular command, because with macros, I can invent (almost) any command I want.

Then press the **Up Arrow** twice to put the cursor in the middle of the paragraph. Now follow these steps to define the Alt-D macro:

Step 1. Press **Macro Def** (Alt-F10) to turn *on* the macro definition mode.

Step 2. Press **Alt-Y** to name the macro.

Step 3. Type Delete an entire line of text and press **Enter** to describe the macro.

Step 4. Define the macro by first pressing **Home, Home, Home, Left Arrow** (to move the cursor to the left edge of the line), **Ctrl-End** (to delete the line), and **Del** (to delete the [HRt] (hard return) or [SRt] (soft return) code so that the text beyond the cursor will move up one line.

Step 5. Press **Macro Def** (Ctrl-F10) to turn *off* the macro definition mode.

To use the macro, just press **Alt-Y**. Try it. As you can see, it deletes a whole line of text, quickly and easily.

Stopping a Macro

Pressing **Cancel** (F1) will abort most macros; however, you should carefully check your text and the status line to see the current condition of your document, since prematurely stopping a macro can yield some unexpected results.

CREATING A GLOSSARY

With macros you can type commonly used words and phrases with just the touch of a key or two. For example, if you were assigned to publish the Ocean Breeze Bookstore newsletter, you might want to set up a glossary of words and phrases that you would have to use over and over again throughout the report. This might be a list of your glossary:

Macro Name	Word or Phrase
Alt-A	Annual Report
Alt-C	Computer Books Department
Alt-O	Ocean Breeze Bookstore
Alt-R	Read A. Page, Bookstore Manager
Alt-U	Used Books Department

If you were the customer relations officer of Ocean Breeze Bookstore in charge of corresponding with customers, you might want to set up the following glossary of commonly used phrases and sentences:

Macro Name	Word or Phrase
NIS (Not In Stock)	The book you ordered is not in stock at this time.
OOP (Out Of Print)	The book you ordered is currently out of print.
AP (Apology)	We are sorry for any inconvenience this may have caused you.
REF (Refund)	If you would like to return the book to our store, we will be happy to give you a complete refund.

These glossary macros are just examples, of course. As you start typing your letters or manuscripts, you will develop your own glossary of words, phrases, sentences, and paragraphs.

DEFINING MACROS FOR USER INPUT

WordPerfect macros have the capability of performing a set of functions and then accepting input from the user before completing other functions. This adds tremendous power and flexibility to macros. It is the beginning of a programming language based on macros (not covered in this book).

As an example, we will define a macro that makes a title (to begin each article in a newsletter). We want the titles to be centered, bold-faced, all-capitalized characters. The start of the macro will contain, of course, such commands as Center and Bold, after which we will want to be able to enter the actual title name, press Enter, and have the macro continue by turning *off* the Bold, capitalizing the letters in the title, etc.

Follow these steps to define a macro that accepts user input:

Step 1. Press **Macro Def** (Ctrl-F10) to turn *on* the macro definition mode.

Step 2. Type title and press **Enter** to give the macro a name.

Step 3. Type Inserts a formatted title, and press **Enter** to give the macro a description.

Step 4. Begin defining the macro by pressing the following keys or commands in the order given: **Enter, Enter, Center** (Shift-F6), **Bold** (F6), and **Macro Commands** (Ctrl-PgUp).

Macro Commands (Ctrl-PgUp) evokes the one-line menu: **1 P**ause; **2 D**isplay; **3 A**ssign; **4 C**omment: **0**. Most of these menu items are used with advanced macros and will not be discussed. For the current macro, you only have to know that **1** (Pause) causes the macro to pause for keyboard input.

Step 5. Press **1** (Pause), type the complete guide to desktop publishing with wordperfect, press **Enter, Bold** (F6, to turn *off* bold), **Block** (Alt-F4, to turn *on* block), **Home, Left Arrow, Switch** (Shift-F3), **1** (Uppercase), **End, Enter, Enter**.

You can type any title you wish in place of the complete guide to desktop publishing with wordperfect, since the macro definition mode replaces this phrase with a pause command for future input.

Step 6. Press **Macro Def** (Ctrl-F10) again to turn *off* the macro definition.

In step 3, **Macro Commands** (Ctrl-PgUp) followed by **1** (**P**ause) tells WordPerfect to pause and wait for user input. When you execute the macro, WordPerfect will execute all of the commands up until the **Macro Commands** (Ctrl-PgUp), at which point it will pause for you to type the new title name and to press **Enter**, then it will execute the other functions in the macro. Note that pressing **Enter** following the pause does *not* put a [HRt] in the text.

Try the macro you have just defined. Clear the WordPerfect screen by typing **Exit** (F7), **N** (No), **N** (no); then press **Macro** (Alt-F10), type title, and press **Enter**. When the macro pauses, type a title such as how to use a computer (in either uppercase or lowercase), and press **Enter**. Notice how the macro automatically centers, capitalizes, and bolds the title.

YOUR MACRO TOOL CHEST

A list of helpful macros is given in Figure 15.1. The Macro Name column lists the name you should type after starting the **Macro Def** (Ctrl-F10). The Macro Description column lists the description you should type after giving the name. And the Macro Definition column lists the keys you must press while **Macro Def** is active. After pressing the Macro Definition keys, press **Macro Def** (Ctrl-F10) again to turn *off* the macro definition mode.

Figure 15.1 should give you enough examples to demonstrate the wide range of possible uses of macros. You will see other examples in subsequent chapters.

MACRO DIRECTORIES AND LIBRARIES

When you defined the macros in this chapter, they were saved to the default directory (e.g., C:\WPFILES) or default disk drive (e.g., B:\). Thus, any time you write a document with this default directory or drive, the macros are ready and waiting to be used.

When you change directories, however, the macros are not available for use. To solve this problem, you can do one of two things:

- Copy the macros from the previous directory to the current one.

  Simply use the **List** (F5), **Mark Files** (*), and **8** (**C**opy) commands.

- Press **Setup** (F1), **7** (**L**ocation of Auxiliary Files), **3** (**K**eyboard/Macro Files) to set the directory containing the macros.

  This causes WordPerfect to *always* look in the same directory for macros, regardless of the current default directory.

Examples of Macros

Macro Name	Macro Description	Macro Definition
DELFOL	Delete from cursor to first of line	**Block** (Alt-F4), **Home, Home, Home, Left Arrow, Del, Y**
Alt-Y	Delete entire line	**Home, Home, Home, Left Arrow, Delete to EOL** (Ctrl-End), **Del**
Alt-W	Delete word left	**Word Left** (Ctrl-Left Arrow), **Delete Word** (Ctrl-Backspace)
Alt-U	Uppercase letter at cursor	**Block** (Alt-F4), **Right Arrow, Switch** (Shift-F3), **1, Left Arrow**
Alt-L	Lowercase letter at cursor	**Block** (Alt-F4), **Right Arrow, Switch** (Shift-F3), **2, Left Arrow**
Alt-R	Reverse characters at cursor	**Del, Right Arrow, Cancel** (F1), **1, Left Arrow, Left Arrow**
Alt-W	Delete from cursor to end of word with space	**Home, Del, Space Bar, Left Arrow**
Alt-E	Delete from cursor to end of sentence	**Block** (Alt-F4), **.** (period), **Del, Y**
UW	Underline word	**Block** (Alt-F4), **Word Right** (Ctrl-Right Arrow), **Left Arrow, Underline** (F8)
BW	Bold word	**Block** (Alt-F4), **Word Right** (Ctrl-Right Arrow), **Left Arrow, Bold** (F6)
CW	Capitalize word	**Block** (Alt-F4), **Word Right** (Ctrl-Right Arrow), **Left Arrow, Switch** (Shift-F3), **1**
IW	Italicize word	**Block** (Alt-F4), **Word Right** (Ctrl-Right Arrow), **Left Arrow, Font** (Ctrl-F8), **2, 4**

Figure 15.1 A list of sample macros.

On the other hand, you may want to define a specialized set of macros that are specific to a small number of documents (such as annual reports). In this case you would simply change the default directory (for example, to C:\REPORTS) and define a set of macros specific to the report documents. As long as the default directory is C:\REPORTS those (and only those) keyboard macros will be available for execution. You just have to make sure the location specification of the keyboard/macro files in Setup is left blank.

Using Macros with the Keyboard Layout Feature

If you like the convenience of the Alt macros but you want the flexibility of using **Alt** with other keys (such as **Alt-1**) or of executing macros with other key combinations (such as **Ctrl-A**), then you should use WordPerfect's keyboard layout feature. For example, suppose you would like to execute the DELFOL macro (defined above) by pressing **Ctrl-T**. Follow these steps:

Step 1. After having defined the DELFOL macro as described earlier in this chapter, press **Setup** (Shift-F1), **5** (**K**eyboard Layout), and **4** (**C**reate), type auxkeys and press **Enter.**

You may give the keyboard layout file any name you want, as long as it is a legal DOS filename. WordPerfect automatically appends the filename extension .WPK.

Step 2. Press **7** (**R**etrieve) to retrieve a defined macro from the disk.

The prompt Key: appears at the bottom of the screen.

Step 3. Press **Ctrl-T** (the key combination that will execute the commands of the DELFOL macro).

The prompt Macro: appears on the screen.

Step 4. Type delfol and press **Enter.**

WordPerfect loads a copy of the macro into the keyboard layout file, which retains the set of keyboard commands recorded in DELFOL but does not use the macro file itself. The DELFOL.WPM file may be deleted.

Step 5. Press **Exit** (F7).

The name of the Keyboard layout file, AUXKEYS, appears on the Setup: Keyboard Layout menu.

Step 6. Press **1** (**S**elect) to activate the keyboard layout file AUX-KEYS and then **Enter** to return to the document screen.

From now on, **Ctrl-T** executes the command that was recorded in DELFOL to delete from the cursor to the left margin.

CHAIN, REPEAT, AND CONDITIONAL MACROS

Suppose you have typed a description of new books at Ocean Breeze Bookstore, similar to the list shown in Figure 15.2, but with fifty books instead of only five. Now, after the list is all typed, you realize that you want a different format:

• Double spacing between paragraphs.

• Unnumbered paragraphs.

• Hanging indented paragraphs.

With a list of only five books, you could probably make these revisions in a minute or two, but if you had a list of 50 books, the revisions might take 10 to 20 minutes—unless you know how to do a repeating chain macro.

Repeating Chain Macros

Follow these steps to write a repeating chain macro that will make the above revisions on every paragraph in your book list:

Step 1. Get into WordPerfect, make sure the screen is clear, type Figure 15.2 exactly as shown, and save it to the disk with the filename BOOKLIST.

Step 2. Move the cursor to the beginning of the document (by pressing **Home, Home, Home, Up Arrow**), then press **Down Arrow** three times to position the cursor on the line just above book #1, and then press **Macro Def** (Ctrl-F8), type the name revise, press **Enter**, type the description Revise list of books, and press **Enter**.

These operations start the Macro Definition of the macro named REVISE. You could have either selected any legal name or opted for no name at all by just pressing **Enter**.

Step 3. Press **Search** (F2), and at the prompt → **Search:**, press **Enter**, and press **Search** (F2) again to initiate the search.

The macro searches for the hard return code [HRt], which precedes each paragraph. The cursor should now be on the left edge of the screen, to the left of 1. Wilde.

NEW BOOKS

at Ocean Breeze Bookstore

   1. Wilde, Foster, <u>Zookeeper's Handbook</u>. This one-of-a-kind volume includes animal husbandry, cage design, care of exotic species, grant proposal writing, and public relations for zookeepers.

   2. Compton, Rowland, <u>Computers on Parade</u>. Are you having difficulty keeping up with the latest computers? This manual presents a comprehensive review of the latest machines, including desktop and laptop computers from Apple, IBM, Compaq, Tandy, Toshiba, etc.

   3. Hardy, B. Moore, <u>Physical Conditioning</u>. Written for coaches, trainers, sports managers, physical therapists, and athletes, this book provides simple step-by-step procedures for getting in shape without the use of special equipment or facilities.

   4. Knight, Chester, <u>How to Play Master Chess</u>. Whether you are a novice or expert, Mr. Knight (an FIDE Grandmaster and United Chess Federation Certified Tournament Director) shows you the tactics and strategy for playing chess at the master level, including powerful principles of the opening, middle, and end game.

   5. Downey, Neil, <u>How to Pray</u>. If your prayers are in a rut and seem never to get past the roof of your home, read <u>How to Pray</u>. The book contains proven techniques for more meaningful prayers and personal spiritual development.

Figure 15.2 Descriptions of new books at Ocean Breeze Bookstore. After typing this list, you realize that you want the list in a different format. You can modify the format using a repeating chain macro.

Step 4. Press **Block** (Alt-F4) to turn *on* block mode and press **Word Right** (Ctrl-Right Arrow) twice.

The highlight covers the number (1.) and the spaces preceding Wilde.

Step 5. Press **Backspace** and **Y** (Yes) to delete the block text and codes.

The tab, number, and spaces preceding the author's name are deleted.

Step 6. Press **Enter** to insert an extra [HRt] into the text.

This produces a double space between paragraphs.

Step 7. Press **Indent** (F4) and **Margin Release** (Shift-Tab).

The key combination **Indent** and **Margin Release** at the beginning of a line produces a hanging paragraph.

Step 8. Press **Macro** (Alt-F10), type revise, and press **Enter**.

This step is the key to the whole procedure: The macro calls itself. In other words, after the macro edits one paragraph, the macro calls itself again to edit the next paragraph and so on until all the paragraphs have been modified. This is called a repeating chain (or recursive) macro; it repeats until a search operation yields a Not Found message, at which point the macro automatically terminates.

Step 9. Press **Macro Def** (Ctrl-F10) to terminate definition of the repeating chain macro.

These nine steps serve to define the macro and edit the first paragraph. Now execute the macro by pressing **Macro** (Alt-F10), typing revise, and pressing **Enter**. After a few moments, all the paragraphs have been revised to the desired format, as shown in Figure 15.3.

Repeating chain macros are among the most powerful techniques available in any word processor. Once you catch on to their use, you will become totally addicted to using them and wonder how you ever survived without them.

The following is another simple (but very useful) repeating chain macro called U2I, for converting all the underlined text in a document to italicized text. Suppose you decide, for example, that the book names in Figure 15.2 should be italicized instead of underlined. You cannot simply replace underline codes [UND] with italics codes [ITALC] (since there is no way to replace the end underline

NEW BOOKS

at Ocean Breeze Bookstore

Wilde, Foster, <u>Zookeeper's Handbook</u>. This one-of-a-kind volume includes animal husbandry, cage design, care of exotic species, grant proposal writing, and public relations for zookeepers.

Compton, Rowland, <u>Computers on Parade</u>. Are you having difficulty keeping up with the latest computers? This manual presents a comprehensive review of the latest machines, including desktop and laptop computers from Apple, IBM, Compaq, Tandy, Toshiba, etc.

Hardy, B. Moore, <u>Physical Conditioning</u>. Written for coaches, trainers, sports managers, physical therapists, and athletes, this book provides simple step-by-step procedures for getting in shape without the use of special equipment or facilities.

Knight, Chester, <u>How to Play Master Chess</u>. Whether you are a novice or expert, Mr. Knight (an FIDE Grandmaster and United Chess Federation Certified Tournament Director) shows you the tactics and strategy for playing chess at the master level, including powerful principles of the opening, middle, and end game.

Downey, Neil, <u>How to Pray</u>. If your prayers are in a rut and seem never to get past the roof of your home, read <u>How to Pray</u>. The book contains proven techniques for more meaningful prayers and personal spiritual development.

Figure 15.3   The revised list of new books after defining and executing the repeating chain macro REVISE.

code [und] with the end italicize code [italc]), so you have to create a repeating chain macro:

Step 1. Move the cursor to the beginning of the document, press **Macro Def** (Ctrl-F10), type u2i, press **Enter**, type Underline to italics, and press **Enter**.

Step 2. Press **Search** (F2), **Underline** (F8) (to produce the underlining code [UND]), and press **Search** (F2) again.

The cursor moves to the first letter of Zookeeper and to the right of the (invisible) [UND] code.

Step 3. Press **Block** (Alt-F4), **Search** (F2), **Underline** (F8), and **Underline** (F8) again.

The codes [UND][und] appear on the search line. We really only want the end underline code [und], but the only way to make it appear on the search line is by pressing **Underline** twice.

Step 4. Press **Left Arrow** (to move past [und]), **Backspace** (to delete [UND]), and **Search** (F2) (to initiate the search).

The cursor moves past the [und] code at the end of the book title, which becomes blocked (highlighted).

Step 5. Press **Font** (Ctrl-F8), **2** (Appearance), **4** (Italc).

The text is now underlined and italicized.

Step 6. Press **Left Arrow** (to move the cursor past the [italc] code), **Backspace**, and **Y** (Yes) (to delete the [und] code).

The first underlined text has been converted to italicized text. We will now make the macro recursive (chaining it to itself) by having it execute itself.

Step 7. Press **Macro** (Alt-F10), type u2i, and press **Enter**.

Step 8. Press **Macro Def** (Ctrl-F10) to terminate the macro definition.

This completes the definition of the U2I (to convert underline to italics). To execute the macro, press **Macro** (Alt-F10), type u2i, and press **Enter**. In a few moments, all the underlined text from the cursor to the end of the document is converted to italics.

Chaining Macros

The above two sample macros are called chained repeating macros because they are chained to themselves. You can also chain a macro to another macro. For example, assume you have already defined the macro CW (to capitalize words) in Figure 15.1 and now want a macro that bolds *and* capitalizes a word. Follow these steps to define the new macro CB:

Step 1. Move the cursor to the beginning of a word, press **Macro Def** (Ctrl-F10) to turn *on* macro definition, enter the macro name cb, and enter the description Caps and bolds word.

Step 2. Press **Block** (Alt-F4) (to turn block *on*), press **Word Right** (Ctrl-Right Arrow) (to highlight the word), **Left Arrow** (to move the cursor to the other side of the space after the selected word), **Bold** (F6), and **Block** (Alt-F4) (to turn block *off*).

This sequence of commands is the same one given above to define the BW (bold word) macro.

Step 3. Press **Word Left** (Ctrl-Left Arrow) (to move the cursor to the start of the original word).

Step 4. Press **Macro** (Alt-F10), type cw, and press **Enter**.

Step 5. This chains the macro CW to the macro currently being defined, but the CW is not executed at this time. (You cannot execute a named macro while defining another one, but you *can* execute an Alt macro while defining another macro.)

Step 6. Press **Macro Def** (Ctrl-F10) to end the definition of the macro CB.

Now try the macro: move the cursor to the first letter of a word, press **Macro** (Alt-F10), type cb, and press **Enter**.

HINTS ON CREATING MACROS

Here are some hints that may help you create and use macros for increasing your word processing productivity:

- If you have to perform a complex editing operation four or more times, you will usually save time by defining a macro to do the job. If you have to perform the operation only two or three times, don't bother with a macro.

- Simple macros are easier to define and are usually easier to use than chain macros. Use chain macros only when you can clearly see an advantage to using them.

- To repeat an editing procedure throughout a document, use a repeating chain macro. Begin the repeating chain macro with a search (either forward or backward), perform the editing procedures, and then end the macro by having the macro execute itself. When you execute the macro, it will repeat until a search fails.

- In defining a repeating chain macro, be sure that the cursor is past (to the right of or below) the newly edited item before the chained macro is invoked; otherwise, the editing procedures will be repeated over and over again at the same item, and never end. If this happens, press **Cancel** (F1) to stop the macro.

- Keep a list of the macros you have defined. By writing down the names and functions of the macros and keeping the list next to your computer, you will save yourself time and frustration.

- Learn how to edit macros, put macros in Keyboard layout files, and use WordPerfect's full programming features. These topics are not treated in this book but are covered in *Working with Word-Perfect* (see Appendix C, "Additional Reading".

SUMMARY

Macros can help you write, edit, and format your WordPerfect documents. The five steps required to define a macro include: (1) Press **Macro Def** (Ctrl-F10) to turn *on* macro definition, (2) type the macro name, (3) type the macro description, (4) press the keys you want to record in the macro, and press **Macro Def** (Ctrl-F10) to turn *off* macro definition. A macro can be defined that accepts user input using the **Macro Command** (Ctrl-PgUp) feature. Macros can chain to other macros and to themselves.

If you spend time defining the macros given in this chapter and practicing some macros on your own, you will find macros an essential tool in desktop publishing.

Chapter 16

Publishing Letters

The purpose of this chapter is to show you the following:

• How to design a letter.

• How to create a letterhead using many of the WordPerfect features described in the early chapters.

• How to use WordPerfect's merge features to generate and print form letters.

DESIGNING A LETTER

The design of a letter conveys as much of a message as the body of the letter. Compare Figures 16.1A, 16.1B, and 16.1C. The text is the same in all three letters, but the overall message is different. The first (handwritten) letter is personal and informal. The second (typewritten) letter is semiformal and "secretarial." The third (desktop-published) letter is formal and professional.

None of the three letter designs is better than the others. Which design you choose depends on the purpose of the letter, on your personality, on the personality of your company, and on the overall message you want to convey.

Before you write a letter, you should determine the overall feeling you want to convey and then design your letter accordingly by considering the following features:

• Production: handwritten (personal), typewritten (semiformal and secretarial), or desktop-published (formal and professional) letter?

• Font: Courier (typewritten look), Helvetica (clean, traditional look), Times Roman (formal, typeset look), or some other font?

• Justification: justified (more formal, less legible) or ragged right (less formal, more legible).

• Letterhead: large or small, formal or informal, traditional or avant garde, plain or fancy?

The remainder of this chapter will give you some examples of each of these features.

DESIGNING YOUR OWN LETTERHEAD

Traditionally, large and small businesses alike have used graphics designers, typesetters, and printers to prepare their letterheads. Now, with desktop publishing, you can design and print your own letterhead and take advantage of the following benefits:

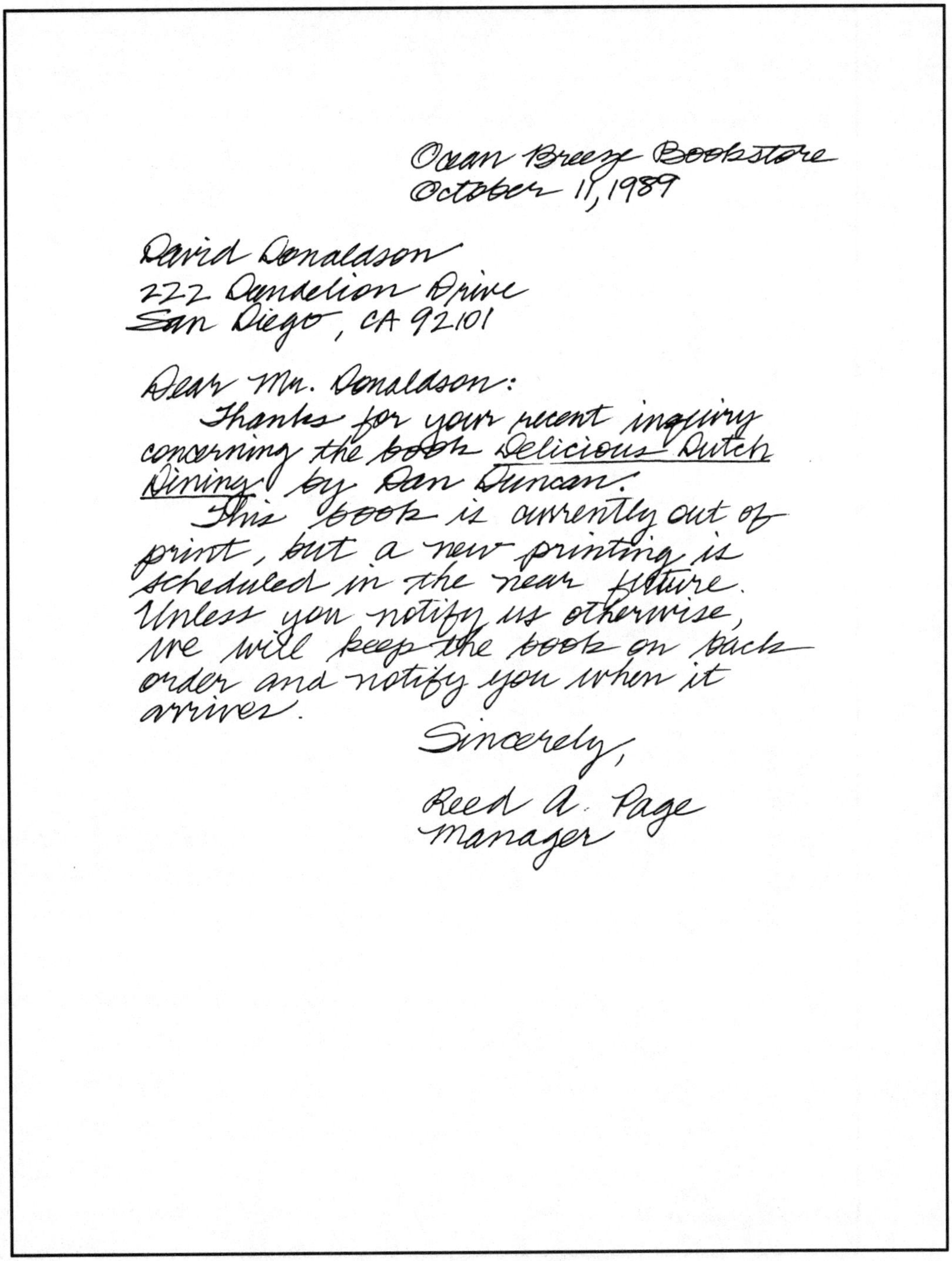

Ocean Breeze Bookstore
October 11, 1989

David Donaldson
222 Dandelion Drive
San Diego, CA 92101

Dear Mr. Donaldson:

Thanks for your recent inquiry concerning the ~~book~~ _Delicious Dutch Dining_ by Dan Duncan.

~~This book~~ is currently out of print, but a new printing is scheduled in the near future. Unless you notify us otherwise, we will keep the book on back order and notify you when it arrives.

Sincerely,

Reed A. Page
Manager

Figure 16.1A A handwritten letter.

```
                                    Ocean Breeze Bookstore
                                    October 11, 1989


        David Donaldson
        222 Dandelion Drive
        San Diego, CA 92101

        Dear Mr. Donaldson:

            Thanks for your recent inquiry concerning the book
        Delicious Dutch Dining by Dan Duncan.

            This book is currently out of print, but a new
        printing is scheduled in the near future. Unless you
        notify us otherwise, we will keep the book on back order
        and notify you when it arrives.

                            Sincerely,



                            Reed A. Page
                            Manager
```

Figure 16.1B A typewritten letter.

**OCEAN BREEZE
BOOKSTORE**

October 11, 1989

David Donaldson
222 Dandelion Drive
San Diego, CA 92101

Dear Mr. Donaldson:

Thanks for your recent inquiry concerning the book *Delicious Dutch Dining* by Dan Duncan.

This book is currently out of print, but a new printing is scheduled in the near future. Unless you notify us otherwise, we will keep the book on back order and notify you when it arrives.

Sincerely,

Reed A. Page
Manager

1212 San Ysidro Ave., San Diego, CA 92101   *Quality service since 1966*

Figure 16.1C A desktop-published letter.

- *Less expense.* Doing the work yourself saves money.

- *Increased flexibility.* You can change a design any time you choose.

- *Convenience.* You can print the letterhead as you print each letter, all in one step using your laser printer.

But designing and printing your own letterhead also has the potential for creating the following problems:

- *Reduced quality.* Graphic design in the hands of a novice may produce unsatisfactory results.

- *Inconsistency and confusion.* Frequent changes in the design of letterheads and other company forms may irritate customers and cause confusion in your correspondence.

- *Increased time.* Printing graphics and text is much slower than printing text alone. Waiting for letters to print can be time-consuming and expensive.

If you are competent in your design abilities and consciously seek to avoid problems, the advantages of desktop publishing will outweigh the disadvantages.

PREPARING A LETTERHEAD

The following sections of this chapter show various letterhead designs for Ocean Breeze Bookstore. Each design was created with WordPerfect using a variety of typefaces, graphics lines, text boxes, graphics figures, and font colors (for reversed text).

The following sections also give a step-by-step explanation of how to create each letterhead. Each letterhead demonstrates an important application of WordPerfect in desktop publishing. Some of the steps in the explanations only give the desired settings necessary to produce the formats, not the complete list of keypresses. If you have questions about certain steps and keystrokes, refer to the appropriate subject in previous chapters in this book.

If you make a mistake while trying to create a letterhead (or any other document in this and future chapters), do one of the following, depending on the severity of the problem:

- Erase your most recent mistake and insert the correct text or code.

- Read back through the steps to make sure the correct window is on your computer screen. For example, if you should be editing a text or graphics box, make sure the cursor is in the proper edit screen or menu and not in the document screen.

*   If you discover an error from several steps earlier, back up and proceed from that step.

*   If you know something is wrong but can't find your error, clear the screen and start over.

*   If you feel you have followed the steps properly but the letter-head still looks wrong, the problem may be differences between your printer and ours. You may have to modify the design to fit your printer and font library. This may require using differ-ent typefaces or smaller fonts.

*   If certain features don't seem to be working properly, you may have an outdated release of WordPerfect. Press **Help** (F3) and look at the release date in the upper right corner. It should be 11/06/89 or later. To receive an interim release, call 1-800-321-4566 or write WordPerfect 5.1 Interim Release, 81 North State Street, Orem, UT 84057.

*   As a last resort, you may have to abandon a procedure altogether. Your printer and type library may simply not work with one or more of the designs.

Keeping It Simple

Figure 16.2 shows a simple but effective letterhead. Follow these steps to create this letterhead:

Step 1.   Clear the document screen: **Exit** (F7), **N** (No), **N** (No).

Step 2.   Set the left and right margins: **Format** (Shift-F8), **1** (**Line**), **7** (**Margins**), 1.5, **Enter** (for a 1.5-inch left margin), 1.5, **Enter** (for a 1.5-inch right margin), **Exit** (F7) (to return to the document screen).

Step 3.   Choose the font: **Font** (Ctrl-F8), **4** (Base Font), select 10-point Times Roman, and return to the document screen.

Step 4.   Choose bold, very large font: **Font** (Ctrl-F8), **1** (Size), **6** (**Vry Large**), **Bold** (F6), and type Ocean Breeze Bookstore.

Step 5.   Press **End** to move the cursor past the codes for bold and very large, then press **Enter** to go to the next line.

Ocean Breeze Bookstore
1212 San Ysidro Avenue
San Diego, CA 92101

Figure 16.2 A simple letterhead design.

Step 6.   Type the return address:

```
1212 San Ysidro Avenue
San Diego, CA 92101
```

Step 7.   Draw a thick vertical line: **Graphics** (Alt-F9), **5** (Line), **2** (Vertical), **1** (Horizontal Position), **4** (Set Position), 1.2, **Enter**, **2** (Vertical Position), **2** (Top), **3** (Length of Line), 0.58, **Enter**, **4** (Width of Line), 0.25, **Enter**, **Exit** (F7).

Step 8.   View the document: **Print** (Shift-F7), **6** (View Document).

Make sure the letterhead design looks correct. If your printer doesn't support Times Roman in the font size Very Large, the letterhead may appear different from Figure 16.2.

Step 9.   Save the letterhead to the disk using any filename you wish.

You can modify this basic design by using a different font typeface, selecting different font sizes, or drawing a vertical line of different length and width.

Reversing and Spacing Text

Figure 16.3 demonstrates reversed (also called *dropout* or *surprinted*) type and WordPerfect's letter spacing feature in a letterhead.

To create the letterhead in Figure 16.2, follow these steps:

Step 1.   With a clear document screen, press **Graphics** (Alt-F9), **3** (Text Box), and **4** (Options); press **1** (Border Style) and **1** (None) four times (for all four borders); press **2** (Outside Border) and enter 0.17 for all four sides; press **3** (Inside Border) and set the left and right borders to 0″ and the top and bottom borders to 0.1″; press **9** (Gray Shading) and set the gray shading to 100% (black). Press **Exit** (F7) to return to the document screen.

Step 2.   Create the text box: **Graphics** (Alt-F9), **3** (Text Box), **1** (Create), and set the **5** (Vertical Position) to 0″, the **6** (Horizontal Position) to **3** (Center), the **7** (Size) to **3** (Both Width and Height) of 6″ × 0.65″, the **8** (Wrap Text Around) to **Yes**, and **9** (Edit).

Step 3.   From the text box edit screen, set the font to 32-point Times Roman: **Font** (Ctrl-F8), **4** (Base Font), and specify Times Roman Bold, 32-point.

Step 4.   Set the text color to white: **Font** (Ctrl-F8), **5** (Print **C**olor), **2** (White), **Enter.**

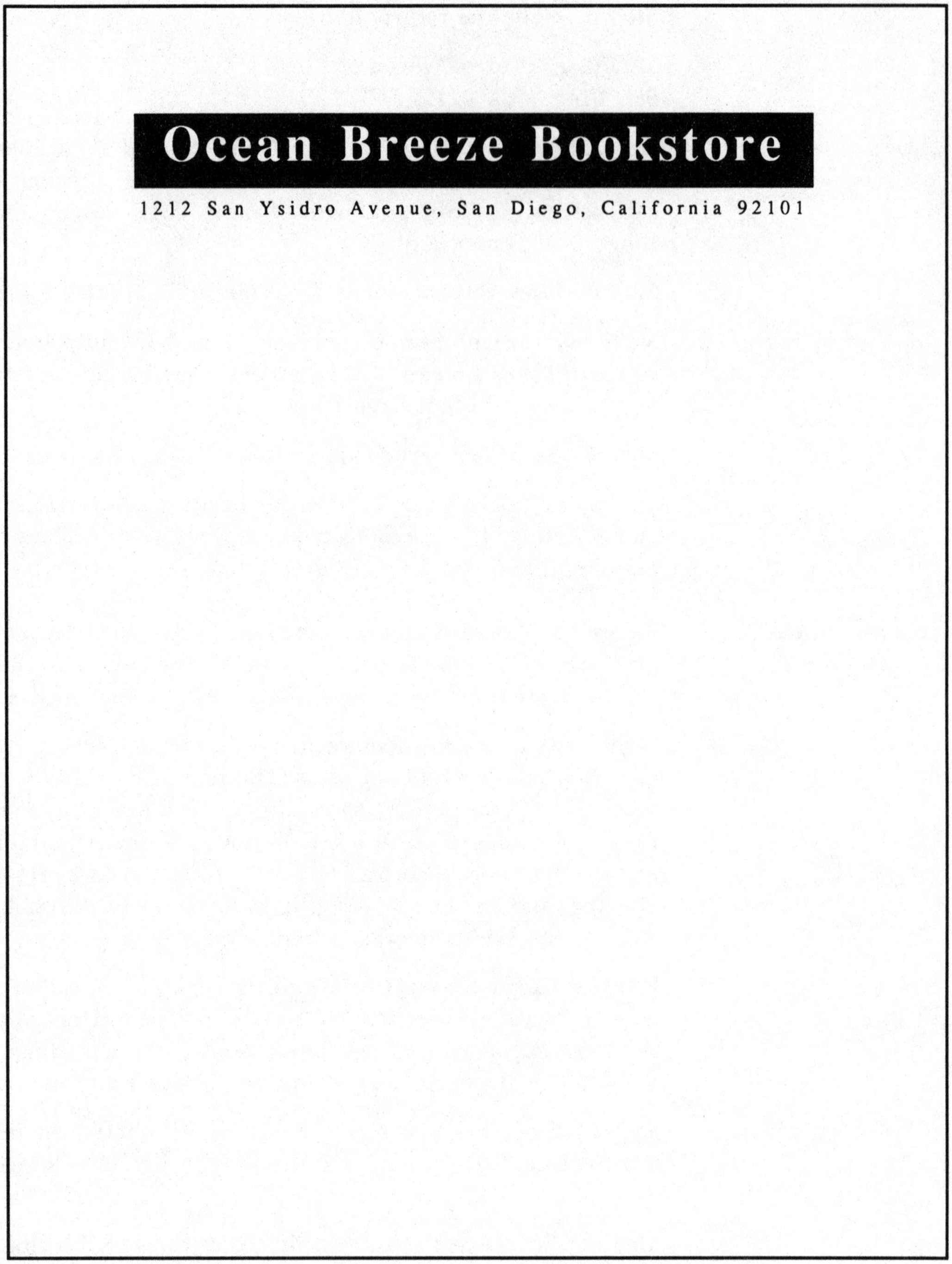

Ocean Breeze Bookstore

1212 San Ysidro Avenue, San Diego, California 92101

Figure 16.3 A letterhead with reversed text and expanded letter spacing.

Step 5. Set the word spacing to spread out the text: **Format** (Shift-F8), **4** (**Other**), **6** (**Printer Functions**), **3** (**Word Spacing**), **3** (**Percent of Optimal**), 115, **Enter** (to set the word spacing to 115%), **3** (**Percent of Optimal**), 115, **Enter** (to set the letter spacing to 115%), and **Exit** (F7) to return to the text box edit screen.

Step 6. Center and type the text: **Center** (Shift-F6), Ocean Breeze Bookstore, **Exit** (F7) (to return to the main document screen).

Step 7. To place the next line of text immediately under the text box, use WordPerfect's Advance Up feature: **Format** (Shift-F8), **4** (**Other**), **1** (**Advance**), **1** (**Up**), 0.15 (to advance up 0.15″), **Enter**, **Exit** (F7).

Step 8. Set the word/letter spacing to 145% of optimal by repeating the commands given above in step 5, except set the word and letter spacing both to 145% of optimal.

Step 9. Center and type the text: **Center** (Shift-F6), 1212 San Ysidro Avenue, San Diego, California 92101, **Enter**, and set the word/letter spacing back to 100% of optimal.

Step 10. Save the letterhead to the disk.

This completes the creation of Figure 16.3.

Using Macros

In creating the attractive letterhead in Figure 16.4, you'll use the same features that you used for Figure 16.3, but this time you will define macros that will save you keystrokes and hence increase your productivity.

Step 1. With a clear document screen, select the 60-point Times Roman font: **Font** (Ctrl-F8), **4** (**Base Font**), and select Times Roman, 60-point.

Step 2. Create a macro called KERN for adjusting the word/letter spacing: **Macro Def** (Ctrl-F10), kern, **Enter**, Adjust word/letter spacing, **Enter**, **Format** (Shift-F8), **4** (**Other**), **6** (**Printer Function**), **3** (**Word Spacing**), **3** (**Percent of Optimal**), **Macro Commands** (Ctrl-PgUp), **1** (**Pause**), 90 (to set the word spacing to 90%), **Enter**, **Enter**, **3** (**Percent of Optimal**), **Macro Commands** (Ctrl-PgUp), **1** (**Pause**), 90 (to set the letter spacing to 90%), **Enter**, **Enter**, **Exit** (F7) (to return to the text box edit screen), **Macro Def** (Ctrl-F10) (to turn *off* macro definition).

OCEAN BREEZE

B O O K S T O R E

1212 San Ysidro Avenue, San Diego, CA 92101

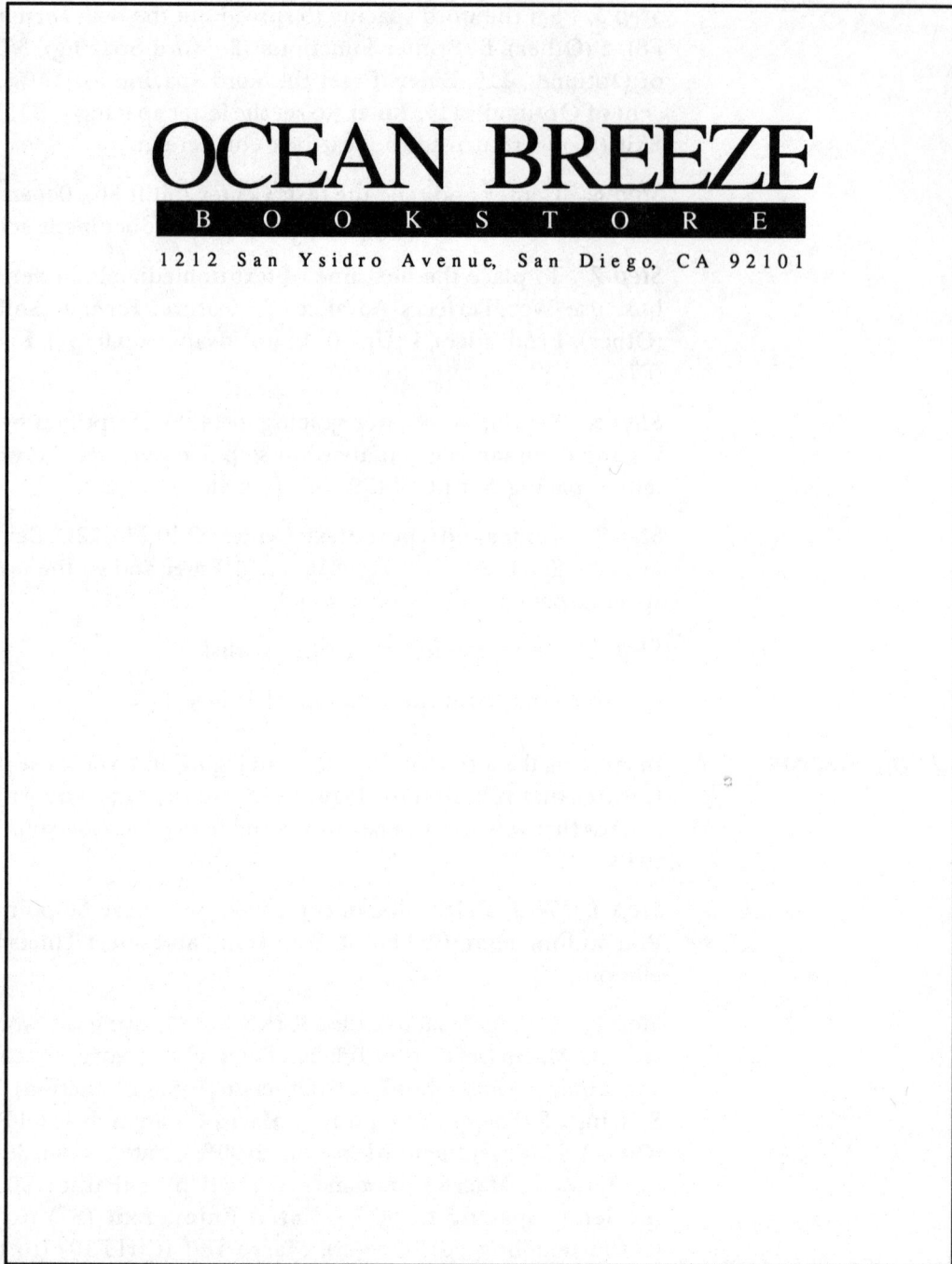

Figure 16.4 Creating this letterhead demonstrates how to define helpful macros.

This completes the macro definition and sets the word/letter spacing to 90% of optimal. As you can see in Figure 16.4, the letters in **OCEAN BREEZE** are kerned (closer together than normal). We will use this macro to expand or compress the word/letter spacing in other phrases. If you know macro programming, you can define the advanced macro KERN (Figure 16.5) that has the same function but gives the same value to both word and letter spacing.

Step 3.   Press **Center** (Shift-F6), type OCEAN BREEZE in all caps, and press **Enter**.

Step 4.   Create a macro called UP to use WordPerfect's Advance Up feature: **Macro Def** (Ctrl-F10), up, **Enter**, Advance up a specified amount, **Enter**, **Format** (Shift-F8), **4** (**O**ther), **1** (**A**dvance), **1** (**U**p), **Macro Commands** (Ctrl-PgUp), **1** (**P**ause), 0.15 (to advance up 0.15″), **Enter**, **Enter**, **Exit** (F7), **Macro Def** (Ctrl-F10) (to turn *off* macro definition).

This completes the macro definition and advances the subsequent text up 0.15″. If you know macro programming, you can define the advanced macro UP (Figure 16.6) that has the same function.

Step 5.   Set the text box options for reversed (dropout) text: **Graphics** (Alt-F9), **3** (Text **B**ox), **4** (**O**ptions); press **1** (**B**order Style) and **2** (**S**ingle) four times (for all four borders); press **3** (**I**nside Border) and set the left and right borders to 0″, the top border to 0.05″, and the bottom border to 0.04″; press **9** (**G**ray Shading) and set the gray shading to 100% (black). Press **Exit** (F7) to return to the document screen.

Step 6.   Create the text box: **Graphics** (Alt-F9), **3** (Text **B**ox), **1** (**C**reate); set the **4** (**V**ertical) position to 0″, the **5** (**H**orizontal) position to **3** (**C**enter), the **6** (**S**ize) to **3** (**B**oth Width and Height) of 5.7″ × 0.3″.

```
Macro name:  KERN
Description: Adjust word/letter spacing

{DISPLAY OFF}
{TEXT}0~{^Q}{^]}Kern percent of optimum: {^\}~
{Format}4633{VAR 0}{Enter}3{VAR 0}{Enter}{Exit}
```

Figure 16.5 The advanced macro KERN, created with the macro editor. If you don't know macro programming, use the simple macro KERN described in the text.

```
Macro name: UP
Description: Advance up 1/2 line

{DISPLAY OFF}
{TEXT}0~{^Q}{^]}Amount advance up: {^\}~
{Format}411{VAR 0}{Enter}{Exit}
```

Figure 16.6 The advanced macro UP. If you don't know macro programming, use the simple macro UP described in the text.

Step 7. Press **8** (**Edit**) to access the text box edit screen and set the font to 16-point Times Roman: **Font** (Ctrl-F8), **4** (Base Font), and specify Times Roman, 16-point. Then set the text color to white: **Font** (Ctrl-F8), **5** (Print Color), **2** (White), **Enter**. Type the text:

B   O   O   K   S   T   O   R   E

with five spaces between each letter. Press **Exit** (F7) to return to the document screen. Finally, set the font to 12-point Times Roman.

The space between each of the letters is too big to use the KERN macro, since the maximum value for the word/letter spacing is 250% of optimal.

Step 8. Prepare the address line in the letterhead: **Enter** (to go down a line), **Macro** (Alt-F10), up, **Enter** (to execute the macro UP), 0.65, **Enter** (to advance up 0.65″), **Macro** (Alt-F10), kern, **Enter** (to execute the macro KERN), 92, **Enter**, 92, **Enter** (to kern to 92% of optimal), **Center** (Shift-F6). Now type the address:

1 2 1 2   S a n   Y s i d r o   A v e n u e ,
S a n   D i e g o ,   C A   9 2 1 0 1

with one space between the letters and two spaces between the words.

Step 9. Press **Enter** and reset the word/letter spacing back to 100% of optimal: **Macro** (Alt-F10), kern, **Enter**, 100, **Enter**, 100, **Enter**.

Step 10. Save the letterhead to the disk.

This completes the creation of the letterhead in Figure 16.4.

Drawing a Gray Line

The simple letterhead with a modern elegant look shown in Figure 16.7 is created as follows:

Step 1. Set the base font to 16-point Avant Garde.

ocean breeze bookstore

1212 San Ysidro Avenue, San Diego, CA 92101

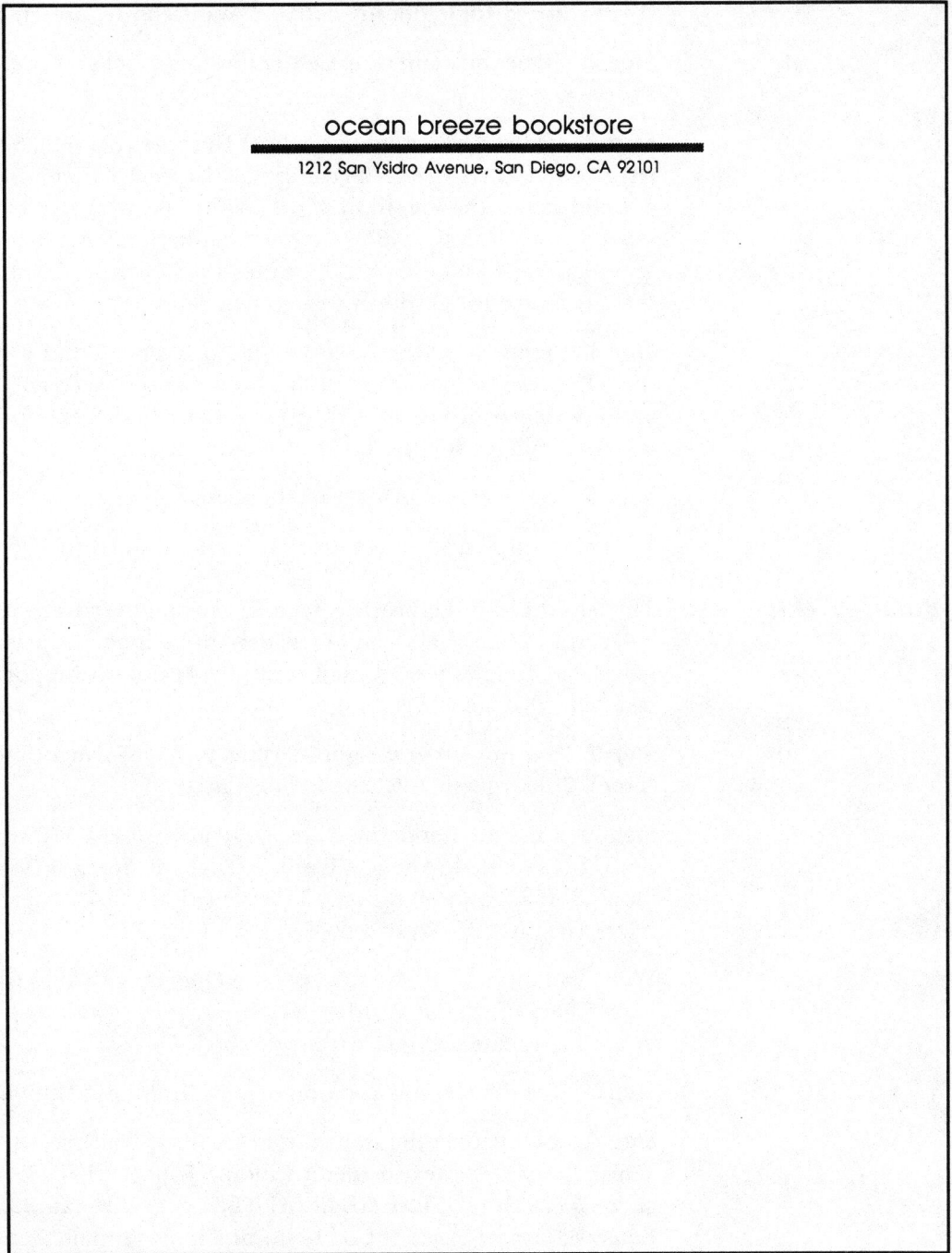

Figure 16.7 A letterhead with a modern look. The font typeface is Avant Garde Gothic Book. The horizontal line has a gray scale of 60%.

If your list of fonts doesn't contain Avant Garde, use Helvetica.

Step 2.   Type the main title: **Center** (Shift-F6), ocean breeze book-store, **Enter**.

Step 3.   Draw a horizontal gray line: **Graphics** (Alt-F9), **5** (Line), **1** (Horizontal), **1** (Horizontal Position), **3** (Center), **3** (Length of Line), **4**, **Enter** (to set the length to 4"), **4** (Width of Line), 0.08, **Enter** (to set the line width to 0.08"), **5** (Gray Shading), 60, **Enter** (to set the gray shading to 60% of black), **Enter** (to return to the document screen), **Enter** (to go down to the next line).

Step 4.   Type the address: Set the font to 10-point Avant Garde, use the UP macro to advance up 0.08", press **Center** (Shift-F6), type the address shown in Figure 16.7, press **Enter**, and set the font to the desired typeface for the body of your letters.

Step 5.   Save the letterhead to the disk.

This completes the creation of the letterhead in Figure 16.7.

Rotating Text

The letterhead in Figure 16.8, with text printed vertically along the left margin, has a modern but conservative look. To prepare this letterhead, follow these steps (if your printer doesn't support rotated text, skip this section):

Step 1.   Set the left and right margins to 1.5": **Format** (Shift-F8), **1** (Line), **7** (Margins), 1.5, **Enter**, 1.5, **Enter**.

Step 2.   Create a user-defined box: **Graphics** (Alt-F9), **4** (User-defined Box), **1** (Create), **4** (Anchor Type), **2** (Page), **0**, **Enter**, **5** (Vertical), **2** (Top), **6** (Horizontal Position), **3** (Set Position), 0.4, **Enter**, **7** (Size), **2** (set Height/Auto Width), **9**, **Enter**, **9** (Edit).

When you set the box size to a specified height with auto width, the height stays fixed, but WordPerfect automatically adjusts the width to accommodate the text within the box.

Step 3.   Set the text to a rotation of 90°: **Graphics** (Alt-F9), **2** (90°).

Step 4.   Create the title: **Font** (Ctrl-F8), **4** (Base Font), select 36-point Times Roman and text box edit window, **Font** (Ctrl-F8), **2** (Appearance), **5** (Outline), **Flush Right** (Alt-F6), Ocean Breeze Bookstore, **Enter**, set a new base font of 14-point Times Roman, **Enter**, **Flush Right** (Alt-F6), 1212 San Ysidro Avenue, San Diego, California 92101, **Exit** (F7) twice (to return to the document screen).

Ocean Breeze Bookstore

1212 San Ysidro Avenue, San Diego, California 92101

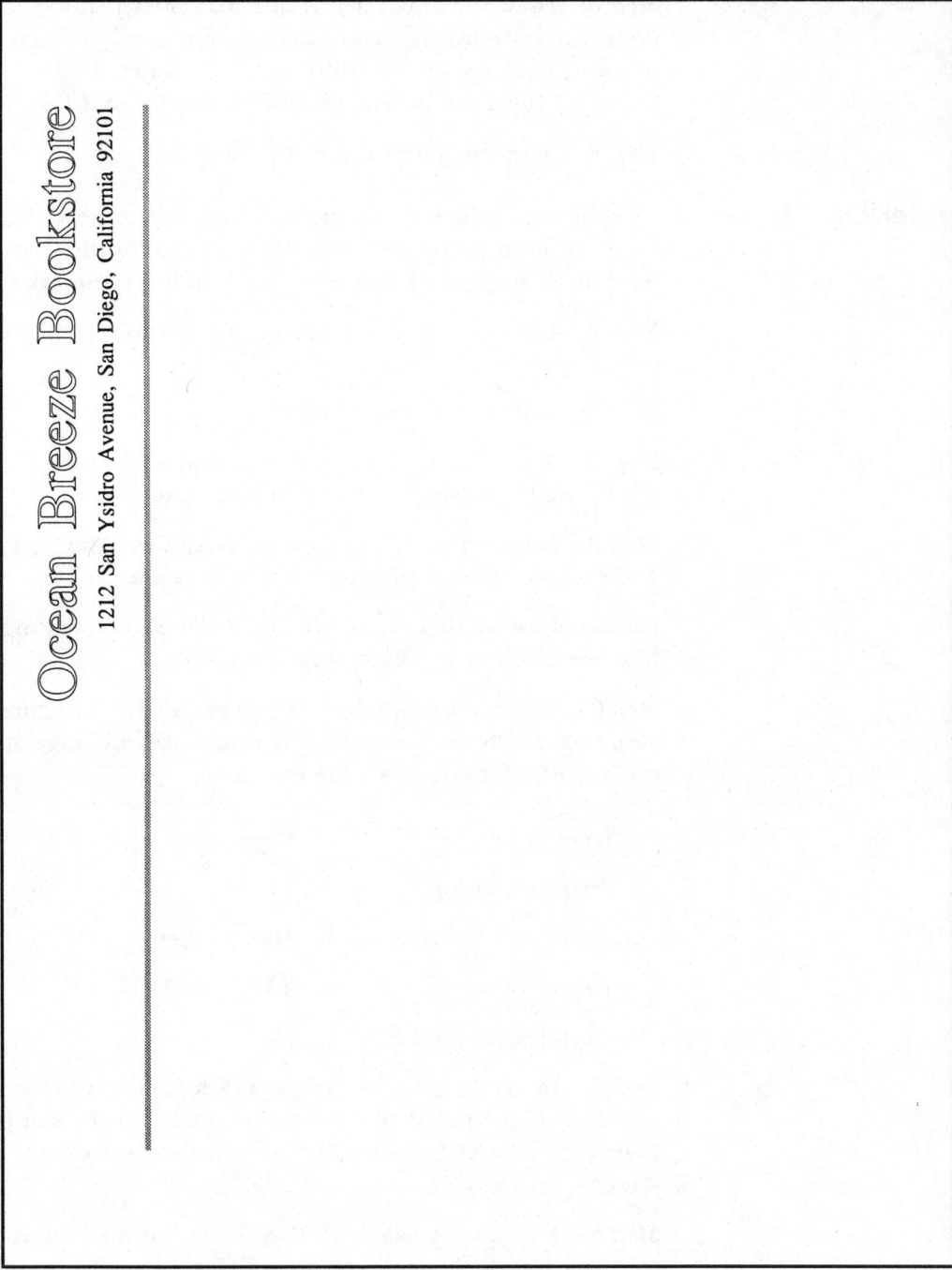

Figure 16.8 A letterhead with rotated text.

Step 5. Draw the gray vertical line: **Graphics** (Alt-F9), **5** (Line), **2** (Vertical), leave the line set to Left Margin and Full Page, **4** (Width of Line), 0.05 (to set the width to 0.05″), **Enter,** **5** (Gray Shading), 20 (to set the gray shading to 20% of black), **Exit** (F7).

Step 6. Save the letterhead to the disk.

Inserting a Logo

Using a logo enhances and personalizes a letterhead. Figure 16.9, for example, displays the book and disk logo of the Ocean Breeze Bookstore. To prepare this letterhead, follow these general steps:

Step 1. Using a graphics program (not WordPerfect), create your letterhead logo.

See Chapter 8, "Creating Graphics."

Step 2. Draw the horizontal line: **Graphics** (Alt-F9), **5** (Line), **1** (Horizontal), and set the width of line to 0.05″.

Step 3. Set the figure box options: **Graphics** (Alt-F9), **1** (Figure), **4** (Options), and set all four borders to None.

For details on setting the figure box options and creating a figure box, see Chapter 9, "Displaying Graphics."

Step 4. Create the figure box: **Graphics** (Alt-F9), **1** (Figure), **1** (Create), and specify the following (the values are only suggestions; use other values for your own logo):

Type:	**Page**
Vertical Position:	**1.08″**
Horizontal Position:	**Margin, Left**
Size:	**2.5″ × 1.75″**
Wrap text around box:	**No**

Step 5. Insert the graphics image: **1** (Filename), type the filename or complete pathname of the file containing the logo, or press **List** (F5) to see a directory listing and retrieve the file from the List Files screen.

Step 6. Edit the logo as desired: **8** (Edit) and then move, scale, rotate, or invert the image; then press **Exit** (F7) to return to the document screen.

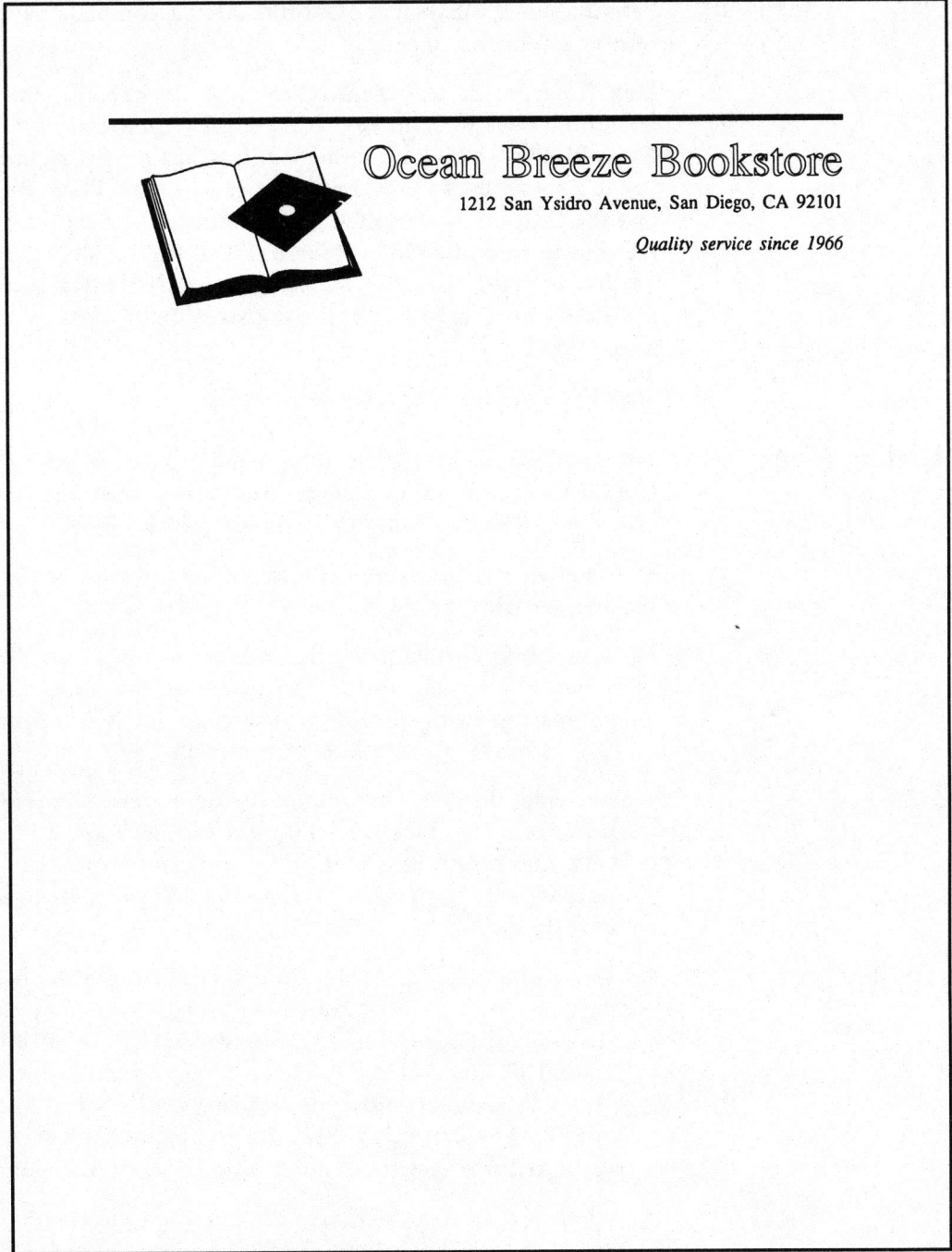

Ocean Breeze Bookstore

1212 San Ysidro Avenue, San Diego, CA 92101

Quality service since 1966

Figure 16.9 Using a logo in a letterhead.

See Chapter 9, "Displaying Graphics," for a complete explanation of how to edit an image.

Step 7. Type the text: **Font** (Ctrl-F8), **4** (Base Font), and specify 30-point Times Roman; **Font** (Ctrl-F8), **2** (Appearance), **5** (**Outln**); **Flush Right** (Alt-F6) (to put the text flush against the right margin); Ocean Breeze Bookstore, **End** (to move past the Flush Right code and the Outline code), **Enter** (to go down to the next line); change the font to 12-point Times Roman, **Flush Right** (Alt-F6), 1212 San Ysidro Avenue, San Diego, CA 92101; **Enter, Enter, Flush Right** (Alt-F6), **Font** (Ctrl-F8), **2** (Appearance), **4** (Italc), Quality service since 1966.

Step 8. Save the letterhead to the disk.

Getting Fancy

The final letterhead (Figure 16.10) includes many of the techniques already demonstrated earlier in this chapter. Make this letterhead on your own by following the explanations given previously.

- The figure in the upper left corner has a default border of thin lines on all four sides.

- The text underneath the figure is all caps, boldface, 14-point Times Roman. The words "Ocean Breeze" are set with word/letter spacing (with the KERN macro) at 140% of optimal, and "Bookstore" is set at 193% of optimal.

- The rules (lines) to the right of the figure have a horizontal position of 3.7", a length of 3.3", and widths from 0.01" to 0.11". (The line height on which the rules are drawn is set to 0.12": **Format** (Shift-F8), **1** (Line), **4** (Line Height), **2** (Fixed), 0.12, **Enter**, **Exit** (F7).)

- To put the horizontal rule (line) and address at the bottom of the page, first set the bottom margin to 0.5" and then use Word-Perfect's Advance to Line feature: **Format** (Shift-F8), **4** (Other), **3** (Line), 10, **Enter**, **Exit** (F7). Then type the address using 10-point Times Roman. Type the motto using italics with **Flush Right** (Alt-F6). After inserting this information, use Advance to Line again to move back up to the position of the text (about 3.25").

When you are finished, save the letterhead to the disk.

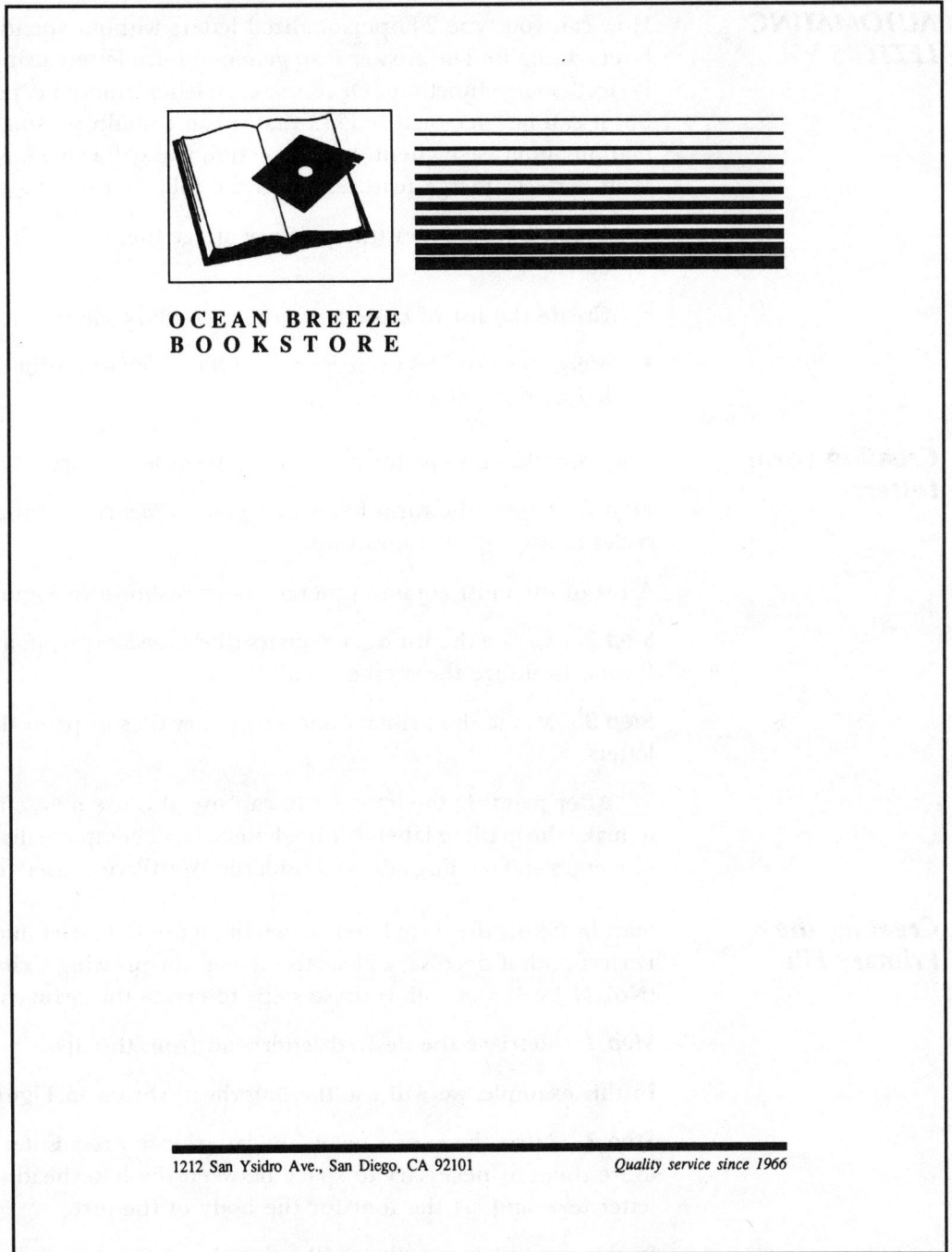

**OCEAN BREEZE
BOOKSTORE**

1212 San Ysidro Ave., San Diego, CA 92101   *Quality service since 1966*

Figure 16.10 A letterhead that uses most of the WordPerfect features discussed earlier in the chapter.

AUTOMATING LETTERS

How can you type 200 personalized letters without spending 200 hours doing it? The answer is to generate form letters using Word-Perfect's merge functions. Of course each letter cannot be "personal," but it can be "personalized," in that it can contain personal information about each client. In this section you will learn how to use WordPerfect's merge features to do the following:

- Create a form letter (the primary merge file) containing merge codes.

- Create the list of customers (the secondary merge file).

- Merge the two files to create a third file which will print the form letters using the list of customers.

Creating Form Letters

The three basic steps for automating form letters are:

Step 1.   Create the form letter (the *primary file*) containing merge codes at appropriate locations.

A list of the most common merge codes is shown in Figure 16.11.

Step 2.   Create the list of customers (the *secondary file*) in a special format to utilize the merge capabilities.

Step 3.   Merge the primary and secondary files to print the form letters.

After printing the letters, you can use also use merge features to make the mailing labels for the letters. For a complete discussion of merges and mailing labels, consult the WordPerfect user's manual.

Creating the Primary File

Start by typing the form letter shown in Figure 16.12. Get into Word-Perfect and, if necessary, clear the screen (by pressing **Exit** (F7), **N** (No), **N** (No)) and follow these steps to create the primary file:

Step 1.   Retrieve the desired letterhead from the disk.

In this example, we will use the letterhead shown in Figure 16.4.

Step 2.   Move the cursor below the letterhead, press **Enter** one or more times as necessary to space between the letterhead and the letter text, and set the font for the body of the text.

In this example, we will use 12-point Courier.

Description of Selected Merge Codes

Code Name	Description
{KEYBOARD}	Pauses for user input from the keyboard; press **End Field** (F9) to continue.
{DATE}	Inserts the current date into the text.
{END RECORD}	Marks the end of a record in a secondary merge file; also press **Merge Codes** (Shift-F9), **2** (End Record) to abort a merge.
{FIELD}*field~*	Inserts the named field from a record of a secondary merge file into the primary merge file.
{CHAIN MACRO}*macname~*	Executes a macro; the macro begins at the end of the merge.
{NEXT RECORD}	Looks for the next record in the secondary file; if no record is found, the merge terminates.
{PROMPT}*message~*	Displays a message on the status line.
{NEXT PRIMARY}*filename~*	Inserts a file; if no *filename* is given, it uses the current primary file.
{QUIT}	Quits the merge (used in a primary or secondary file).
{END FIELD}	Indicates the end of a field in a secondary merge file; also press **End Field** (F9) after a pause (in response to {PROMPT}) to cause the merge to continue.
{PRINT}	Outputs the text merged to that point to the printer.
{REWRITE}	Rewrites (updates) the screen during the merge.
{MRG CMNDS}	Transfers a merge code from the primary file into the file being created, using the syntax {MRG CMNDS}*command*{MRG CMNDS}

Figure 16.11 WordPerfect merge codes.

OCEAN BREEZE
B O O K S T O R E
1212 San Ysidro Avenue, San Diego, CA 92101

```
                            {DATE}

{FIELD}Title~ {FIELD}First~ {FIELD}Last~
{FIELD}Address~
{FIELD}City~, CA {FIELD}Zip~

Dear {FIELD}Title~ {FIELD}Last~:

     Ocean Breeze Bookstore wishes to announce an exciting new
service. As one of our preferred customers, {FIELD}Title~
{FIELD}Last~, you may place telephone orders on any book in our
store  by  calling  our  toll-free  number,  1-800-BOOKBUY.  A
representative will be in the {FIELD}City~ area one day a week to
make free deliveries and to accept new orders.

     We are looking forward to hearing from you.

                         Sincerely,


                         Reed A. Page
                         Manager

{PRINT}{NEXT RECORD}{NEXT PRIMARY}~
```

Figure 16.12   The primary file (FORM.LET), which consists of the form letter with merge codes.

Step 3. Press **Tab** six times; then press **Merge Codes** (Shift-F9) and **6** (**More**).

The Merge Codes window appears in the upper right corner of the screen.

Step 4. Move the cursor, by pressing **Down Arrow**, down to the {DATE} code, and press **Enter**.

The date code is inserted into the document. During the merge, WordPerfect inserts the *current* date at this location in the letter.

Step 5. Press **Enter** three times to leave space between the date and the inside address.

Each record of the secondary file (which you will type later) contains the following fields of client information, with the name of the field in italics:

1. The *last* name.

2. The *first* name(s).

3. The personal *title* (Miss, Ms., Mrs., Mr., Dr.).

4. The company and/or street *address*.

5. The *city*.

6. The *zip* code. No field for the state is necessary in the secondary file since all of the clients are in California (in or near San Diego).

Step 6. Insert the merge code for the *title* field: **Merge Codes** (Shift-F9), **1** (**Field**), *Title*, **Enter** and tilde (~). Press **Space Bar** and insert the merge code for field *First* (using the same method as for field *Title*). Press **Space Bar** again and insert the merge code for field *Last* (using the same method as for fields *First* and *Title*). Now press **Enter**, insert the code for field *Address*, press **Enter** again, insert the code for field 5, type a comma (to separate city and state), type CA (for California), press **Space Bar** to separate state and zip code, and finally, insert the merge code for field 6.

Step 7. Continue typing the letter as shown in Figure 16.12, inserting the merge codes at the appropriate places.

As you can see, the salutation (Dear . . .) contains the *Title* field and the *Last* field (the last name) separated by a space. This same sequence of codes is repeated in the second line of the body of the letter. The *City* is inserted into the fifth line of the letter body.

Step 8. At the end of the letter, after typing Manager, press **Enter** to move the cursor down a line, and then insert four merge codes: **Merge Codes** (Shift-F9), **6** (**More**), select {PRINT}, **Merge Codes** (Shift-F9), **6** (**More**), select {NEXT RECORD} **Merge Codes** (Shift-F9), **6** (**More**), select {NEXT PRIMARY}, **Enter** (no filename). These merge codes have the following meanings:

{PRINT} sends the previous merge to the printer (rather than to the screen). Technically, this command prints from the beginning of the current document to the position of the cursor (usually at the end of the document).

{NEXT RECORD} tells WordPerfect to get the next record in the secondary file. If it does not find the record, the merge ends.

{NEXT PRIMARY} inserts another file (with the specified filename) from the disk into the document. If no filename is specified—which is the case in this example—WordPerfect uses the current primary file.

For a partial list of merge codes and their definitions, see Figure 16.11.

Step 8. Save the primary file to the disk by pressing **Save** (F10), typing form.let, and pressing **Enter**.

This completes the creation of the form letter, which in this case is the primary merge file.

By Way of Explanation

Whenever you merge to the printer, you obviously need to include the {PRINT} code (which tells WordPerfect to send the merge to the printer), but you also need {NEXT RECORD}{NEXT PRIMARY} ~

These codes at the end of the primary file are necessary because normally, at the end of a merge between the primary file and a record of the secondary file, WordPerfect inserts a hard page code [HPg] and then goes to the next record in the secondary file. But we don't want this [HPg] code, since the printer automatically does a form feed (advances the paper) after printing each letter. If we allowed the [HPg], the printer would create a blank page between each letter. The {NEXT RECORD} tells WordPerfect to go to the next record of the secondary file, and {NEXT PRIMARY} ~ tells WordPerfect to start the merge over again. In this way, the primary document never ends (until the secondary file runs out of records), and the merge continues without having WordPerfect generate a hard page.

Creating the Secondary File

The secondary file contains information on each client—his or her surname, given name(s), title, address, city, and zip code. The information for this address list is shown in Figure 16.13.

```
{FIELD NAMES}Last~First~Title~Address~City~Zip~~{END RECORD}
================================================================
Lockhardt{END FIELD}
Laura{END FIELD}
Ms.{END FIELD}
555 La Lapiz Lane{END FIELD}
Linda Vista{END FIELD}
92111{END FIELD}
{END RECORD}
================================================================
Olsen{END FIELD}
Oliver O.{END FIELD}
Mr.{END FIELD}
Oriental Clothing Outlet
777 Oscar Dr.{END FIELD}
Ocean Beach{END FIELD}
92107{END FIELD}
{END RECORD}
================================================================
Eldridge{END FIELD}
Eric{END FIELD}
Mr.{END FIELD}
222 Elmira Ave.{END FIELD}
Encanto{END FIELD}
92114{END FIELD}
{END RECORD}
================================================================
Partridge{END FIELD}
Patricia P.{END FIELD}
Mrs.{END FIELD}
Peoples Park N' Pay
333 Paloma Place{END FIELD}
Pacific Beach{END FIELD}
92109{END FIELD}
{END RECORD}
================================================================
```

Figure 16.13 The secondary file (CLIENTS), which contains the information on each client and merge codes.

To type Figure 16.13, first clear the document screen and then follow these steps to create the secondary file:

Step 1. Enter the information and merge codes given in Figure 16.13.
After each field, press **End Field** (F9), and after each record, press **Merge Codes** (Shift-F9), **2** (End Record).

Step 2. When you are through typing Figure 16.13, save the document using the filename CLIENTS.

You may have hundreds of clients to whom you wish to send a letter. Use the same procedure regardless of the number of clients. You are limited only by the disk space.

Executing the Merge

Merging to the printer (rather than to the screen) has two advantages:

- It saves a step in the merge by automatically printing the newly created file.

- It avoids potential out-of-memory errors that would result from the merge file being too big for the available disk space.

To merge the primary and secondary files, follow these steps:

Step 1. Clear the WordPerfect document screen by pressing **Exit** (F7), **N** (No), **N** (No).

Step 2. Turn *on* your printer and adjust the paper.

Step 3. Press **Merge/Sort** (Ctrl-F9) and **1** (Merge).

WordPerfect displays the prompt **Primary file:**.

Step 4. Enter the name of the primary file, in this case, `form.let`.

WordPerfect displays the prompt **Secondary file:**.

Step 5. Enter the name of the secondary file, in this case, `clients`.

WordPerfect now prints the "personalized" letters to your clients. A sample letter is shown in Figure 16.14.

OCEAN BREEZE
B O O K S T O R E
1212 San Ysidro Avenue, San Diego, CA 92101

October 11, 1989

Ms. Laura Lockhardt
555 La Lapiz Lane
Linda Vista, CA 92111

Dear Ms. Lockhardt:

Ocean Breeze Bookstore wishes to announce an exciting new service. As one of our preferred customers, Ms. Lockhardt, you may place telephone orders on any book in our store by calling our toll-free number, 1-800-BOOKBUY. A representative will be in the Linda Vista area one day a week to make free deliveries and to accept new orders.

We are looking forward to hearing from you.

Sincerely,

Reed A. Page
Manager

Figure 16.14 The merged "personalized" form letter created by combining the primary and secondary files.

SUMMARY

In this chapter you have learned how to design and create letterheads by using many of WordPerfect's special features: graphics, advance, word/letter spacing, lines, color (for reversed or gray text), rotated text, macros, and so forth.

You have also learned how to create a form letter as a primary merge file and a list of addressees as a secondary merge file, using the merge commands {FIELD} (which inserts the field *n* from the secondary file into the primary file), {DATE} (which inserts the current date), {PRINT} (which sends the previous merge to the printer), {NEXT RECORD} (which tells WordPerfect to get the next record in the secondary file), and {NEXT PRIMARY}*filename* ~ (which inserts another file from the disk into the document or, if no filename is specified, uses the current merge file).

Chapter 17

Publishing Flyers

Publishing flyers and other types of advertisements requires the same principles of design as other documents, with one exception: advertisements usually have more flamboyance and pizazz. In this chapter you will see three flyers of increasing flamboyance, yet all three remain within the bounds of good taste. These flyers will also demonstrate (among other things) the following WordPerfect features:

- Drawing rules (lines).

- Changing font typefaces, sizes, and appearances.

- Displaying graphics.

- Typing a hanging-indented paragraph.

- Making text right justified, with a ragged left margin.

- Adjusting the word and letter spacing (kerning).

You may not be able to reproduce all aspects of the examples given in this chapter, depending upon your software (graphics, clip art, and fonts) and your printer. If you can't follow a step or create an effect, use what you have to come as close as possible.

BEING CONSERVATIVE

The first sample flyer is shown in Figure 17.1. This flyer has the following features:

- A two-inch margin on both left and right.

- Horizontal lines with the Horizontal Position set to Left & Right, line width of 0.03″, and 100% gray shading (all black).

- The heading **BOOK SALE** typed with 12-point Times Roman set to bold Extra Large, with a space between each letter, two spaces between the words, and the Word/Letter Spacing set to 170% of optimal so that the title fits exactly between the left and right margins.

- The book titles set with 12-point Times Roman italic, the book description with 12-point Times Roman normal, and the price line set with 12-point Helvetica.

- The Ocean Breeze Bookstore title placed flush right in Very Large font, the address and motto also flush right but in normal 12-point Times Roman. This creates text with a ragged left edge.

B O O K S A L E

Computers on Parade by Rowland Compton. This is a combination tutorial and buyer's guide dealing with all popular brands of personal computers for home and business. Reg. $8.95. Sale **$6.29**.

Encyclopedia of Computers by Noah Ahl and Chip Hacking. This huge volume includes descriptions and definitions of all aspects of micro-, mini-, and main-frame computers. Reg. $117.50. Sale **$57.95**.

How to Play Master Chess by Chester Knight. A complete guide to tournament chess, written by a popular United States Chess Federation Certified Tournament Director. Includes opening, middle game, and end game tactics and strategy. Reg. $21.95. Sale **$16.29**.

How to Pray by Neil Downey and Theo Goodsell. For the religious and nonreligious alike, this book is a collection of twelve interesting essays and five amazing anecdotes on prayer, written by well known evangelists, scientists, and ordinary people. Reg. $12.95. Sale **$8.29**.

You will find many more outstanding titles now on sale, 10% to 50% off. All software in the store is discounted 10% to 20%. Hurry while supplies last.

Ocean Breeze Bookstore
1212 San Ysidro Avenue, San Diego, CA 92101

Quality service since 1966

Figure 17.1 Book Sale announcement, a conservative flyer from Ocean Breeze Bookstore.

- Advance Down specified at 0.1″ at the beginning of the title line to leave extra space between the top horizontal line and the title.

- The figure options set to the following:

Border Style:	**None** (on all four sides)
Outside Border Space:	**0.17″** (on all four sides)
Inside Border Space:	**0″** (on all four sides)
Gray shading:	**0%**

- The Ocean Breeze Bookstore logo (book and disk) set as a figure with the definition:

Filename:	**BOOK.PCX** (from PC Paintbrush); you could use BOOK.WPG on the WordPerfect Graphics disk.
Caption:	(none)
Type:	**Paragraph**
Vertical Position:	**0″**
Horizontal Position:	**Left**
Size:	**1.5″ wide ″ × ″ high**
Wrap:	**No**

By carefully inspecting Figure 17.1 and using the above features, you could probably reproduce the flyer on your own. For this example, however, we will give the step-by-step procedure for creating the flyer. This will serve as a review of the WordPerfect commands covered earlier in this book.

Setting the Margins and Drawing a Line

Step 1.   Set the margins to 2″: **Format** (Shift-F8), **1** (Line), **7** (Margins), **2**, **Enter**, **2**, **Enter**, **Exit** (F7).

Step 2.   Draw the top line: **Graphics** (Alt-F9), **5** (Line), **1** (Horizontal), **4** (Width of Line), 0.03, **Enter**, **Exit** (F7) (to return to the document screen), **Enter** (to go down to the next line).

Creating the Title

Step 1.   Set the font: **Font** (Ctrl-F8), **4** (Base **F**ont), move the cursor to Times Roman and set the font size to 12-point.

Some printers (such as the Hewlett-Packard LaserJet) give the base font as 12-pt Times Roman and do not have you specify the font size separately from the font itself. Other printers (such as the Apple LaserWriter) give the base font typeface without a point size and then you must specify the size in a separate step.

Step 2.   Advance down 0.1 ″: **Format** (Shift-F8), **4** (Other), **1** (Advance), **2** (**D**own), 0.1, **Enter**, **Exit** (F7).

Step 3.   Set font to extra large and bold: **Center** (Shift-F6), **Font** (Ctrl-F8), **1** (**S**ize), **7** (Ext Large), **Bold** (F6).

Step 4.   Set the Word/Letter Spacing to 170% of optimal: **Format** (Shift-F8), **4** (**O**ther), **6** (Printer Functions), **3** (Word Spacing), **3** (Percent of Optimal), 170, **Enter**, **3** (Percent of Optimal), 170, **Enter**, **Exit** (F7).

If you created the KERN macro in Chapter 16, "Publishing Letters," you can use the macro in this step instead of the procedure given here.

Step 5.   Type the title, with one space between each letter and two spaces between the words: **Caps Lock**, B O O K   S A L E, **Caps Lock** (to turn *off* the caps lock), **End** (to move past the [bold] and [ext large] codes, **Enter** (to go down a line).

Step 6.   Reset the word/letter spacing back to 100% of optimal by repeating step 4 above, except type 100 instead of 170.

Now draw another line exactly as you did above in step 2 under "Setting the Margins and Drawing a Line," and press **Enter** three times to triple-space after the second line.

Typing the Book Descriptions

Step 1.   Create a hanging-indented paragraph: **Indent** (F4), **Left Margin Release** (Shift-Tab).

This makes the first line of the paragraph flush with the left margin but indents the subsequent lines of the paragraph.

Step 2.   Type the book title, by-line, and description: **Font** (Ctrl-F8), **2** (Appearance), **4** (Italc), Computers on Parade, **Right Arrow** (to move past the italics code and return to normal appearance), by Rowland

Compton. This is a combination tutorial and buyer's guide dealing with all popular brands of personal computers for home and business.

Step 3.   Type the price line: **Space Bar**, **Font** (Ctrl-F8), **4** (Base Font), select 12-point Helvetica, Reg. $8.95. Sale, **Space Bar**, **Bold** (F6), $6.29, **Bold** (F6) (to turn *off* bold), period (.), **Enter** twice (to double-space between book descriptions).

Step 4.   Return the base font to Times Roman: **Font** (Ctrl-F8), **4** (Base Font), and select 12-point Times Roman.

Step 5.   Repeat steps 1 through 4 for the other three books.

Step 6.   After the last book description, triple-space (press **Enter** three times) and then type the final paragraph that begins You will find many more outstanding titles.

Setting the Figure Options

Step 1.   Access the Figure Options menu: **Graphics** (Alt-F9), **1** (Figure), **4** (Options).

Step 2.   Set the border style: **1** (Border Style), **1** (None) four times.

Step 3.   Press **Exit** (F7) to leave the other options with their default values.

Inserting the Figure

Step 1.   Create a figure: **Graphics** (Alt-F9), **1** (Figure), **1** (Create).

The Definition: Figure menu appears on the screen.

Step 2.   Retrieve the graphics file: **1** (Filename), type the name of the file, and press **Enter**; or press **List** (F5) to get a listing of the current directory, select a new directory if necessary, and retrieve the desired graphics file.

Step 3.   Keep the vertical position at its default value (1 ″) and set the horizontal position: **5** (Horizontal Position), **1** (Left).

Step 4.   Set the figure size: **6** (Size), **3** (Both Width and Height), 1.5, **Enter**, 1.0, **Enter**.

Step 5.   Turn *off* Wrap Text Around Box: **7** (Wrap Text Around Box), **N** (No).

Step 6.   Edit the figure as desired: **8** (Edit), and then move, scale, rotate, or invert the image; when done, press **Exit** (F7) twice to return to the document screen.

Typing the Address and Motto

The company name, address, and motto are flush right with a ragged left edge. To create this effect, follow these steps:

Step 1. Change the font to 10-point Times Roman.

Step 2. Type the company name: **Format** (Shift-F8), **1** (Line), **3** (Justification), **3** (Right), **Exit** (F7), (to put the text against the right margin), **Font** (Ctrl-F8), **1** (Size), **6** (Vry Large), Ocean Breeze Bookstore, **End** (to move past the codes), **Enter** (to go down to the next line).

Step 3. Type the address: 1212 San Ysidro Avenue, San Diego, CA 92101, **Enter** twice (to go down two lines).

Step 4. Type the motto: **Font** (Ctrl-F8), **2** (Appearance), **4** (Italc), Quality service since 1966.

This completes the creation of the flyer in Figure 17.1. You should now save the file to the disk and print the document.

PUBLISHING WITH PIZAZZ

The advertisement in Figure 17.2 is still conservative, but it's more eye-catching than Figure 17.1: The heading and graphics are larger, the type is Bookman (less conservative than Times Roman), and the writing is livelier.

The features of Figure 17.2 follow. We will not give you a step-by-step procedure for creating these effects but will rather give you references, where appropriate, to those chapters of the book that explain the features.

• Justification is turned *off* (set to Left Justification). See "Justifying Text" in Chapter 4, "Formatting Documents."

• The figure options are left at their default settings. See Chapter 9, "Displaying Graphics."

• The figure of the stacks of money in the upper left corner of Figure 17.2 has the following definition features:

Filename:	**MONEY.PLT**, a clip art image from Harvard Graphics. The figure BILLS from CURRENCY.SYM was exported in HPGL format.
Caption:	(none)

HOW TO SAVE A BUNDLE ON THE BOOKS YOU BUY.

For a limited time only, Ocean Breeze Bookstore will send you three books for three bucks. Any books in stock. No questions asked. No obligations.

Here's how it works. Come into Ocean Breeze Bookstore and pick out your three books* and pay only $3.00. Then, each month you will receive the *Ocean Breeze Bulletin* describing our Book of the Month selection and other books of special interest, all at 10% off the retail price. If you want the book of the month, do nothing. We will send you the book automatically. If you want another selection or no selection at all, just return a postcard to let us know your desires. It's just that easy.

*For a book to qualify, it must have a minimum retail price of $8. A book between $20 and $30 counts as two books. A book over $30 counts as all three of your book selections.

Ocean Breeze Book Club
1212 San Ysidro Ave., San Diego, CA 92101
Phone 1-800-BOOKBUY

Figure 17.2 An Ocean Breeze Book Club advertisement.

Type:	**Paragraph**
Vertical Position:	**0″**
Horizontal Position:	**Left**
Size:	**3.25″ wide × 2.74″ (high)**
Wrap:	**Yes**

For information on creating graphics and using clip art, see Chapter 8, "Creating Graphics."

• The second figure (in the right, middle position on the page) has the following definition features:

Filename:	**BOOK.WPG**, from the Publisher's PicturePak included with WordPerfect.
Caption:	(none)
Type:	**Paragraph**
Vertical Position:	**0″**
Horizontal Position:	**Right**
Size:	**3.25″ wide × 2.25″ (high)**
Wrap:	**Yes**

See Chapter 9, "Displaying Graphics."

• The headline (**HOW TO SAVE A BUNDLE ON THE BOOKS YOU BUY**) has the following attributes:

Font:	**Helvetica Narrow, 48-point**
Word/Letter Spacing:	**90% of Optimal** (to kern the characters closer together)
Justification:	**No**

The main body of text has the following attributes:

Font:	**Bookman Light, 12-point**
Word/Letter Spacing:	**100% of Optimal**
Justification:	**Left**

See Chapter 4, "Formatting Documents," and Chapter 11, "Using Fonts."

- The footnote (marked with * under the body of the text) is 10-point Times Roman.

- The company name has the following attributes:

Font:	**Helvetica Narrow, 48-point**
Word/Letter Spacing:	**95% of Optimal**
Position:	**Centered left to right**

- The address and phone number are 14-point Bookman Light and centered left to right.

This completes the description of features for Figure 17.2.

FASHIONING FLAMBOYANT FLYERS

Figure 17.3 is the most eye-catching of the three flyers: It has an enormous headline in an unusual type (Adobe's Revue), and the text was written more for effect than for information.

Yet the design and message are simple and clear, and except for an oversized headline, the flyer follows the basic elements of design given in Chapter 3, "Designing Documents."

Figure 17.3 has the following features:

- The headline is 140-point Revue (a PostScript font available from Adobe Systems Incorporated).

- The figure options are the defaults, except that the border style is **None** on all four sides.

- The figure has the following definition settings:

Filename:	**BOOK.WPG** (a clip art image from the Publisher's PicturePak supplied with WordPerfect)
Type:	**Page**
Vertical Position:	**2.5"**
Horizontal Position:	**3.25"**
Size	**3.5" wide × 2.42" (high)**
Wrap Text Around Box:	**No**

READ A BOOK

Read about agriculture, airplanes, alpacas, armies, automobiles, banking, baseball, billiards, biology, blood, cancer, candy, carpentry, cats, chess, cities, danger, delicatessens, depression, desire, dogs, . . . widows, willows, wind, windows, wisdom, X chromosomes, x-rays, xenon, xerography, xylophones, yachts, Yankees, yawning, Yugoslavia, yuletide, zebras, zinc, Zionism, zodiac, zoology.

Get the full story. The details. The inside scoop. The romance. The passion. Get them from a book.

A message from

Ocean Breeze Bookstore
1212 San Ysidro Ave., San Diego, CA 92101. Quality service since 1966.

Figure 17.3 The "Read A Book" flyer, showing an oversized headline.

- The font of the main body of text is 10-point Bookman Light with kerning turned *on*.

    To turn *on* kerning, press **Format** (Shift-F8), **4** (**O**ther), **6** (**P**rinter Function), **1** (**K**erning), **Y** (Yes).

- The bookstore name is centered, extra large (from a base font of 10-point Bookman), outline text.

- The address and motto are 10-point Times Roman.

This completes the specifications for the flyer in Figure 17.3.

SUMMARY

In this chapter you have seen how to create three flyers using a wide variety of WordPerfect features, including: drawing lines; changing font typefaces, sizes, and appearances; displaying graphics; typing a paragraph with a hanging indent; making ragged left text with the Flush Right feature; and adjusting the word and letter spacing (kerning).

Chapter 18

Publishing Forms

PUBLISHING AN ORDER FORM
  Creating the Title
  Creating the Fill-in Blanks
  Making the "For Bookstore Use Only" Box
  Typing the Name and Address Blanks
  Creating the Check Box
  Drawing the Bottom Line

PUBLISHING A JOB APPLICATION

PUBLISHING A QUESTIONNAIRE

SUMMARY

Businesses and individuals require many forms: order forms, check registers, daily planners, meeting planners, schedules, financial statements, invoices, travel itineraries, travel reports, telephone logs, job applications, surveys, questionnaires, . . . and the list goes on.

Producing these forms yourself is an excellent use of desktop publishing. There is no need to wait for an outside publisher, no need to fuss with mail orders, and no need to ever run out of forms. You can design, create, print, modify, and reprint the forms quickly and efficiently, all within your own office. In this chapter you will see three example forms: a book order form, a job application, and a questionnaire. These forms give examples of the following desktop publishing tasks:

- Creating interesting titles and headlines.

- Making check lists and check boxes.

- Producing "Do not write in this space" boxes.

PUBLISHING AN ORDER FORM

To create the order form in Figure 18.1, use the following procedures.

Creating the Title

Step 1.   Set the margins: **Format** (Shift-F8), **1** (Line), **7** (Margins), **1.5**, **Enter**, **1.5**, **Enter**, **Exit** (F7).

Step 2.   Draw the top line: **Graphics** (Alt-F9), **5** (Line), **1** (Horizontal), **4** (Width of Line), **0.03**, **Enter**, **Exit** (F7) (to return to the document screen), **Enter** (to go down to the next line).

Step 3.   Set the figure options so that the company logo (book and disk) has no border: **Graphics** (Alt-F9), **1** (Figure), **4** (Options), **1** (Border), **1** (None) four times (for each of the four sides of the figure), **Exit** (F7) (to return to the document screen).

Step 4.   Create the logo (book and disk): **Graphics** (Alt-F9), **1** (Figure), **1** (Create), **1** (Filename), type the name of the figure (you can use BOOK.WPG, supplied with WordPerfect as a clip art image from Publisher's PicturePak, or any other figure you have created), **Enter**, **5** (Horizontal Position), **1** (Left), **6** (Size), **3** (Both Width and Height), **1.5**, **Enter**, **1.5**, **Enter**, **8** (Edit) (to move, scale, rotate, or invert the figure as desired), **Exit** (F7) (to return to the Definition: Figure menu), **Exit** (F7) (to return to the document screen), **Enter** (to go down a line).

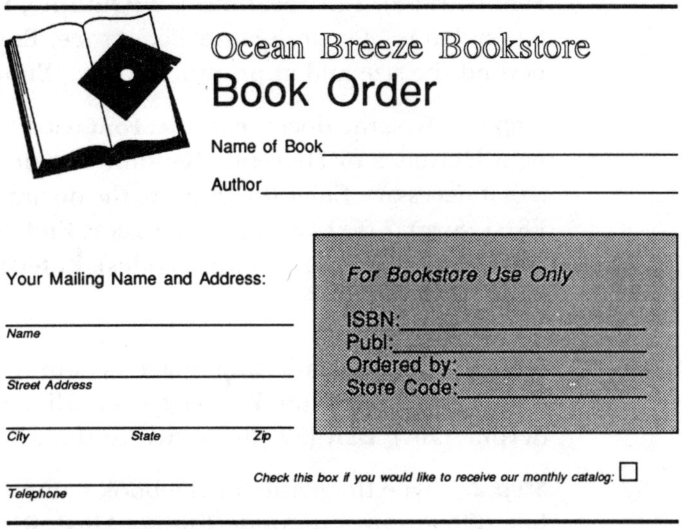

Ocean Breeze Bookstore
Book Order

Name of Book_____

Author_____

Your Mailing Name and Address:

_____
Name

_____
Street Address

_____
City   *State*   *Zip*

_____
Telephone

For Bookstore Use Only

ISBN:_____
Publ:_____
Ordered by:_____
Store Code:_____

Check this box if you would like to receive our monthly catalog: ☐

Figure 18.1 A sample order form.

Step 5. Type the company name: **Font** (Ctrl-F8), **4** (Base Font), highlight Times Roman or Times Roman 12-point, **1** (Select), type the point size (12) if necessary, **Enter** (to return to the document screen), **Font** (Ctrl-F8), **2** (Appearance), **5** (Outline), **Font** (Ctrl-F8), **1** (Size), **6** (Vry Large), Ocean Breeze Bookstore, **End** (to move the cursor beyond the size and appearance codes), **Enter** (to go down a line).

Step 6. Type the document title: **Font** (Ctrl-F8), **4** (Base Font), highlight Helvetica or Helvetica 10-point, **1** (Select), type the point size (10) if necessary, **Enter** (to return to the document screen), **Font** (Ctrl-F8), **1** (Size), **7** (Ext Large), Book Order, **End** (to move the cursor beyond the size and appearance codes), **Enter** twice (to go down two lines).

Creating the Fill-in Blanks

Step 1. Set the Underline Space/Tabs to on: **Format** (Shift-F8), **4** (Other), **7** (Underline), **Y** (Yes) (to underline spaces), **Y** (Yes) (to underline tabs), **Exit** (F7) (to return to the document screen).

Step 2. Type the blank for the book name: Name of Book, **Underline** (F8), (to turn on underlining), **Flush Right** (Alt-F6) (to draw a line to the right margin), **End** (to move past the flush right and underline code), **Enter** twice (to go down two lines).

Step 3. Type the blank for the author: Author, **Underline** (F8), **Flush Right** (Alt-F6), **End**, **Enter** three times (to move the cursor below the logo figure box).

Making the "For Bookstore Use Only" Box

Step 1. Set the text box options: **Graphics** (Alt-F9), **3** (Text Box), **4** (Options), **1** (Border Style), **2** (Single) four times (to set the border to single lines), **3** (Inside Border Space), 0.25 and **Enter** four times (to set the inside border space to one-quarter inch on all four sides), **9** (Gray Shading), 20, **Enter** (to set the gray shading to 20%), **Exit** (F7) (to return to the document screen).

Step 2. Create the text box: **Graphics** (Alt-F9), **3** (Text Box), **1** (Create), **6** (Size), **1** (Width), **3**, **Enter**, **8** (Edit).

Step 3. Type the text in the box: **Font** (Ctrl-F8), **4** (Base Font), select 12-point Helvetica, **Font** (Ctrl-F8), **2** (Appearance), **4** (Italc), For Bookstore Use Only, **Right Arrow** (to move past italics code), **Enter**, **Enter**, ISBN:, **Format** (Shift-F8), **4** (Other), **7** (Underline), **Y** (Yes), **Y** (Yes), **Exit** (F7), **Underline** (F8), **Flush Right** (Alt-F6) (to draw a blank line), **End** (to move past the underline and flush right codes), **Enter**, Publ:,

Underline (F8), Flush Right (Alt-F6), End, Enter, Ordered by:, Underline (F8), Flush Right (Alt-F6), End, Enter, Store Code:, Underline (F8), Flush Right (Alt-F6), Exit (F7) twice (to return to the document screen), Enter twice (to go down two lines).

Typing the Name and Address Blanks

Step 1. Your Mailing Name and Address:, **Enter**, **Enter**.

Step 2. **Underline** (F8), **Flush Right** (Alt-F6) (to draw a blank line from the left margin to the text box on the right), **End** (to move past the codes), **Enter**, **Font** (Ctrl-F8), **1** (Size), **4** (Small), **Font** (Ctrl-F8), **2** (Appearance), **4** (Italc), Name, **End** (to move the cursor past the codes), **Enter** twice (to go down two lines).

Step 3. Repeat step 2 twice, but instead of typing Name, type Street Address the first time and City, **Tab**, **Tab**, State, **Tab**, **Tab**, Zip the second time.

Step 4. Type the telephone number blank: **Underline** (F8) and **Tab** three times, **End**, **Enter**, **Font** (Ctrl-F8), **1** (Size), **4** (Small), **Font** (Ctrl-F8), **2** (Appearance), **4** (Italc), Telephone.

Creating the Check Box

Step 1. Press **Up Arrow** to move the cursor to the line containing the blank space for the telephone number.

Step 2. **End** (to move the cursor past the blank line and associated codes), **Tab**, **Font** (Ctrl-F8), **1** (Size), **4** (Small), **Font** (Ctrl-F8), **2** (Appearance), **4** (Italc), Check this box if you would like to receive our monthly catalog:, **End** (to move past codes).

Step 3. Set the text box options for the check box: **Graphics** (Alt-F9), **3** (Text Box), **4** (Options), **1** (Border Style), **2** (Single) four times (to set the border to single lines), **9** (Gray Shading), **0**, **Enter** (to set the gray shading to 0%, white), **Exit** (F7) (to return to the document screen).

Step 4. Create the check box: **Space Bar** twice (to space between the text and the check box), **Graphics** (Alt-F9), **3** (Text Box), **1** (Create), **3** (Type), **3** (Character), **6** (Size), **3** (Both Width and Height), 0.15, **Enter**, 0.15, **Enter**, **Exit** (F7) (to return to the document screen).

Drawing the Bottom Line

Step 1. Move the cursor to the end of the document: **Home, Home, Down Arrow**.

Step 2.   Draw the line:, **Enter, Enter** (to double-space between text and the bottom line), **Graphics** (Alt-F9), **5** (Line), **1** (Horizontal), **4** (Width of Line), 0.03, **Enter, Exit** (F7) (to return to the document screen).

This completes the creation of Figure 18.1. You may now save and print the document.

PUBLISHING A JOB APPLICATION

The front page of the job application in Figure 18.2 demonstrates two special desktop publishing techniques:

- Creating a two-part headline.

  Notice that the headline in Figure 18.2 has two lines on the left (for **JOB APPLICATION**) and three lines on the right (for the company name and address) within the same vertical dimensions. The trick to creating this effect is to use WordPerfect's columns feature.

- Creating left-margin headings.

  Notice that the headings (**Application, Applicant, Education**, and **Experience**) are in the left margin. The trick to creating this effect is to use WordPerfect's **Left Margin Release** (Shift-Tab) command and a simple macro.

The job application in Figure 18.2 has the following characteristics:

- The heading was creating with WordPerfect's column feature: **Math/Columns** (Alt-F7), **4** (Column **D**ef), **Enter** (to accept all the column definition defaults and return to the document screen), **3** (**C**olumn On/Off) (to turn on column mode).

- The title **JOB APPLICATION** is 25-point Helvetica.

- The three lines of the company name and address are typed with the **Flush Right** (Alt-F6) command. You could also use Right Justification (ragged left).

- The company name Ocean Breeze Bookstore has the base font of 12-point Times Roman, with the size set to Very Large and the appearance set to Outline. See Chapter 11, "Using Fonts," for a description of how to set the font typeface, size, and appearance.

- The address is normal 12-point Times Roman.

JOB APPLICATION

Ocean Breeze Bookstore
1212 San Ysidro Avenue
San Diego, CA 92101

Application

Today's date_____
Type of job (check one):
_____Custodian   _____Accounting
_____Stock/freight/labor   _____Purchasing
_____Sales clerk   _____Marketing/Advertising
_____Section manager   _____Corporate management

Applicant

Name_____
Address_____
City_____State_____Zip_____
Telephone_____

Friend or relative with a different telephone number where you can be contacted:

Name_____
Telephone_____

Education

Check highest level of education:
_____No diploma   _____M.S. or equivalent
_____H.S. diploma   _____Ph.D. or equivalent
_____Associate degree   _____Other. Specify:
_____B.S./B.A. or equivalent   _____

Major or specialty_____
Please attach transcript of grades and copy of your diploma.

Experience

Please list your work experience during the past 10 years. Give your most recent employment first. Make sure all time periods are accounted for.

Starting date_____Ending date_____
Job title/Description_____
Company/Institution_____
Supervisor_____Telephone_____
May we contact this supervisor?   _____Yes   _____No
Reason for leaving job_____

Figure 18.2 The front page of a job application.

- The heading was terminated by turning off column mode: **Math/Columns** (Alt-F7), **3** (**C**olumn On/Off).

- The thick horizontal line underneath the title has a vertical position of 1.74 (use WordPerfect's advance feature to move the cursor to that position before drawing the line). See "Positioning Text: Advance" in Chapter 4, "Formatting Documents."

- The line under the title has the horizontal position set to **Left & Right**, the line width to 0.05″, and the gray shading to 100%. See Chapter 7, "Drawing Lines and Boxes," for a description of how to draw a horizontal line.

- The body of the document has a left margin of 2.5″, a right margin of 1″, and tab stops at every 0.5″ except 1.5″ and 2″. See Chapter 4, "Formatting Documents," for a description of how to set the margins and the tabs.

- The headings in the left margin were created with the following macro: **Macro Def** (Ctrl-F10), head (the macro name), **Enter**, Create heading (the macro description), **Left Margin Release** (Shift-Tab), **Font** (Ctrl-F8), **4** (**B**ase Font), **N** (**N**ame Search), helvetica bold, **Enter**, **Enter**, 14, **Enter** (or whatever steps are required to set the font to 14-point Helvetica Bold), **Macro Commands** (Ctrl-PgUp), **1** (**P**ause), Application, **Enter**, **Font** (Ctrl-F8), **4** (**B**ase Font), **N** (**N**ame Search), times roman, **Enter**, **Enter**, 12, **Enter** (or whatever steps are required to set the font to 12-point Times Roman), **Indent** (F4), **Font** (Ctrl-F8) (to turn off macro definition). Execute this macro to create the other three headings: **Macro** (Alt-F10), head **Enter**, type the heading, **Enter**.

- The rules (blank lines) were drawn by setting the Underline Spaces/Tabs to on: **Format** (Shift-F8), **4** (**O**ther), **7** (**U**nderline), **Y** (**Y**es), **Y** (**Y**es). You can then type the text and blank lines using **Underline** (F8), **Flush Right** (Alt-F6), and **Tab**, as required.

Although the previous description of the document in Figure 18.2 is only an outline, you should be able to create the document (or others like it) from the information you learned earlier in this book.

PUBLISHING A QUESTIONNAIRE

Figure 18.3 shows the first page of a questionnaire (or survey). The document has several unique features:

- The title QUESTIONNAIRE is reversed (also called surprinted or dropout) text.

- The thick lines surrounding half the title and the entire company name and address is a special application of a graphics (text) box.

- The check boxes demonstrate two features: boxes with thick border lines on the right and bottom, and the use of styles.

To create the document in Figure 18.3, follow this procedure (check previous chapters in the book for the detailed key commands):

Step 1. Set the top and bottom margins to 0.5″.

Step 2. Specify the user-defined box options for the thick-lined box that surrounds the company address: **Graphics** (Alt-F9), **4** (User-defined box), **4** (**O**ptions), and then set the following:

Border Style:	**Thick** (on all four sides)
Outside and Inside Border Styles:	**0″** (for both on all four sides)
Gray shading:	**0%**

Step 3. Create the box: **Graphics** (Alt-F9), **4** (User-defined Box), **1** (**C**reate), then set the following attributes:

Type:	**Page**
Vertical Position:	**0.88″**
Horizontal Position:	**1.75″**
Size:	**5″ wide × 1.13″ high**
Wrap Text Around Box:	**No**

After specifying the attributes, press **Exit** (F7) to return to the document screen. In general, if you want boxes to appear on top of or in front of another box (as in Figure 18.3), create the bottom one first and the top one last. Make the boxes of type Page so that they can occupy the same or overlapping areas on the page.

QUESTIONNAIRE

OCEAN BREEZE BOOKSTORE
1212 San Ysidro Avenue, San Diego, CA 92101

At Ocean Breeze Bookstore, *quality service* is more than a motto; it is our way of doing business. Would you please take a moment to answer a few questions to help us serve you better?

Check only one box for each question unless asked to do otherwise.

What is the distance from your home to the nearest Ocean Breeze Bookstore?
- [ ] Less than 2 miles.
- [ ] 2 or more but less than 5 miles.
- [ ] 5–10 miles.
- [ ] Greater than 10 miles.

What is the distance from your workplace to the nearest Ocean Breeze Bookstore?
- [ ] Less than 2 miles.
- [ ] 2–5 miles.
- [ ] Greater than 5 but less than 10 miles.
- [ ] Greater than 10 miles.

How many books do you purchase each year *for yourself?*
- [ ] Fewer than 2 books.
- [ ] 2–5 books.
- [ ] More than 5 but fewer than 10 books.
- [ ] More than 10 books per year.

How many books do you purchase each year *for others?*
- [ ] Fewer than 2 books.
- [ ] 2–5 books.
- [ ] More than 5 but fewer than 10 books.
- [ ] More than 10 books per year.

Figure 18.3 The first page of a questionnaire.

Step 4. Set the base font to 12-point Times Roman.

Step 5. Specify the text box options for the reversed text of the title:

Border Style:	**None** (on all four sides)
Outside Border Space:	**0″** (on all four sides)
Inside Border Space:	**0.1″** on left, right, and bottom; **0.2″** on top
Gray Shading:	**100%**

Step 6. Create the text box of the reversed title with the following attributes:

Type:	**Paragraph**
Vertical Position:	**0″**
Horizontal Position:	**Center**
Size:	**4.25″ wide × 0.76″ (high)**
Wrap Text Around Box:	**Yes**
Edit	Specify **Extra Large, White, Centered, Bold** text for QUES-TIONNAIRE

For information on creating text boxes, see Chapter 7, "Drawing Lines and Boxes." For information on font sizes, appearances, and colors, see Chapter 11, "Using Fonts."

Step 7. Type the company name using the base font of 12-point Times Roman, Very Large size, Outline appearance, all caps and centered.

Step 8. Type the inside address in normal 12-point Times Roman, with a word/letter spacing (kerning) of 120% of optimal: **Format** (Shift-F8), **4** (**Other**), **6** (**Printer Functions**), **3** (**Word Spacing**), **3** (**Percent of Optimal**), **120**, **Enter**, **3** (**Percent of Optimal**), **120**, **Enter**, **Exit** (F7) (to return to the document screen).

Step 9.   Type the body of the questionnaire in 12-point ITC Bookman Light (or some other typeface of your choice). Be sure to return
the word/letter spacing to 100% of optimal before starting to type
the first paragraph.

Step 10.   When you get to the first question ("What is the distance
from your home . . ."), set the line height: **Format** (Shift-F8), **1** (**Line**),
4 (**Line Height**), **2** (**Fixed**), 0.22 (to set a fixed line height of 0.22"),
Enter, **Exit** (F7) (to return to the document screen).

We want a line height a little greater than the default to space the
questionnaire items slightly more apart and to leave space between
the check boxes (which will be 0.20" × 0.20").

Step 11.   When you get to the first check box, begin the creation
of a WordPerfect style as follows: **Style** (Alt-F8), **3** (**Create**), **1** (**Name**),
Check Box, **Enter**, **2** (**Type**), **2** (**Open**), **3** (**Description**), Draws a small
box, **Enter**, **4** (**Codes**).

The Style Codes window appears on the screen.

Step 12.   From within the Styles Codes window, press **Indent** (F4),
Graphics (Alt-F9), **4** (**User-defined box**), **4** (**Options**), and set the options to the following:

Border Style:	**Single, Thick, Single, Thick**
Outside Border Space:	**0"** (on all four sides)
Inside Border Space:	**0"** (on all four sides)
Gray Shading:	**0%**

Then press **Exit** (F7) to return to the Styles: Edit window.

Step 13.   Create the check box: **Graphics** (Alt-F9), **4** (**User-defined
Box**), **1** (**Create**), and specify the following attributes:

Type:	**Character**
Vertical Position:	**Top**
Size:	**0.2" wide × 0.2" high**
Wrap Text Around Box:	**Yes**

Then press **Exit** (F7) to return to the Styles: Edit window.

Step 14. Press the **Space Bar** to insert a space after the user-defined text box (the check box), and press **Exit** (F7) to return to the Styles: Edit menu, **Exit** (F7) again to return to the Styles menu, and **1** (**On**), to insert the first text box.

Step 15. Finish typing the questionnaire.

When you want to insert a check box, press **Style** (Alt-F8) and **Enter**, and then type the answer item.

This completes the description of how to create the questionnaire in Figure 18.3. You may wish to save the document to the disk and print it.

SUMMARY

In this chapter you have seen how to publish forms by creating an order form, a job application, and a questionnaire. In the process, you have also seen how to create blank lines using the Underline (F8) key with Underline Spaces/Tabs set to on, how to create "For Office Use Only" (or "Don't Write in This Space") boxes, how to create titles or headlines with special features, how to generate headings in the left margin, how to create check boxes, and how to use macros and styles to assist in document preparation.

Chapter 19

Publishing Newsletters

Your home or company newsletter may never be able to compete with the *Washington Post* or the *Los Angeles Times*. But with WordPerfect you will be able to create attractive newsletters that will fascinate your friends and impress your boss.

In this chapter you will see three sample newsletters that demonstrate how to produce the following desktop publishing features with WordPerfect:

- Strong titles and headlines.

- Enlarged initial letters.

- Vertical lines between newspaper-type columns.

- Columns of equal length.

- Columns of unequal width.

- Two or more text boxes or graphics boxes superimposed.

- Rotated text (to read vertically instead of horizontally).

Many of the other techniques required to produce a newsletter have been covered previously in this book.

CREATING THE NEWSLETTER

Before we discuss the specific procedures and techniques of publishing a newsletter, let's review the general steps for creating a newsletter. These suggested steps give the order of production (after you have made the pencil design for the document and created the graphics) that we have found to be most convenient.

The Order of Production

Step 1. Create the title.

Step 2. Define the columns and turn *on* column mode.

Most newsletters are formatted with two or three columns per page. If your newsletter doesn't use multiple columns, skip this step.

Step 3. Create the macros and/or styles for the headlines.

This step often involves specifying a different typeface (such as Helvetica) and a different font size from the base font.

Step 4. Type (or retrieve) the written copy for the body of the newsletter.

Step 5.   Insert headlines, graphics, horizontal rules (lines), sidebars, pull quotes, page numbering, headers or footers, table of contents, and index, as desired; check the spelling; proofread the text; polish the prose.

At this stage, *all* text and graphics (except vertical lines) should be in your newsletter just as you want them, edited and polished. The final three steps (6 through 8) add the final touches.

Step 6.   Set the hyphenation zone, turn *on* hyphenation, and move the cursor to the end of the document.

WordPerfect will hyphenate (or help you manually hyphenate) each word that spans the hyphenation zone. You will save yourself time by leaving hyphenation *off* until all the text is typed, edited, and polished.

Step 7.   Adjust the column lengths as desired.

For aesthetic reasons, you will want columns on the same page to be the same length. You can adjust the column length by several methods, as explained below.

Step 8.   Draw the vertical lines.

Wait until the very end before drawing vertical rules (lines) so you will know exactly how long they need to be. If you try to draw the lines (for example, to separate columns) before the column lengths are known, you will have to edit the lines once the column lengths are set.

The order of these steps isn't crucial until you get to steps 6, 7, and 8, which should be the third-to-the-last, the next-to-the-last, and the last steps in your newsletter production.

Techniques for Adjusting Column Lengths

You will need to adjust the length of newsletter columns for two main reasons:

- To fill a page or a region of the page with text.

  Awkward blank space in your newsletter is unattractive; designed white space is attractive (see Chapter 3, "Designing Documents").

- To make columns even at the bottom of the page.

Use one of the following techniques to adjust the column length:

* Add or delete copy.

  This may not be as difficult as you think. If the column needs to be longer, you can usually think of one more tidbit of information that could be inserted. You could add a pull quote (a short quote from the article) or filler (a short joke, proverb, or adage, added after an article).

* Change the bottom margin.

  You can change the bottom margin by trial and error until the columns on a page are even. (See Chapter 6, "Generating Columns.") This technique works best if the newsletter is one page in length or is on the last page of a multiple-page newsletter. This technique does not work well on a middle page of a news-letter, since you usually want the margins of all the middle pages to be the same.

* Change the line height.

  Small changes in the line height can lead to significant changes in the column length.

* Use WordPerfect's Advance Up and Advance Down feature.

  For example, use advance up or advance down to put headlines and text closer together or farther apart to make subtle adjust-ments in the position of the beginning and ending of an article.

* Keep the text unjustified (ragged right) and then use a hard return where you want one column to end and another one to begin.

  This technique does not work with justified text, since the last line of the column (the line that ends with a hard return) will not be justified).

PRODUCING THE OCEAN BREEZE BANNER

The *Ocean Breeze Banner* newsletter (Figure 19.1)—for customers of the Ocean Breeze Bookstore—is simple but exemplifies many im-portant desktop publishing techniques.

Ocean Breeze Banner

San Diego, California, February 1989

Published by Ocean Breeze Bookstore   Volume 5 Number 3

Autograph Signing

Ocean Breeze Bookstore is pleased to announce an autograph signing party to be held February 8, 1989, to honor local author Grace Fuller. A former member of the Southern California Civic Ballet, Ms. Fuller will be on hand to autograph her new book, *Dance, Ballerina, Dance*, published by Turner Press and currently a national best-seller.

Children's Story Hour

Take advantage of Children's Story Hour, every Friday from 2:00 to 3:00 p.m. at the Central City Public Library. This month Stella Torrey will read children's fairy tales. Parents attending the story hour with their children will receive a coupon worth 10% off the price of any children's book at Ocean Breeze Bookstore.

Summer Reading Contest

Ocean Breeze Bookstore, Double Decker Ice Cream Store, and several school districts within the San Diego area are sponsoring a Summer Reading Contest. Elementary School students who set and reach summer reading goals will receive a free ice cream cone from Double Decker and are eligible to participate in a drawing for over $400 in books, software, and school supplies at Ocean Breeze Bookstore. The drawing is August 10, 1989. Information concerning the Summer Reading Contest and entry blanks are available at your local elementary school or at Ocean Breeze Bookstore.

Home Delivery

Do you need that special birthday book but don't have time to go to the store and pick it up? Are you anxious to start reading the latest best seller but don't have transportation to the bookstore? Do you want a book title but don't know where to find it?

If the answer to any of these questions is *yes*, then the new Ocean Breeze Bookstore Home Delivery Service is for you!

We will find your book and deliver it to your home within three working days, at no extra charge.

Just call our toll-free number 1-800-BOOKBUY and give us the title (and if possible the author and publisher) of the book you want. A representative from our store will make a free delivery to your home. You will be billed for the book later.

Figure 19.1 A simple version of the *Ocean Breeze Banner*.

Creating the Title

Follow these steps to create the title of the newsletter:

Step 1.   Set the font to 48-point Helvetica Narrow Bold.

If your printer doesn't support this typeface or font size, select the largest Helvetica font you have. If you have a question about how to set the font, see Chapter 11, "Using Fonts."

Step 2.   Type the title: **Center** (Shift-F6), Ocean Breeze Banner, **Enter**.

Step 3.   Change the base font to 12-point Times Roman.

Step 4.   Type the subheading: **Center** (Shift-F6), San Diego, California, February 1989, **Enter** three times (to triple space).

Step 5.   Set Underline Spaces/Tabs to *on*: **Format** (Shift-F8), **4** (**Other**), **7** (**Underline**), **Y** (**Yes**), **Y** (**Yes**).

Step 6.   Draw the top horizontal rule: **Underline** (F8), **Flush Right** (Alt-F6), **Enter** (to move the cursor past the underline and flush right codes), **Enter** (to go down a line).

Step 7.   Type the line of text: Published by Ocean Breeze Bookstore, **Flush Right** (Alt-F6), Volume 5 Number 3, **End**, **Enter**.

Step 8.   Draw the second horizontal rule: **Underline** (F8), **Flush Right** (Alt-F6), **End**, **Enter**.

Step 9.   Turn *off* justification: **Format** (Shift-F8), **1** (**Line**), **3** (**Justification**), **N** (**No**), **Exit** (F7).

Defining and Turning On Columns

Step 1.   Define the columns as newspaper type, with 0.25″ between each column, so that the column margins are 1″–3″, 3.25″–5.25″, 5.5″–7.5″, and then turn *on* column mode.

If you have questions on how to define and turn *on* columns, see Chapter 6, "Generating Columns."

Step 2.   Set the tab stops as − 1″, 0″, + 0.25″, + 2.25″, + 2.5″, + 4.5″, and + 4.75″.

Setting tab stops is discussed in Chapter 4, "Formatting Documents."

Creating a Headline and Enlarged Initial Letter

Step 1.   Type the first headline: Change the font to 12-point Helvetica, and use font size Large, **Bold** (F6), **Center** (Shift-F6), Autograph, **End** (to move the cursor past the codes), **Enter**, **Center** (Shift-F6), Signing, **End**, **Enter**, **Enter**.

Step 2. With the base font still at 12-point Helvetica, create the box options for the enlarged initial letter: **Graphics** (Alt-F9), **4** (User-defined Box), **4** (Options), **2** (Outside Border Space), **0**, **Enter**, **0**, **Enter**, **0**, **Enter**, **0**, **Enter** (to set all four outside borders to 0″), **Enter** (to return to the document screen).

Step 3. Create the user-defined box for the enlarged initial letter: **Graphics** (Alt-F9), **4** (User-defined Box), **1** (Create), **5** (Horizontal Position), **1** (Left), **6** (Size), **3** (Both Width and Height), 0.33, **Enter**, 0.36, **Enter** (to make the size 0.33″ × 0.36″), **8** (Edit), **Font** (Ctrl-F8), **1** (Size), **7** (Ext Large), **Bold** (F6), **O** (capital O, not zero), **Exit** (F7) twice (to return to the document screen).

The graphics box used to create an enlarged initial letter can be a figure, table, text box, or user-defined box. Just make sure the box is of type Paragraph and the horizontal position is Left. Specify a box size that is slightly larger than the letter within the box. Set the box option so that the inside and outside border space is 0″. Caution: If the box size is too small and you turn *on* hyphenation, WordPerfect will append a hyphen to the enlarged letter in an effort to make it fit within the box. The cure, of course, is to make the box size slightly bigger than the initial letter.

Typing the Body of the Newsletter

Step 1. Set the base font back to 12-point Times Roman.

Step 2. Type the first news item, starting with cean Breeze Book-store is pleased to announce an autograph signing party . . . . (The **O** in Ocean is the enlarged initial letter, so don't re-type it.)

Step 3. When you get to the end of the first article (. . . a national best-seller.), press **Enter** and draw the short horizontal rule: **Graphics** (Alt-F9), **5** (Line), **1** (Horizontal Line), **1** (Horizontal Position), **3** (Center), **2** (Length of Line), 1.25, **Enter**, **Exit** (F7) (to return to the document screen), **Enter** twice (to double-space to the next headline and news item).

Step 4. Type the remainder of the newsletter, using the procedures given above to create headlines, enlarged initial letters, and horizontal rules that separate new items.

The easiest way to create the other enlarged letters (since they are all about the same size, is to copy (using WordPerfect's block move feature) the user-box code and then edit the box with the new initial letter.

Setting the Hyphenation Zone and Hyphenating Words

Step 1. Set the hyphenation zone to 5%, 2%: **Format** (Shift-F8), **1** (Line), **2** (Hyphenation Zone), **5**, **Enter**, **2**, **Enter**.

Decreasing the left and right values of the hyphenation zone increases the amount of hyphenation and decreases the amount of raggedness along the right margins of the columns. See "Hyphenating Words" in Chapter 4, "Formatting Documents."

Step 2. With the Format: Line menu still on the screen, turn *on* hyphenation: **1** (Hyphenation), **2** (Manual), **Exit** (F7) (to return to the document screen).

Step 3. Press **Home, Home, Down Arrow** to move the cursor to the end of the document.

WordPerfect stops at words that need hyphenation and asks you to press **Cancel** (F1) if you don't want the word hyphenated, **Left Arrow** and **Right Arrow** to change the location of the hyphenation, or **Esc** to permit hyphenation and to move to the next word. In this example (Figure 19.1), most words suggested by WordPerfect for hyphenation should not be hyphenated.

Aligning the Bottoms of the Columns

Since Figure 19.1 is a short, one-page newsletter, the columns should be aligned at the bottom.

Step 1. Move the cursor to the beginning of the line that you want in column 2.

In Figure 19.1, move the cursor to the **r** in **receive a coupon**.

Step 2. Press **Hard Page** (Ctrl-Enter) to force the text to the next column.

Step 3. Move the cursor to the beginning of the line that you want in column 3, and press **Hard Page** (Ctrl-Enter).

In Figure 19.1, this position is just before the headline "Home Delivery."

Step 4. Since the second column is slightly longer than the first and third columns, use Advance Up to align the columns: move the cursor to the left of the code for user box 3 (**[Usr Box:3;;]**, the third enlarged initial letter), **Format** (Shift-F8), **4** (**O**ther), **1** (**A**dvance), **1** (**U**p), 0.08, **Enter**, **Exit** (F7).

This adjustment moves the text slightly closer to the headline in the article "Summer Reading Contest," significantly improving the overall appearance of the newsletter.

Drawing the Vertical Rules

You should have your newsletter completely prepared before drawing vertical rules (lines) so that you'll know exactly how long they need to be. To get the correct length, you sometimes have to use trial and error; or you can print the document without the lines, make the necessary horizontal and vertical measurements, and then insert the lines. In this example, follow these steps:

Step 1. Move the cursor to the immediate right of the code [**Col On**] that turns *on* column mode.

Step 2. Draw the vertical line between the first and second columns: **Graphics** (Alt-F9), **5** (**L**ine), **2** (**V**ertical Line), **1** (**H**orizontal Position), **3** (**B**etween Columns), **1**, **Enter** (to place the line to the right of column 1), **2** (**V**ertical Position), **5** (**S**et Position), 3.4, **Enter** (to begin the line 3.4″ from the top, the measured distance to the top of the columns), **3** (**L**ength of Line), 5.6, **Enter**, **Exit** (F7).

Step 3. Draw the vertical line between the second and third columns: **Graphics** (Alt-F9), **5** (**L**ine), **2** (**V**ertical Line), **1** (**H**orizontal Position), **3** (**B**etween Columns), **2**, **Enter** (to place the line to the right of column 2), **2** (**V**ertical Position), **5** (**S**et Position), 3.4, **Enter** (to begin the line 3.4″ from the top, the measured distance to the top of the columns), **3** (**L**ength of Line), 5.6, **Enter**, **Exit**.

This completes the preparation of Figure 19.1. You may now save the document to the disk and print the newsletter.

IMPROVING THE OCEAN BREEZE BANNER

The version of *Ocean Breeze Banner* in Figure 19.1 is simple and attractive, but the same headline size and same column width for all four news items is monotonous. The version of the *Ocean Breeze Banner* in Figure 19.2, on the other hand, creates excitement. The title is bold and attractive, the column widths vary, and the headlines appear in different sizes and weights.

Ocean Breeze BANNER

Volume 5 • Number 3 • February 1989

Autograph Signing

Ocean Breeze Bookstore is pleased to announce an autograph signing party to be held February 8, 1989, to honor local author Grace Fuller. A former member of the Southern California Civic Ballet, Ms. Fuller will be on hand to autograph her new book, *Dance, Ballerina, Dance*, published by Turner Press and currently a national best-seller.

Ocean Breeze Banner

Editor Ronald Rowan
Assoc. Editor Janice Jaynes

Technical Ed. Sam Simms
Copy Editor Alice Ahl

Marketing Malanie Moore
Book Reviews Bob Boren

Ocean Breeze Banner is a monthly publication of Ocean Breeze Bookstore, 1212 San Ysidro Ave., San Diego, CA 92101, (800) 266-5289 (1-800-BOOKBUY).

Summer Reading Contest
Children Encouraged to Read During the Summer

Ocean Breeze Bookstore, Double Decker Ice Cream Store, and several school districts within the San Diego area are sponsoring a Summer Reading Contest. Elementary School students who set and reach summer reading goals will receive a free ice cream cone from Double Decker and are eligible to participate in a drawing for over $400 in books, software, and school supplies at Ocean Breeze Bookstore. The drawing is August 10, 1989. Information concerning the Summer Reading Contest and entry blanks are available at your local elementary school or at Ocean Breeze Bookstore.

The rules for the contest are simple. Just have your child go to the office of your school or come into Ocean Breeze Bookstore and pick up the entry blank. Write the student's name, address, phone number, parent or guardian's name, school, grade, and teacher's name. Then indicate the reading goal for the summer—the number of pages or number of books. A parent or guardian *and* a school teacher must sign the entry blank to make sure that the reading goal is realistic. Guidelines for appropriate goals at each grade level appear on the entry form.

Children's Reading Hour at the Library

Take advantage of Children's Story Hour, every Friday from 2:00 to 3:00 p.m. at the Central City Public Library. This month Stella Torrey will read children's fairy tales. Parents attending the story hour with their children will receive a coupon worth 10% off the price of any children's book at Ocean Breeze Bookstore.

Figure 19.2 A more complex version of the *Ocean Breeze Banner.*

Creating the Title

The *Ocean Breeze Banner* title in Figure 19.2 has the following attributes:

- The outline of the large banner (but not the characters or graphics within the banner) was created with Harvard Graphics. You could use almost any graphics package to create the banner.

- The graphics figure options have the following settings:

Border Style:	**None** (on all four sides)
Outside Border Space:	**0″** (on all four sides)
Inside Border Space:	**0″** (on all four sides)
Gray Shading:	**0%** (white)

- The banner outline has the following settings:

Filename:	**BANNER.PLT** (created with Harvard Graphics, saved in HPGL format).
Caption:	(none)
Type:	**Page**
Vertical Position:	**Top**
Horizontal Position:	**1″**
Size:	**6.5″ wide × 2.5″ high**
Wrap Text Around Box:	**No**
Edit:	The scale of the banner outline should be expanded to fill the entire graphics box.

- "Ocean Breeze" is centered, 36-point, outline Times Roman.

- The Ocean Breeze Bookstore logo (book and disk) has the same figure options as the banner outline but has the following settings:

Filename:	**BOOK.PCX** (created with PC Paintbrush)
Type:	**Character**
Vertical Position:	**Center**
Size:	**0.7″ × 0.6″**
Wrap Text Around Box:	**Yes**

- The word "BANNER" in the title is a text box. Use Advance Down 0.1″ to leave white space between the Ocean Breeze Bookstore logo and the box. The text box has the following option settings:

Border Style:	**None** (on all four sides)
Outside Border Space:	**0.17″** (on all four sides)
Inside Border Space:	**0.1″** on left, right, and top; **0.3″** on bottom
Gray shading:	**65%**

- The text box itself has the following settings:

Type:	**Paragraph**
Vertical Position:	**0″**
Horizontal Position:	**Center**
Size:	**4.5″ wide × 0.8″ high**
Wrap Text Around Box:	**No**

The trick to creating complex titles such as the one in Figure 19.2 is to superimpose two or more graphics images or two or more text boxes. You can, in fact, superimpose as much text and graphics as you wish by making the boxes of type Page, setting Wrap Text Around Box to *No*, and specifying the desired horizontal and vertical positions.

- To create the text in the box, do the following: Set the font to 60-point Times Roman, the font color to White, and the font appearance to Bold; advance right 0.2″ to make the word more accurately centered in the text box; Set the word/letter spacing (kerning) to 115% of optimal before the **B** in **BANNER**, to 120% after the **B** and before the **A**, to 130% after the **A** and before the first **N**, and to 125% after the first **N** in **BANNER**.

The individual kerning within the word **BANNER** creates an even amount of space between the letters. Notice that in Figure 19.3A the **A** in **BANNER** has too much space around it, while in Figure 19.3B the letters are more aesthetically spaced.

- The volume, number, and date are in 12-point Times Roman, centered on the page, with word/letter spacing set to 140% of optimal. The black dot (bullet) separating the items is the Word-Perfect special character 4,0: **Compose** (Ctrl-V), 4,0, **Enter**.

Creating the Body of Text

The main body of text in Figure 19.2 has the following characteristics:

- The base font is 12-point Times Roman.

- Kerning is turned *on* and the word spacing justification limits are set: **Format** (Shift-F8), **4** (**Other**), **6** (Printer Functions), **1** (Kerning), **Y** (Yes), **4** (Word Spacing Justification Limits), 60, **Enter**, 150, **Enter**, **Exit** (F7).

- The tab settings are as follows: $-1''$, $-0.5''$, $0''$, $+0.25''$, $+2.25''$, $+2.5''$.

- The columns settings are as follows: Newspaper type with margins for the first column at $1''$ and $3''$, and for the second column at $3.25''$ and $7.5''$.

- The first and third headlines are 18-point Helvetica.

A: **BANNER**

B: **BANNER**

Figure 19.3 (A) Mathematically spaced letters; (B) Aesthetically spaced letters.

- The second headline (**Summer Reading Contest**) has a base font of 12-point Helvetica, with a font size of Very Large. The subheading is normal size 12-point Helvetica.

Creating the Masthead

The masthead in Figure 19.2 — the gray box in the lower left corner of the page — has the following characteristics:

- The text box options have the following settings:

    Border Style: **Single** (on all four sides)

    Outside Border Space: **0″** (on all four sides)

    Inside Border Space: **0.1″** (on all four sides)

    Gray Shading: **10%**

- The text box of the masthead has the following settings:

    Type: **Paragraph**

    Vertical Position: **0″**

    Horizontal Position: **Center**

    Size: **2″ wide × 2.83″ (high)**

    Wrap Text Around Box: **Yes**

- The text within the masthead box is 10-point Times Roman. The horizontal rules were created with Underline Spaces/Tabs turned *on* and with the **Underline** (F8) and **Flush Right** (Alt-F6) commands.

This completes the description of the *Ocean Breeze Banner* in Figure 19.2.

CREATING THE OCEAN BREEZE BULLETIN

The most complex document in this chapter (and in the entire book) is shown in Figure 19.4, the first page of the *Ocean Breeze Bulletin*, a newsletter for employees of Ocean Breeze Bookstore. But don't be intimidated by the complexity. It arises from the application of a large number of well-known WordPerfect features, not from any new, fancy WordPerfect commands.

The following is a list of the major features of the newsletter in Figure 19.4.

OCEAN BREEZE BULLETIN

Volume 5 • Number 11 • November 1988

How to Buy a Personal Computer

So you want to buy a personal computer but don't know where to start? Well, start right here at the Ocean Breeze Bookstore. Ask around. Find out what your fellow employees like and *don't* like about their computers.

Then, list the things you will do with your computer. Possible uses include word processing (at the top of most people's list), game playing (more important than most people admit), accounting, database management, telecommunications, and programming. With your list in hand (and your friends' recommendations in mind), visit your local computer stores. Talk to the sales personnel about what the computer can do to meet your specific needs rather than about the technical specifications of the hardware. Then match your needs with the equipment available in your price range.

Bookstore Posts Record Month

Store Reaches $240,000 in Sales in September

What started out as a trickle ended as an avalanche. Sales during the first week of September at Ocean Breeze Bookstore were anything but spectacular. But by month's end employees knew they had a record. "We were simply swamped most of the month, especially during the last week," reported William Wordsworth, sales manager in the Trade Books Department. "Many people in the company are responsible for this amazing sales record."

The record month, however, shouldn't have come as a surprise. September is always a big-volume month because of the influx of college students at the beginning of a new school year and because parents and children alike are reading more.

Computer book sales were especially brisk. This seems in part due to the increased popularity of personal computers and to the purchase of new computers at this time of the year. The best-selling book of the month was *Working with WordPerfect, Third Edition: The Complete Guide to Word Processing and Desktop Publishing* by Beverly and Scott Zimmerman. This handy book contains all you need to know about using *WordPerfect*, the most popular and most powerful word processor available. The book guides you through all the ordinary word processing features but also contains tutorials on WordPerfect's latest capabilities, including graphics, macro programming, merges, math functions, styles, font sizes and appearances, and expanded printer support. If you use *WordPerfect*, buy this book.

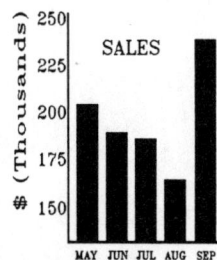

SALES

(Thousands)
250
225
200
175
150

MAY JUN JUL AUG SEP

Gross Income from sales, 1988.

Employee of the Month: Barbara Bookspan

A fellow worker described Barbara Bookspan as "having that winning combination: a passion for books and a love of people." For her dedication and conscientious service, the Ocean Breeze board of directors has selected Barbara as its Employee of the Month for September.

Barbara is originally from St. George, Utah, where her mother is a professor of English at Dixie College. She moved to La Jolla to attend UCSD, where she received a B.S. in marketing. Barbara has worked at Ocean Breeze Bookstore for three years.

Figure 19.4   The first page of the newsletter, the Ocean Breeze Bulletin.

- The title along the left edge of the page was created using three text boxes—one for each font size—rotated 90°.

  You could easily use two text boxes rather than three. To rotate text, create a text box, type the text within the box, and (while still in the text box) press **Graphics** (Alt-F9) and select **1** (0°), **2** (90°), **3** (180°), or **4** (270°).

- The thick gray line is a vertical line, a full page in length, 0.3″ in width, and 50% gray shading.

- The first figure (an IBM PS/2 computer) was drawn with Mac-Paint on a Macintosh computer and ported to an IBM-compatible computer through a local area network.

- The second figure (sales from May through September) was drawn with PC Paintbrush.

- The base font of the first text column is 10-point Times Roman; the base font of the (wider) second column is 11-point Times Roman.

- The third news item ("Employee of the Month") spans both columns and was created by simply turning *off* column mode.

- The headlines are Helvetica or Helvetica bold.

Based on this information and what you learned earlier in this chapter and in this book, and depending on the capabilities of your printer, you should be able to create the entire newsletter in Figure 19.4.

SUMMARY

This chapter has presented a suggested order for creating newsletters and has described how to do the following:

- Make strong titles and headlines by applying different font sizes, appearances, rotations, and shadings and by using graphics.

- Insert enlarged initial letters (see Figure 19.1) by creating text boxes containing only one large character.

- Draw vertical lines between newspaper-type columns (see Figures 19.1 and 19.2).

- Adjust column lengths by one of the following techniques: (1) adding or deleting copy; (2) changing the bottom margin; (3) changing the line height; (4) using Advance Up or Advance Down; and (5) using Hard Page (Ctrl-Enter) with unjustified text.

- Create columns of unequal width (see Figure 19.2).

- Superimpose two or more text or graphics boxes to create complex titles and figures (see Figure 19.2).

- Rotate text by pressing Graphics (Alt-F9) in the text box edit screen.

You can use the techniques learned in this chapter and throughout this book to create virtually any kind of publication you desire.

Appendix A

Troubleshooting

Your Computer Dealer
Computer Clubs and Users' Groups
The WordPerfect Support Group
Friends and Fellow Workers
Computer Camps and Workshops
The WordPerfect User's Manual
The WordPerfect Help Menus
The WordPerfect Workbook
Other Books and Magazines
WordPerfect Customer Support

Working with computer hardware and software can be frustrating. Every computer user—beginner and expert alike—needs help in solving problems. This appendix lists some of your main sources of help.

Your Computer Dealer

Your hardware and software dealers should back their products. If you have problems getting your equipment and programs to work properly, consult the retailer who sold them to you.

Realistically, however, few dealers can give the type or amount of help you need. Most people have to rely on other sources of help after the initial warranty period.

Computer Clubs and Users' Groups

Many universities, colleges, large businesses, and communities have an IBM users' group or computer club. Members of these groups are unlimited sources of advice and help in solving tough problems. Call the Computer Services, the Computer Science, or the Information Management department at your local university for information on user's groups.

The WordPerfect Support Group

The WordPerfect Support Group is an independent users' group, not affiliated with WordPerfect Corporation, designed to help support users of the WordPerfect word processor and other WordPerfect Corporation software. *The WordPerfectionist*, the newsletter of the Support Group, provides tips, techniques, instructions, and examples on a wide range of technical subjects.

Write WordPerfect Support Group, P.O. Box 1577, Baltimore, MD 21203.

Friends and Fellow Workers

Don't be afraid to ask questions of friends and fellow workers. They may be willing to answer questions on the telephone or even come to your house and give some hands-on help.

Computer Camps and Workshops

Attending a computer camp or a computer workshop is a good way to learn about computers and to get to know others with problems similar to yours. Computer instructors are often willing to give you personal help with your applications.

The WordPerfect User's Manual

Your WordPerfect User's Manual actually contains answers to most of your questions. Even if you "don't understand technical manuals," you may find that carefully reading this manual will help you considerably, especially if you already have had some experience with WordPerfect.

The WordPerfect Help Menus

If you have a question about a function, or you don't know what function to use for a particular need, press **Help** (F3) and then press the first letter of a feature or a function key. For example, if you can't remember how to create columns, press **Help** (F3) and **C** (the first letter of *columns*). The screen shows that pressing **Math/Columns** (Alt-F7) allows you to turn columns *on* and *off*. Press **Enter** or the **Space Bar** to exit the menu screen. Press **Help** (F3) and **Math/Columns** (Alt-F7) to get more information on the math and columns functions.

The WordPerfect Workbook

The *WordPerfect Workbook*, which comes with WordPerfect 5.1, is a valuable source of information about many of the WordPerfect features. Read the explanations and work through the examples.

Other Books and Magazines

See Appendix C, "Additional Reading."

WordPerfect Customer Support

WordPerfect Corporation is the best in the business for supporting customers. If you have read your user's manual and have worked through the lessons but still have questions on a particular subject, write or call WordPerfect Technical Support, 1555 Technology Way, Orem, UT 84057. Call one of the following numbers (the 800 numbers are toll-free; the 801 numbers have a toll charge):

General features	800-541-5096 or 801-226-7900
Graphics	800-321-3383 or 801-226-4770
Printers	800-541-5097 or 801-226-7977

We suggest that you have your software license number available when you call (although the WordPerfect technical consultants usually do not ask for the number). You should be sitting at your computer with WordPerfect on the screen when you make the call.

Appendix B

Using Your Printer

Printer Problems
Testing Your Printer
PTR: The Printer Program

Configuring your computer and software to your printer can be one of the most baffling and upsetting experiences in all of computing. To assure that your printer works with WordPerfect, do the following:

- Make sure you configure WordPerfect for your printer by following the steps in "Configuring Your Printer" (Chapter 2, "Using WordPerfect").

- If your printer is not among the dozens listed on the Word-Perfect Printer disks, call WordPerfect Technical Support at 1-800-541-5097 or 1-801-226-7977; these numbers are specifically assigned for questions about printers. The WordPerfect technical personnel may be able to send you a disk containing your printer's specifications. If they don't have your specifications on a disk, they may know if another printer configuration will work with your printer.

- If your printer specifications are not on the WordPerfect Printer disk and you want to try to configure your own printer, follow the procedure given in the section "PTR: The Printer Program" below. Be forewarned, however, that defining your printer for WordPerfect is highly technical. Before attempting it, make sure you understand printer and ASCII codes, know how printers and computers communicate with each other, and understand hexadecimal and binary numbers.

Printer Problems

Even after configuring WordPerfect to your printer, you may still have problems. Carefully go through the items in the "Printer Checklist" given in Chapter 5, "Printing Documents," before giving up on your printer.

If your printer still has problems, carefully go through the section "Printer Troubleshooting" in the appendix of the WordPerfect user's manual.

If your printer still doesn't work, you should contact your dealer or the printer manufacturer.

Testing Your Printer

WordPerfect provides three printer test files to help you understand the capabilities and limitations of your printer. You should print each of them by following these steps:

Step 1.   From within WordPerfect, clear the WordPerfect document screen (if necessary) by pressing **Exit** (F7), **N** (No), **N** (No).

Step 2. Place the Conversion disk in one of your disk drives, press **List** (F5) from within WordPerfect, enter the disk drive (A: or B:, for example), use the arrow keys to highlight the file PRINTER.TST, and press **1** (**R**etrieve).

The two-page printer text document is loaded from the disk onto the document screen.

Step 3. Press **Font** (Ctrl-F8) and **4** (Base **F**ont), use the arrow keys to highlight the desired font, press **Enter** to select the font, and type the point size if requested to do so.

Step 4. Press **Print** (Shift-F7) and **1** (**F**ull Document) to print the printer test document.

Step 5. Repeat steps 1 through 4 for any other font that you want to test, selecting a different base font in step 3.

Step 6. Repeat the above steps, but in step 2 replace PRINTER.TST for the file CHARACTR.DOC.

PTR: The Printer Program

If you feel confident about your knowledge of printer/computer communications and decide to configure your own printer, you will need the following items:

- A copy of the WordPerfect PTR Program disk or the PTR.EXE file on your hard disk.

- The directory or disk that contains the printer definition file most like your printer.

  You should follow the steps in Chapter 2, "Using WordPerfect," to define the printer that you think might be most like yours. If you don't know or can't guess what printer it might be, just use the Standard Printer. After configuring the printer, write down the name of the printer definition file for later reference. You will use this file as a pattern for defining your printer.

- A copy of the *Printer Manual* (documentation for defining your own printer), available from WordPerfect Corporation for $19.95. Phone (800) 222-9409 to order the Printer Manual.

- Your printer user's manual.

- A list of the decimal equivalents ASCII codes (American Standard Code for Information Interchange). Many printer manuals contain such a list.

Now do the following:

Step 1.   At the DOS prompt, type ptr and press **Enter** to run the Printer Program.

The Printers window appears on the screen. The window probably contains no printer names at this point. The one-line menu **1** Add; **2** Delete; **3** Rename; **4** Copy appears underneath the Printers window.

Step 2.   Press **Retrieve** (Shift-F10) and enter the filename of the printer definition file that you want to use as a pattern for defining your printer.

You should choose a printer definition file that is as close to your printer as possible. For example, if you are defining a dot matrix printer, choose a definition file of a similar dot matrix printer.

Step 3.   Press **3** (Rename), type My Printer (or whatever your printer name happens to be), and (if prompted to do so) press **1** if it is a standard printer or **2** if it is a PostScript printer.

The new printer name appears in the Printers window.

Step 4.   With the cursor next to the new printer name, press **Enter**.

The list of printer features appears in the Printer window. You can now use the cursor-movement keys to highlight the desired printer feature.

Step 5.   With **Initialize and Reset** highlighted, press **Enter**.

The Initialize and Reset window appears on the screen, with the function name on the left and the expression (string of printer codes) on the right. You can use the cursor-movement keys to highlight the desired initialize or reset feature.

Step 6.   For example, press **Down Arrow** to move the cursor to **Initialize at Start of Print Job**, and press **Enter** or **Right Arrow**.

Step 7.   Type the expression.

Control character codes are typed as decimal numbers in brackets, for example, [27] and [13] for ESC and CR. Normal keyboard characters are enclosed in quotes, for example, "a" and "C". You can also use variable names, such as PAPERLENGTH, as described in the WordPerfect Printer Manual. While editing the expression, you can use most of the normal WordPerfect cursor movement keys.

Step 8.   Set all the required Initialize and Reset expressions.

Most printers do not require that all the functions contain an expression. Consult your printer's user manual.

Step 9.   Press **Exit** (F7) to return to the Printer window with the list of printer features.

Step 10.   Follow the steps above to go through all the printer features as explained in the WordPerfect Printer Manual, setting the expressions for each item in the features menus.

Step 11.   Press **Exit** (F7) to return to the Printers window with the list of printers and press **Exit** (F7) again.

You are asked if you want to save the new printer definition file.

Step 12.   Press **Y** (Yes), enter a new legal filename (with the filename extension .PRS; don't use the old filename), and press **Y** (Yes) to exit the Printer Program after the file has been saved to the disk.

These steps are, of course, only the general outline of what is required to define a printer. Read the WordPerfect Printer Manual for details.

Appendix C

Additional Reading

Suggested Books on General WordPerfect Features
Other Books on Desktop Publishing with WordPerfect
Recommended General Books on Desktop Publishing
Recommended Magazines
Books on Writing

Suggested Books on General WordPerfect Features

Acerson, Karen. *WordPerfect: The Complete Reference, Series 5 Edition.* Berkeley, Calif.: Osborne/McGraw-Hill, 1988.

Zimmerman, Beverly B., and Zimmerman, S. Scott. *Working with WordPerfect, Third Edition.* Glenview, Ill.: Scott, Foresman and Company, 1989.

Other Books on Desktop Publishing with WordPerfect

Parker, Roger C. *Desktop Publishing with WordPerfect.* Chapel Hill, N.C.: Ventana Press, 1988.

Tevis, Jim. *Desktop Publishing with WordPerfect 5.0.* New York: Wiley, 1989.

Will-Harris, Daniel. *WordPerfect 5: Desktop Publishing in Style.* Berkeley, Calif.: Peachpit Press, 1988.

Recommended General Books on Desktop Publishing

Lichty, Tom. *Design Principles for Desktop Publishers.* Glenview, Ill.: Scott, Foresman and Company, 1988.

Parker, Roger C. *Looking Good in Print: A Guide to Basic Design for Desktop Publishing.* Chapel Hill, N.C.: Ventana Press, 1987.

White, Jan V. *Graphic Design for the Electronic Age: The Manual for Traditional and Desktop Publishing.* New York: Watson-Guptill Publications, 1988.

Recommended Magazines

Personal Publishing, P. O. Box 3240, Harlan, IA 51593-2420. This magazine covers all types of hardware and software for desktop publishing.

Publish!, PCW Communications, Inc., 501 Second St., San Francisco, CA 94107. This magazine covers all types of hardware and software for desktop publishing, with slightly more emphasis on the Macintosh than on IBM compatibles.

WordPerfect, The Magazine, WordPerfect Publishing Corporation, 288 W. Center Street, Orem, UT 84057. This excellent publication covers WordPerfect in general but has many articles directly applicable to desktop publishing.

Books on Writing

Among the hundreds of books on writing, two stand out:

Strunk, William, Jr., and White, E. B. *The Elements of Style.* 3rd ed. New York: Macmillan, 1979. Must reading for all desktop publishers and writers.

Zinser, William. *On Writing Well.* 3rd ed. New York: Harper & Row, 1985.

Appendix D

Directory of Products

Laser Printers
Graphics Software
Fonts
Clip Art
Scanners
Mouse Input Devices

The following is a short list of popular hardware and software products and their manufacturers. For more information, consult your local computer dealers.

Laser Printers

- Acer LP-76
  Acer Technologies Corp.
  401 Charcot Ave.
  San Jose, CA 95131

- Apple LaserWriter Plus, IInt, and IIntx
  Apple Computer Inc.
  20525 Mariani Ave.
  Cupertino, CA 95014

- AST TurboLaser/PS
  AST Research Inc.
  2121 Alton Ave.
  Irvine, CA 92714

- Hewlett-Packard LaserJet Series II
  Hewlett-Packard Co.
  1820 Embarcadero Road
  Palo Alto, CA 94303

- Panasonic KX-P4450 Laser Partner
  Panasonic Industrial Co.
  Two Panasonic Way
  Secaucus, NJ 07094

- Toshiba PageLaser 12, TurboLaser PS
  Toshiba American Inc.
  Information Systems Division
  9740 Irvine Blvd.
  Irvine, CA 92718

Graphics Software

- Adobe Illustrator (for the IBM)
  Adobe Systems Inc.
  P. O. Box 7900
  Mountain View, CA 94039-7900

- Draw Applause
  Ashton-Tate
  20101 Hamilton Ave.
  Torrance, CA 90502

- DrawPerfect
  WordPerfect Corp.
  1555 N. Technology Way
  Orem, UT 84057

- Harvard Graphics
  Software Publishing Corporation
  P. O. Box 7210
  Mountain View, CA 94039-7210

- Lotus 1-2-3, Freehand Plus
  Lotus Development Corp.
  55 Cambridge Parkway
  Cambridge, MA 02142

- PC Paintbrush, Paintbrush Plus
  ZSoft Corporation
  440 Franklin Rd., Suite 100
  Marietta, GA 30067

Fonts

- Adobe Type Libraries
  Adobe Systems Incorporated
  P.O. Box 7900
  Mountain View, CA 94039-7900

- Bitstream Fontware
  Bitstream Inc.
  Athenaeum House
  215 First Street
  Cambridge, MA 02142

- Glyphix Fonts
  Swfte International
  P. O. Box 219
  Rockland, DE 19732

- SoftCraft LaserFonts
  SoftCraft
  16 N. Carroll Street, Suite 500
  Madison, WI 53703

Clip Art

- Desktop Art
  Dynamics Graphics, Inc.
  P. O. Box 1901
  Peoria, IL 61656-9975

- Harvard Graphics (includes clip art library)
  Software Publishing Corporation
  P. O. Box 7210
  Mountain View, CA 94039-7210

- Metro ImageBase
  Metro ImageBase, Inc
  18623 Ventura Blvd., Suite 210
  Tarzana, CA 91356

- Publisher's PicturePak
  Marketing Graphics Inc.
  4401 Dominion Blvd., Suite 210
  Glen Allen, VA 23060-3379

Scanners

- AST TurboScan
  AST Research, Inc.
  2121 Alton Ave.
  Irvine, CA 92714

- Cannon IX-12
  Cannon, Inc.
  One Cannon Plaza
  Lake Success, NY 11042

- The Complete Hand Scanner
  The Complete PC, Inc.
  521 Cottonwood Dr.
  Milpitas, CA 95035

- Handy Scanner
  Diamond Flower Electric Instrument Co.
  2544 Port Screet
  West Sacramento, CA 95691

Mouse Input Devices

- Genius Mouse
  Kye International Corp.
  769 Pinefalls Ave.
  Walnut Creek, CA 91789

- ClearCase Mouse, HiREZ Mouse, Logitech Mouse
  Logitech
  6505 Kaiser Drive
  Fremont, CA 94555

- Microsoft Mouse
  Microsoft Corp.
  Box 97017
  Redmond, WA 98073-9717

- M-Mouse, E-Mouse, S-Mouse
  Mitsubishi International Corp.
  520 Madison Ave.
  New York, NY 10022

- PC Mouse II, OmniMouse
  MSC Technology, Inc.
  47505 Seabridge Dr.
  Fremont, CA 94538

Index